British Children's Literature and
Material Culture

Bloomsbury Perspectives on Children's Literature

Bloomsbury Perspectives on Children's Literature seeks to expand the range and quality of research in children's literature through publishing innovative monographs by leading and rising scholars in the field. With an emphasis on cross and inter-disciplinary studies, this series takes literary approaches as a starting point, drawing on the particular capacity for children's literature to open out into other disciplines.

Series Editor
Dr Lisa Sainsbury, Director of the National Centre for Research in Children's Literature, Roehampton University, UK

Editorial Board
Professor M. O. Grenby (Newcastle University, UK), Dr Marah Gubar (University of Pittsburgh, USA), Dr Vanessa Joosen (Tilburg University, The Netherlands)

Titles in the Series
Adulthood in Children's Literature, Vanessa Joosen
The Courage to Imagine: The Child Hero in Children's Literature, Roni Natov
Ethics in British Children's Literature: Unexamined Life, Lisa Sainsbury
Fashioning Alice: The Career of Lewis Carroll's Icon, 1860–1901, Kiera Vaclavik
From Tongue to Text: A New Reading of Children's Poetry, Debbie Pullinger
Literature's Children: The Critical Child and the Art of Idealisation, Louise Joy
Rereading Childhood Books: A Poetics, Alison Waller
Irish Children's Literature and the Poetics of Memory, Rebecca Long

Forthcoming Titles
Activist Authors and British Child Readers of Colour, Karen Sands-O'Connor
The Dark Matter of Children's "Fantastika" Literature, Chloé Germaine Buckley
British Children's Literature in Japanese Culture, Catherine Butler

British Children's Literature and Material Culture

Commodities and Consumption 1850–1914

Jane Suzanne Carroll

BLOOMSBURY ACADEMIC
LONDON • NEW YORK • OXFORD • NEW DELHI • SYDNEY

BLOOMSBURY ACADEMIC
Bloomsbury Publishing Plc
50 Bedford Square, London, WC1B 3DP, UK
1385 Broadway, New York, NY 10018, USA
29 Earlsfort Terrace, Dublin 2, Ireland

BLOOMSBURY, BLOOMSBURY ACADEMIC and the Diana logo are trademarks
of Bloomsbury Publishing Plc

First published in Great Britain 2022
Paperback edition published 2023

Copyright © Jane Suzanne Carroll, 2022

Jane Suzanne Carroll has asserted her right under the Copyright, Designs and
Patents Act, 1988, to be identified as Author of this work.

For legal purposes the Acknowledgements on pp. x–xi constitute an
extension of this copyright page.

Cover design: Eleanor Rose
Cover image: Detail of an illustration from *The Tale of Two Bad Mice* by Beatrix Potter,
courtesy of Alamy.

All rights reserved. No part of this publication may be reproduced or transmitted in any
form or by any means, electronic or mechanical, including photocopying, recording,
or any information storage or retrieval system, without prior permission
in writing from the publishers.

Bloomsbury Publishing Plc does not have any control over, or responsibility for, any
third-party websites referred to or in this book. All internet addresses given in this
book were correct at the time of going to press. The author and publisher regret any
inconvenience caused if addresses have changed or sites have ceased to exist, but
can accept no responsibility for any such changes.

A catalogue record for this book is available from the British Library.

Library of Congress Cataloging-in-Publication Data
Names: Carroll, Jane Suzanne, author.
Title: British children's literature and material culture /
Jane Suzanne Carroll, Trinity College Dublin, Ireland.
Description: London ; New York : Bloomsbury Academic, 2022. |
Series: Bloomsbury perspectives in children's literature |
Includes bibliographical references and index.
Identifiers: LCCN 2021018058 (print) | LCCN 2021018059 (ebook) |
ISBN 9781350201781 (hardback) | ISBN 9781350201798 (ebook) |
ISBN 9781350201804 (epub)
Subjects: LCSH: Children's literature, English–History and criticism. |
Children's literature, English–Irish authors–History and criticism. |
Material culture in literature. | Children–Books and reading–Great
Britain–History–19th century. | Children–Books and reading–Great
Britain–History–20th century. | Child consumers–Great
Britain–History–19th century. | Child consumers–Great
Britain–History–20th century. | LCGFT: Literary criticism.
Classification: LCC PR990 .C374 2022 (print) | LCC PR990 (ebook) | DDC 820.9/9282–dc23
LC record available at https://lccn.loc.gov/2021018058
LC ebook record available at https://lccn.loc.gov/2021018059

ISBN: HB: 978-1-3502-0178-1
PB: 978-1-3502-0182-8
ePDF: 978-1-3502-0179-8
eBook: 978-1-3502-0180-4

Series: Bloomsbury Perspectives on Children's Literature

Typeset by Newgen KnowledgeWorks Pvt. Ltd., Chennai, India

To find out more about our authors and books visit www.bloomsbury.com
and sign up for our newsletters.

To my parents – Linda and Fran

Contents

List of Figures	ix
Acknowledgements	x

	Introduction: 'Devoured by a desire to possess': Children's literature, commodities and consumption	1
	Children's books as commodities and vehicles for consumerism	3
	Children's books and the creation of new products	7
	Reading objects	11
	Structure of this book	14
1	'Remarkable and perplexing items': Children and the Great Exhibition	17
	Learning to look	22
	Getting lost	27
	Guiding children	30
	Head, hand and heart	37
	The world of goods	42
	Conclusion	49
2	'The wonders of common things': Worldly goods in the nineteenth century	53
	The history of the it-narrative	56
	Children's it-narratives	61
	The History of a Pin and the circulation of domestic goods	64
	The Story of a Needle: Worldly goods at home	67
	Various values in 'A China Cup'	73
	'The wonders of common things'	77
	Conclusion	81
3	'A hailstorm of knitting needles': Other-worldly goods and domestic fantasy	83
	Commodity fetishism	90
	Spiritualism and fiction	95
	The rise of domestic fantasy	99

	Lewis Carroll, Spiritualism and domestic fantasy	102
	Speaking Likenesses and friendly furniture	109
	The Cuckoo Clock as trance novel	112
	Conclusion	119
4	'A disgraceful state of things': Bad consumers and bad commodities	123
	Bad consumers in E. Nesbit's work	127
	Bad things in Nesbit's work	132
	The Enchanted Castle and the live thing	135
	Bad mice and crooked sixpences: Material deviance in Beatrix Potter's work	142
	The (mis)adventures of Mr Toad	148
	Conclusion	154
Conclusions: Failed palaces and magic cities		157
Notes		167
References		169
Index		185

Figures

0.1	Children as empowered and confident consumers	6
0.2	The commercial and cultural value of children's literature	10
1.1	Bored and hungry children at the Great Exhibition	21
1.2	A child engaging with the exhibits in the Chinese Court by both looking and touching	25
1.3	A young visitor to the Great Exhibition reaches out to touch a display	26
1.4	Making the unseen labour behind commodities visible	44
2.1	Talkative commodities appear in advertisements as well as fiction	59
2.2	The nineteenth-century parlour, and its occupants, swathed in fabric	68
3.1	Ordinary furniture endowed with new life in the aftermath of a séance	89
3.2	Children present at a séance	97
3.3a	'Where the noise came from, she couldn't make out …'	106
3.3b	Spirit hands making a racket	107
3.4	The child and the object on friendly terms	110
3.5	Griselda presented as a ghostly figure in the parlour	117
4.1	As 'live things', the Ugly-Wuglies threaten the boundary between object and subject	139
4.2	'Then Tom Thumb lost his temper. He put the ham in the middle of the floor, and hit it with the tongs and with the shovel – bang, bang, smash, smash!'	146
4.3	Toad's material deviance finds its fullest expression in the motor car	153
C.1	Children leading the way to the Exhibition	159

Acknowledgements

This book was started when I lived and worked in one place and ended when I lived and worked in another and I have been lucky to be helped by many people over the course of this project. My first thanks are to my colleagues at the University of Roehampton and my colleagues in the School of English at Trinity College Dublin; to Kate Teltscher, who talked me through the very early ideas for this book, to Laura Peters, who put me on to the bizarre story about the boy getting lost in 1851, to Gillian Lathey, who shared my curiosity about Samuel Prout Newcombe, to Pádraic Whyte, my partner in children's literature, to Clare Clarke and Bernice Murphy – traybakers forever! – for their unfailing support and humour. I also owe heartfelt thanks to my students in the Material Culture in Children's Literature module who helped me cultivate this topic through discussion, debate and digressions about pins.

In all stages of research and writing, I have been supported by friends and by colleagues who have become friends – Trish Ferguson and Helen Conrad-O'Briain who read early chapters, Beth Rodgers, who allowed me to test this material as a talk at Aberystwyth, Dara Downey, who was so generous with her knowledge about Victorian spiritualism, and Katja Bruisch who reminded me often that it is better to write after tea. I am enormously indebted to Alison Waller, who gave such thoughtful and generous feedback on this book and held me to writing deadlines. I want especially to thank Lisa Sainsbury, who provided both clear-headed logic and boundless enthusiasm when I needed both. Her passion, attention to detail and encouragement have made working with her again a true pleasure. I am also grateful to Franziska Kohlt who shared unpublished work with me, and to Ben Phillips who shared his knowledge about Feliks Volkhovskii.

This project could not have been completed without the help of the many librarians in archives and special collections I consulted throughout my research, including the staff at the Royal Commission for the Great Exhibition, the Victoria and Albert Museum, the National Archives, and the librarians and archivists at the University of Roehampton. I owe special thanks to the staff of Early Printed Books at Trinity College Dublin, especially Lydia Ferguson, Helen McGinty and Simon Lang.

Acknowledgements

I am grateful to the Victoria and Albert Museum, to the National Archives and to the Bodleian Library for granting permission to reproduce images from their collections here.

In preparing this book, I received a Sassoon Visiting Fellowship from the Bodleian Library, Oxford. I want to thank Julie Anne Lambert, curator of the John Johnson Collection, for generously sharing her expertise and insight. During my time in Oxford, Lincoln College was extraordinarily kind in accommodating me (and a growing bump). I am especially grateful to Mel Marshall, Peter McCullough and the members of the senior common room for giving me such a warm welcome.

I owe huge thanks to my parents, Linda and Fran, who are to blame for everything. I'm sure when they introduced me to Mr Jackson, Alfie and all the others, they had no idea I'd make reading children's books into a career. Thanks are due too to my sister, Laura, the architect, who did absolutely nothing to help but reminds me often that I am boring. It keeps me humble.

Above all, I want to thank Karl Kinsella, my beloved, for everything, but perhaps most of all for listening to me talk about this stuff constantly, and for all the tea and frips and the timely reminders that I should probably be writing. His deep support, patience and kindness have guided me through rough waters. And Beatrix, thank you for setting a deadline that I couldn't wriggle out of and for napping sometimes.

Finally, I'd like to thank Roland Barks for early morning walks and for not chewing up *all* of the books I was working with.

Introduction: 'Devoured by a desire to possess': Children's literature, commodities and consumption

In 1851, a small girl decided that what she wanted most in all the world was a book about flowers. Frances Eliza Hodgson (later Hodgson Burnett) was 'devoured by a desire to possess' a book and declared to the adults around her that 'a book, and only a book, would satisfy her impassioned cravings' (Burnett 1893: 26–7). Where these cravings came from, or how she had gleaned the idea that there was such a thing as what she called a 'Little Flower Book', the girl didn't quite know, and the adult woman looking back on her childhood could not quite understand it either. Nevertheless, the trip to the shop to make this purchase stands out in her memory. Chaperoned by her grandmother,

> she was taken herself to buy the book. It was a beautiful and solemn pilgrimage. Reason suggests that it was not a long one, in consideration for her tiny and brief legs, but to her it seemed to be a journey of great length principally past wastes of suburban brick-fields, which for some reason seemed romantic and interesting to her, and it ended in a tiny shop on a sort of country road. (27)

Her recollection of the actual moment of purchase is vague. Burnett recalls that she has no memory of the interior of the shop, 'only the outside, which had one small window, with toys and sweet things in glass jars' (27). She is not sure whether she ever actually entered the shop but is absolutely sure that 'there the Flower Book was bought (I wonder if it really cost more than sixpence); from there it was carried home under her arm' (27). Frances Hodgson's experiences give us some important insights into children's experiences of consumer culture and their interactions with commodities. In some respects, her power as a consumer is very limited: she does not have her own money to spend and she is guided, physically and presumably figuratively, by an adult who oversees the purchase. On the other hand, there are hints here that the girl – and by extension many children like her – had some agency. When she first conceives of her desire for a book, 'a suggestion was tentatively made by [her grandmother] that perhaps a doll would finally be found preferable to a book' (26). That the girl can reject her grandmother's suggestion indicates that even at a very young age – the exact date of this incident is not clear but she may have been not quite three years old – her own ideas and fancies are treated as important. Furthermore, while the girl may not have been the one to physically hand over the money in exchange for the book, she was the instigator of the purchase and the ultimate user of the commodity. The episode around its purchase holds hints of a kind of commodity fetishism: her desire for the book is presented as a kind of overwhelming passion and the journey to acquire the book is overlaid with religious symbolism. It is a sort of 'pilgrimage'. But it may also be considered as a rite of passage. By identifying and then fulfilling her desire for a particular commodity, the girl is initiated into the realm of Victorian consumer culture.

While there is a pervasive notion that children's consumer culture is a twentieth-century phenomenon (Trentmann 2017: 486), Burnett's account of her own childhood purchases and her interactions with commodities attests to the fact that children were active, engaged, agent consumers long before the twentieth century. Denis Denisoff argues that consumer culture and childhood have always been inextricably linked, noting that 'consumer culture and the dominant modern concepts of the child arose in Western society at roughly the same time and place' (2016: 9). The late nineteenth century and early twentieth century was a period of unprecedented consumption of commodities, including children's books: at the same time that commodities were being 'produced at unprecedented rates, exchanged in unprecedented numbers, and consumed in unprecedented volumes' (Lindner 2003: 4), there was a corresponding rise in the number of children's books produced. As Claudia Nelson observes, 'propelled by rising literacy rates and ever-cheaper print technology, children's literature boomed, both in quantity and quality' (2016: 137). This period is sometimes referred to as the first 'golden age' of children's literature. The temporal boundaries of this period are up for debate; Humphrey Carpenter identifies it as the period between the publication of *Alice's Adventures in Wonderland* (1865) and *Winnie-the-Pooh* (1921) (2012: x), but Marah Gubar acknowledges that Catherine Sinclair's *Holiday House* (1839) is often seen as a 'harbinger' (2009: 5) of the golden age. Nevertheless, the notion of a golden age is a useful way to identify this period in British social history, which is marked by the effects of the Industrial Revolution, an influx of goods from sovereign and colonized territories, a newly youthful population and a rise in publication to cater to the tastes of this emergent youth (Denisoff 2016: 5).

In this book, I take the Great Exhibition of 1851 as my starting point because, as I argue in Chapter 1, the Exhibition marks a turning point in British consumer culture, changing the ways that objects were displayed and marketed to consumers, and making ordinary consumers more aware of where and how their goods were made. I have chosen 1914 as the end point of my study, not only because the First World War disrupted the production, trade and consumption of commodities but also because it marks the date of another great exhibition – this time, one that never took place. The Universal Exhibition, which was expected to attract at least four million visitors, was scheduled to open in Nottingham in May 1914, but it never did ('Nottingham's Exhibition: Big Scheme on a Business Basis', 5 November 1913: 3). While adverts were placed in newspapers from 1913 calling for exhibitors, and there was a grand ceremony when the first sod was cut on the site in November 1913, the exhibition was cancelled due to a lack of interest from industry ('Nottingham Exhibition: The Enterprise Abandoned for This Year', 24 March 1914: 3). Far from being a unified period then, the 'golden age' is a period in which attitudes towards material goods shifted dramatically, moving from celebration to suspicion or even indifference. These shifting attitudes are reflected in contemporary British children's literature, as authors used their texts to uphold or challenge contemporary attitudes towards commodity culture.

Children's books as commodities and vehicles for consumerism

Children's books, themselves mass-produced and 'repeatable cultural commodit[ies]' (Kline 1993: 97), play a vital role in enculturing child consumers and are important sites for recording and reflecting young people's material experiences. Robin Bernstein argues that 'the union of literature and material culture has defined children's literature since 1744', noting that Newbery's *A Little Pretty Pocket-Book Intended for the Instruction and Amusement of Little Master Tommy, and Pretty Miss Polly*, widely regarded as the first modern book for child readers, was marketed with a pair of objects: a ball and a pincushion (2013: 459). Although Newbery's preface indicates that the ball and the pincushion were not for the child to play with, but for the parent or nursemaid to use as educational tools (the parent was instructed to hang up the pincushion and stick pins into it to chart the child's good or bad behaviour), this innovative publication nevertheless introduced a close, even symbiotic, relationship between children's literature and commodities. This relationship becomes all the more important in the nineteenth century when children's literature emerged as a key consumer product, one that influenced and shaped children's views of and relationships with other kinds of commodities and, ultimately, whetted the appetite for further commodities.

As Christopher Parkes argues persuasively in his study of children's literature and capitalism, the narratives produced by many Victorian and Edwardian writers are 'fundamentally concerned with redefining the relationship of the child to the marketplace in order to accommodate the child within capitalist society' (2012: 1). Parkes contends that, unlike the Romantic period at the end of the eighteenth century and the beginning of the nineteenth century, this new age of capitalism 'required the child to be a figure that could participate in commercial activity and yet remain innocent and uncorrupted' (3). Crucially, the ideal capitalist child is not a producer or a labourer, but a middle-class consumer of the products produced by others. Parkes traces this emerging capitalism to Maria Edgeworth's *Practical Education* (1801), identifying her work as germinal in creating the notion that 'the child's playroom should be a training ground for participation in capitalist society' (5). Edgeworth recommends giving children toy bricks and working models of industrial machines but, implicitly, also recommends giving children a certain kind of book: books that will foster in the child the necessary values and ideas that will prepare them for active, agent consumption. In the nineteenth century, children's literature becomes ever more entangled with commodities and consumption. That is not to say, of course, that all authors were entirely successful in coaching their young readers in good consumer practices. As Gubar points out, golden-age authors 'generally conceive of child characters and child readers as socially saturated beings, profoundly shaped by the culture, manners, and morals of their time', but while children may be 'enabled and inspired' by this culture, they may also rebel against it (2009: 5). Nevertheless, children's books became important sites for educating young readers about commodities and inducting them into their roles as consumers in the late nineteenth and early twentieth centuries.

Parkes's work is part of a growing movement towards centring the child, and children's literature, in discussions of material culture. This work is necessary because, as Daniel Thomas Cook notes, 'studies of consumer society either ignore children and childhood completely or see children as appendages or adjuncts to the central claims, preoccupations and problems of this field of study' (2014: 63). Many sociological and historical discussions about children as consumers assume a linear trajectory by which a naïve and unsophisticated consumer grows into a discerning and economically shrewd one, usually as a result of didactic intervention by an experienced or adept consumer (Cook 2014: 69). These dual positions – naïveté and shrewdness – are simplistically mapped on to polarized ideas about childhood and adulthood whereby childhood is seen as 'a structured becoming' (Jenks 1996: 12) that culminates in, and only finds meaning within, adulthood. But seeing the child consumer as unsophisticated and the adult consumer as adept overlooks a number of crucial issues. First, to be adult is not necessarily to be expert: consumers learn continually and as new products and new technologies come to market, the savvy consumer is one who continually educates themselves. Second, consumers may be adept in only a few specialized areas: the shopper who knows exactly what to look for in a grocer's may be overwhelmed in a haberdasher's; the connoisseur who knows a lot about fine art may be a hopelessly inexperienced buyer of lumber. Third, the assumption that consumers are socialized by means of a simple top-down pedagogy overlooks the complex systems of consumerism that are particular to children – those schoolyard practices of exchange, barter, gifting, lending, making and stealing that are carried out by children, among children and for children. Children may introduce their parents to new products and bring new kinds of products into the home. Children are not passive oblates waiting to be taught how to engage with the commodities around them but are subjects within consumer culture in their own right. Cook suggests that we adopt the term 'commercial enculturation' in place of 'consumer socialization', as the former enables us to acknowledge the pre-existing 'multiple, layered and overlapping webs of meaning' that surround every consumer and every commodity and places renewed emphasis on the 'social relationships with and through goods and their associations' (2014: 70). The child is already participating within consumer culture through the clothes they wear, the toys they play with, the food they eat, the furniture they sit on and, crucially, the books they read.

Children's books enculture children as consumers by depicting child characters as being actively engaged in commodity culture and making considered decisions about their spending. In contrast to the inexperienced child shoppers depicted in early-nineteenth-century texts, such as Rosamond in Edgeworth's 'The Purple Jar' (1801–2) and Julia in Sherwood's *A Drive in a Coach through the Streets of London* (1818), who are easily beguiled by fancy goods on display, and learn hard lessons about 'vain and frivolous materialism' (Norcia 2013: 29), the young shoppers in children's books from the mid-nineteenth century onwards demonstrate greater awareness of their economic potential and their role as consumers. Children's texts from the period often show child characters engaged in consumption – in desiring, choosing and using commodities – and so they normalize the role of the child as consumer and model good consumer practices for the young reader. For example, E. V. Lucas and F. D. Bedford's *The Book of Shops* (1899) presents a complex view of the child as shopper (see Figure 0.1). Some of Bedford's illustrations of the shops depict children as in need of education or enculturation – they are led, sometimes literally by the hand, around the shops by adult figures. In the illustrations showing the Booksellers, the Fishmongers and the Poulterer, children remain passive participants within the scene and the buying power rests squarely with the adults they accompany. In the Watchmaker's, by contrast, children are depicted as unruly and unfocused shoppers, with one boy hiding inside the case of a grandfather clock and the others paying attention to his antics rather than to the goods on display or to the stern-looking staff. However, the text also

Figure 0.1 Children as empowered and confident consumers. *Source: The Book of Shops* (Lucas 1899: 3a), illustration by F. D. Bedford, *The Confectioner's*.

shows that children can be adept and independent consumers: in the illustration of the Confectioner's, three children sit together at a table eating cake and one summons a waitress, who comes towards them – bearing a tray of drinks. They are independent, commanding and capable: these children have both economic and social power. There is a clear invocation of class here too: though the usual aetonormative hierarchies would place adults above children, these children's status as middle-class consumers allows them to have power over the working-class staff at the confectioner's.

Perhaps most significantly, the half-title shows a young girl reading Lucas and Bedford's *The Book of Shops*. She perches on a high-backed wooden chair, her feet propped on a footstool, a doll lying discarded on the floor beside her: significantly, the plaything is abandoned in favour of the book, which offers enculturation in a predominantly adult world of consumerism. This image shows the idealized child reader as burgeoning consumer, eager for experiences that extend beyond the playroom and the nursery, using the book to learn about what each of the typical high-street shops sell. Immediately after this image, the real reader is presented with a page of advertisements of other books offered by Grant Richards: in this way, the book serves as both an educational tool and as a medium for advertisement. These texts use successful child consumers to model proper consumer behaviours and promote these behaviours to the young reader.

Children's books and the creation of new products

The development of children's books intersects with the rise of advertising ephemera in the nineteenth century. Julie Anne Lambert points out that many advertisers made use of 'novelties' in the form of paper puzzles, jigsaws and movables. These novelties make use of techniques that are commonly associated with nineteenth-century movable books, using volvelles, lift-the-flap panels and dissolving or 'window-blind' views that required the reader to pull a tab to shift between the intersecting illustrations (Field 2019: 1–24). That they share these same strategies suggests that children's books and many advertisements had the same intended audience. Indeed, Lambert notes that 'children were often the hidden target of persuaders, and many novelties were produced with them in mind, whether educational … or recreational' (2020c: 121) and that some advertisers even produced storybooks and colouring books aimed at young consumers. Children's books also led directly to the creation of new products in this period. While Newbery's *Little Pretty Pocket-Book* was sold with the gimmick of a ball or a pincushion, neither of these objects played any significant role within the narrative. One of the great innovations of the golden age of children's literature was the creation of new commodities that were inspired by – or even directly lifted from – popular children's books, extending the reader's imaginative and financial engagement with the text. For example, Kate Greenaway's illustrations inspired a line of children's clothing sold by Liberty's department store as 'Artistic Dress for Children' (Cluckie 2008: 133), as well as a range of 'sanitary' washable wallpaper based on her illustrations of the months of the year, printed by David Walker & Co., a company based in Lancashire (Saunders 2002: 130). In 1903, Beatrix Potter made a Peter Rabbit 'doll' and secured a patent (Patent No. 423888) in order to protect her creation from the ravages of the free market (Lear 2007: 172). In this manner, children's literature drove the production and consumption of new commodities and provided a ready-made market for them. Although adults, and especially parents, were likely the purchasers of these items just as they were likely the purchasers of Greenaway's and Potter's books, the dresses and the dolls, like the books, were ultimately destined for the nursery and for child audiences. It is worth noting that children's consumption of commodities is not limited to items that they purchase for themselves: they consume directly and by proxy, deliberately and accidentally, sometimes buying, taking or making items for themselves and sometimes receiving the goods that are bestowed or foisted upon them by adults. Just as many children's books address multiple audiences, many of the commodities that materialized in response to these texts have a dual or even double audience, with both children and adults consuming – or being invited to consume – these items in different ways.

Perhaps the text that generated the greatest number of commodities was Lewis Carroll's *Alice's Adventures in Wonderland*. On 6 June 2001, Sotheby's auctioned a huge collection of memorabilia associated with Alice Liddell and with *Alice's Adventures in Wonderland*. Some of the big-ticket items included photographs and first editions of works by Carroll, whose real name was Charles Lutwidge Dodgson. However, the sale also included a strange array of items including personal effects belonging to Alice Hargreaves (nee Liddell). Lot 90 was a pair of silver buttons in a small presentation box that proclaimed they were 'worn from childhood up to the date of her death' – which is unlikely, considering they were made by the silversmiths George Nathan and Ridley Hayes in Chester in 1896, when Alice was forty-four years old. Despite this obvious oversight, the buttons were expected to make between £1,000 and £1,500. Even stranger was Lot 105: three of Mrs Hargreaves's handkerchiefs. All three bore Alice's initials 'APH', but they were not in good condition. The catalogue notes that one was 'stained and torn', one was 'stained' and the third had 'several darns'. Nevertheless, the catalogue suggested they might fetch £3,000–£5,000. Although silver is, weight-for-weight, more valuable than cotton, and although the craftsmanship on the buttons was finer and more detailed than the machine-made edging around the handkerchiefs, these three soiled hankies were more highly prized. The value of the items is not solely a material one, nor a monetary one but something far more ephemeral. The value that clings to these items stems in part from Alice's celebrity, in part from her association with a famous and well-beloved book. While Carroll's books are lauded as works of fantasy fiction, they were, first and foremost, commercial ventures. As Clayton Tarr observes, 'although Carroll could be neglectful of his financial accounts, he was meticulous about the value and the cost of his books' (2018: 37). The first edition of *Alice's Adventures in Wonderland* was priced at 7s 6d, later reduced to 6s (Lastoria 2019: 196–225). This was the same as an engineer's daily wage at this time (Porter 1998: 176). Though the first printing was unsatisfactory to both Tenniel and Carroll due to the muddy illustrations, Carroll cannily sold these second-rate copies to an American publisher and so recouped at least some of his initial investment. Later, he lamented having to reduce the price of *The Nursery Alice* from 4s to 1s, complaining in a preface to the book that it was

> now to be had on the same terms as the ordinary shilling picture books – although I feel sure that it is, in every quality ... greatly superior to them. Four shillings was a perfectly reasonable price to charge, considering the very heavy initial outlay I had incurred. ... I am selling it at a price which is, to me, much the same thing as *giving* it away. (Carroll [1898] 1920: n. p., emphasis in original)

Carroll kept a close eye on the market value of the Alice books and on the objects that were sold as tie-ins to his literary products, tightly controlling his authorization of this merchandise. Jan Susina details some of the more unusual items including E. Stanley Leathes's *Alice's Wonderland Birthday Book* (1884), The Wonderland Postage-Stamp Case (1890) and a 'Mad Tea-Party' tablecloth (2009: 67–8). On 7 January 1892, Carroll wrote to Alice (Liddell) Hargreaves to offer her a parasol with an ivory handle representing the figures of Tweedledum and Tweedledee (Carroll [1892] 1989: 216). The same year, Jacob & Son produced a 'Through the Looking Glass Biscuit Tin'. Carroll allegedly 'did not like the idea that he was endorsing a brand of biscuit, but was largely pacified by the fact that the manufacturer gave him as many of them (without the biscuits) as Carroll wanted' (Sotheby's 2001: 149). Perhaps most striking is an 1877 advert for Pears

Soap that borrows words and illustrations from Carroll's *Alice's Adventures in Wonderland* to promote Pears as the 'soap of the morning' (Figure 0.2).

Figure 0.2 The commercial and cultural value of children's literature. *Source:* 'Beautiful Soap' Pears Soap advertisement (1871), John Johnson Collection: Soap 7 (11a) © Bodleian Library, University of Oxford 2010.

By using children's literature to advertise soap, the Pears advert implicitly recognizes the commercial value of children's texts. It assumes the consumer is a culturally literate one, familiar with Carroll's text and Tenniel's illustrations, who will instantly recognize the verse and the images used and enjoy the playful intertext. This advert speaks to the child consumer, both as a reader of literature and, potentially, as a user of soap. Through these products and numerous others developed by British companies in the years after their publications, the Alice books become the centre of a complex commercial milieu and gather a nexus of commodities around them. While many children's books did not attain this level of commercial success, it is nevertheless important to acknowledge that the books produced for young readers intersect with, influence and are, in turn, impacted by broader trends in consumer culture. Indeed, similar factors drive the market for both children's reading material and other kinds of consumer goods: in late Victorian Britain, the middle classes enjoyed both an increase in disposable income and an increase in leisure time in which to spend this income. Middle-class children emerged as a distinct market group, and manufacturers and publishers alike were keen to cater to, and to cultivate, the appetites of these new consumers.

Reading objects

While this book sometimes discusses the commodities that surrounded children's literature between 1851 and 1914, my primary interest is in the objects depicted inside the texts, in the ways that ordinary commodities are represented on the page, and in the function of these fictional objects. Reading fictional objects does not always come easily. Like Rudyard Kipling's Kim learning to play the Jewel Game, we have to learn how to pay attention to material goods. Kim is an astute observer of human character, able to remember and imitate the mannerisms, gestures and speech patterns of the many people he encounters on his adventures. Yet when faced with 'a half-handful of clattering trifles' on a copper tray, he is bewildered and unable to remember the objects accurately, and the young boy who plays the Jewel Game against him easily wins ([1901] 2011: 228). Kim is outraged, and insists that they try the game again, '"with common things such as he and I both know"' (230). But this makes no difference and Kim is forced to accept that he needs to learn how to observe objects as closely as he observes people if he is to ever win the Jewel Game. Like Kim, we have to practice giving our attention to objects in literary texts, to take note of their properties and qualities, to recognize their value among other elements of a narrative. This can be difficult because, as Elaine Freedgood argues, 'we have learned to understand [material objects] as largely meaningless: the protocols for reading the realist novel have long focused us on subjects and plots; they have implicitly enjoined us not to interpret many or most of its objects' (2010: 1). As Cynthia Wall notes, we can be tempted to see fictional objects as nothing more than 'visual detail, as pieces of description, and as spatial and narrative markers' (2006: 97). Fictional objects perform various functions: they can appear in texts as narrative devices, as metaphors or as external signs of a character's inner qualities. Descriptions of objects, especially richly ekphrastic descriptions, may lend a sensual, haptic quality to a narrative, or provide a sense of verisimilitude that Roland Barthes terms the 'reality effect' ([1975] 1989: 141–8). Narratives may also call the reader's attention to a particular object, setting it apart from the morass of commodities for special consideration: this may be an object of exceptional material or symbolic value, as in E. Nesbit's *The Story of the Amulet* (1906), or an object around which the axis of a plot turns, as in Robert Louis Stevenson's *Treasure Island* (1883).

For the most part, we are used to having the significance of these special objects made explicit to us by the narrator or by the characters. Like Kim, we are accustomed to and comfortable in reading character, and fall into the habit of seeing objects merely as mute stand-ins for characters. In Brenda's *Froggy's Little Brother* (1875), for example, there is a brief outline of items among which Froggy must choose to sell to the pawnbroker:

> There was the little mattress on which Froggy used to lie when he was Benny's age, and an old waistcoat of father's, and a fur cap, and some shirts in the old deal box, and something else, wrapped up very carefully in a cotton handkerchief, which was very, very sacred, and over which Froggy sometimes shed a flood of tears. This was mother's Sunday best bonnet; the one she had always worn and which Froggy cried over, because he said, 'It looked so like mother!' (1875: 101–2)

As the final item in the litany of objects, the bonnet becomes the culmination of Froggy's collection. Brenda's repeated use of 'very' intensifies the significance of the bonnet; that it is a 'sacred' item amongst mundane items lends it the quality of a relic and, in this way, transforms Froggy's dead mother into a kind of saint. Yet we know nothing about the physical features of the bonnet; we do not know what colour it is, what materials it is made from, whether it is plain or decorated, or whether it retains the scent of the woman who owned it. We know that it provokes an intense physical reaction in Froggy, and that he treasures it so dearly that he would rather face starvation than pawn it. Just as Froggy sees the bonnet as looking 'so like mother', readers may regard any number of fictional objects as mere symbols of the cultural and economic status of a character, or as outward and visible signs of their inner qualities. The habit of reading objects in literary texts as symbols or metaphors distracts us from their quotidian function, and from their true, complex significance. Freedgood's work urges us to re-evaluate fictional objects by 'taking a novelistic thing materially or literally and then following it beyond the covers of the text' (2010: 16). This method of reading allows us to acknowledge both the textual and material properties of the object, to see it simultaneously as a literary and a literal object. Looking at fictional objects in this manner allows us to understand these items within their appropriate historical, social, cultural and economic milieu and affords us a greater appreciation of the intersection between literature, material culture and contemporary attitudes towards children as material subjects.

My focus in *British Children's Literature and Material Culture: Commodities and Consumption 1850–1914* is, therefore, not objects as symbols, or metaphors, or as placeholders for character traits. I am not interested in special, valuable and remarkable objects. I am interested in commodities and their function as commodities within children's books, in the quotidian, fungible items made by mass production and made in such numbers that they become part of the unnoticed background of our lives and the lives of fictional characters. In order to situate these fictional commodities within a broader cultural milieu, I read children's fiction alongside historical documents, shop catalogues, lost property records, and advertisements, and trace connections between fictional objects and the real items that child consumers desired, bought, used, cherished, loathed, broke and threw away. As I am interested in both literary and literal commodities, my primary sources are a mixture of historical and literary texts. This book is made possible by the scholarship that has gone before, not only the interdisciplinary anthologies such as Arjun Appadurai's *The Social Life of Things* (1986) and Tilley, Keane, Kuechler, Rowlands and Spyer's *The Handbook of Material Culture* (2006), but more specifically the collections of essays that speak to and about material cultures of childhood, including Denisoff's *The Nineteenth-Century Child and Consumer Culture*, and David Buckingham and Vebjorg Tingstad's *Childhood and Consumer Culture*. Christopher Parkes's work on the intersections of children's literature and capitalism and Claudia Nelson's work on the impact of capitalism on children's books are especially important to my project, though this book breaks new ground by moving the discussion away from wider economic systems and focusing on fictional children's consumption of commodities in children's literature. My methodology builds upon Bill Brown's work, which reaffirms the quiddity of fictional objects, in order to 'render objects legible' (2003: 15), and Freedgood's, which 'rejoin[s]' (29) the literary and the literal and traces the connections between real, historical objects and their fictional counterparts. By giving fresh attention to the intersections between the real and the fictional, the material and the imagined in British children's books, I offer a new appreciation and understanding of the intimate, even symbiotic, relationship between children's literature and consumer culture.

Structure of this book

Chapters 1–4 trace the changing attitudes towards consumer culture in children's literature, from the celebration of commodities in the mid-nineteenth century, through a period in the latter half of the nineteenth century when both scientific and spiritualist ideas impacted the representation and role of objects in children's literature, to an increasing interest in Fabianism and Marxism that led to a growing unease with consumerism and consumption in the early twentieth century. The chronological structure of the book allows the chapters to trace the development of children's consumer culture in the golden age of children's literature, while also allowing for focused insights into particular groups of texts and authors.

Chapter 1, '"Remarkable and perplexing items": Children and the Great Exhibition', argues that the Great Exhibition of 1851 held in Hyde Park in London was a catalyst in the creation of a new awareness of the child as consumer. While the organizers did not anticipate a significant child audience, enormous numbers of children attended the Exhibition – creating a new market for children's books about the event. I examine the souvenir books and guides produced for child audiences, along with the lost property records for the Exhibition, and argue that these documents reveal that children existed outside of contemporary material culture and had to be inducted into the correct attitudes and approaches to the world of goods. These books cultivated the child visitor to the Exhibition as an informed, discerning and sophisticated consumer of goods. The texts examined here, including *The World's Fair: Or, Children's Prize Gift Book of the Great Exhibition of 1851* (1851), *Uncle Nimrod's First Visit to the Crystal Palace* (n.d.) and Samuel Prout Newcombe's *Little Henry's Holiday at the Great Exhibition* (1851a), served as 'object lessons' that were used to induct child readers into the social, moral and cultural codes of nineteenth-century consumption.

Chapter 2, '"The wonders of common things": Worldly goods in the nineteenth century', explores the ways in which the it-narrative, a genre predominantly associated with the eighteenth century, was revitalized by nineteenth-century authors, who used the genre as a vehicle for scientific education. Though these children's it-narratives have some of the hallmarks of their eighteenth-century predecessors, I argue that they constitute a distinct subgenre, one that firmly situates the child reader among a world of goods. Alongside well-known texts such as A.L.O.E.'s *The Story of a Needle* (1858) and E. M. Stirling's *The History of a Pin; or, The Changes and Chances of an Eventful Life* (1861), I examine lesser-known texts, including Felix Volkhovsky's 'A China Cup' (1898) and Annie Carey's *Wonders of Common Things* (1880). I support my readings of these texts with information drawn from technical manuals, advertisements and descriptive pieces about the manufacture and sale of goods in periodicals, including *Household Words*.

Chapter 3, '"A hailstorm of knitting needles": Other-worldly goods and domestic fantasy', argues that, in the children's fantasy literature of the late nineteenth century, ordinary domestic items are often infused with magical powers. Magical objects, and objects that are animated by supernatural properties, offer a tangible connection between the real world and the fantastic world and, in texts like Carroll's *Through the Looking Glass, and What Alice Found There* (1871), it is the odd behaviour of apparently mundane objects that gives the first indication that the protagonist has crossed over into another world. While modern critical discussions of domestic fantasy identify the genre in terms of its mechanical plot devices (moving from the primary world to the secondary world and back again), I argue that the presence of household items with other-worldly powers are a crucial factor in successful domestic fantasy. This chapter discusses the role of mundane objects in fantasy world building in Carroll's work and in Christina Rossetti's *Speaking Likenesses* (1874) and Mary Louisa Molesworth's *The Cuckoo Clock* (1877). The literary texts examined in this chapter are read alongside historical sources attesting to a growing interest in magic and the supernatural in late-nineteenth-century Britain, particularly the phenomenon of 'table turning', which saw ordinary parlours and sitting rooms transformed into supernatural spaces.

Chapter 4, '"A disgraceful state of things": Bad consumers and bad commodities', charts the growing suspicion of commodity culture in the last years of the nineteenth century and the early years of the twentieth century. As well as an increasing concern about the physical dangers posed by certain items, there is also a growing moral concern for what the object might be and how it might affect the consumer. In the literature of the period, I note the increasing portrayal of commodities as 'things' rather than 'goods'. While objects were inherently passive, *things* could be beguiling, treacherous, even dangerous. In children's literature, this anxiety is reflected in the increased tension between child characters and things. Child characters prove to be ineffective consumers, unable to master the commodities around them. Child characters are seen to break and abuse objects, and objects are seen to damage and hurt their owners. Drawing on Brown's 'Thing Theory' and concentrating on the work of Kenneth Grahame, Beatrix Potter and E. Nesbit, herself a prominent member of the Fabian society, this chapter examines texts in which child characters and things come into direct – and sometimes violent – conflict.

The final chapter of this book, 'Failed palaces and magic cities', uses two exhibitions, the Children's Welfare Exhibition of 1913 and the failed Nottingham Exhibition of 1914, as a means of contextualizing the enormous shifts in children's consumer culture that had taken place in the sixty-odd years since the Great Exhibition of 1851. Many of the authors associated with the golden age of children's literature were themselves young children at the time of that exhibition or grew up in its shadow, immersed in a world that was cluttered with commodities. Their attitudes towards children's consumption and towards children's books as commodities in their own right continued to influence young readers' views of and relationships with other kinds of commodities into the twentieth century. These two final exhibitions – one a bizarre mixture of commercialism and philanthropy and the other an outright failure – exemplify the shifting attitudes towards commodity culture, from celebration to a growing unease, and provide a fitting end point to this study.

1

'Remarkable and perplexing items': Children and the Great Exhibition

Between 1 May and 15 October 1851, the lost property desk in the police station at the Prince's Gate, Hyde Park, took in a remarkable number of items. On 14 January 1852, Superintendent Nicholas Pearce compiled a list of items which remained unclaimed. The 'List of Articles and Money Found in the Exhibition, Hyde Park, Remaining Unclaimed in Possession of the Police' includes

> purses (41), keys (285), handkerchiefs silk & cotton (78) and handkerchiefs, white (719), parasols (363), umbrellas (72), petticoats (2), bustles (2), eye glasses, various (17), opera glasses (2), camp stools (3), bracelets, various (213), spectacles (43), catalogues (87), brooches (500), shawls (43), lockets (22), penknives (16), pencil cases, ivory fasteners for shawls (10), studs (12), watch ornaments (30), shoes and boots (4 ½ pair), silk and other bags (60), silk neck ties (131), sticks and canes (97), capes (13), pairs of gloves (101), pockets and reticules (76), veils, various sorts (150), thimbles (2), pins (25), bustles (2), carpenters rulers (2), clock pendulums (2), tea caddy (1), bayonet (1), toothpick (1). (National Archives, Kew, MEPOL 2/106)

These items were lost by people attending the Great Exhibition of the Works of Industry of All Nations. These forgotten objects were handed in by well-meaning members of the public or gathered by Exhibition staff at the end of each day and brought to the police station at the Prince's gate. There, the items were logged and stored, waiting to be reclaimed by their owners.

Pearce's lost property records offer a counterpoint to the Official Catalogue of the Great Exhibition. Inside the Crystal Palace, thousands of items from all over the world were carefully selected for display, considered, discussed, examined closely by members of the public and the Exhibition jury alike. In the police station, a few yards away, a no less miscellaneous collection of items had been forgotten, overlooked and abandoned. The distance of a few yards is all that seems to separate the three prize-winning brooches exhibited by Messrs Ellis & Son of Exeter and the five hundred brooches kept in a box under the desk in the police station. The *Official Catalogue of the Great Exhibition of the Works of Industry of All Nations* singles out the brooches for special attention as they 'exhibit a great amount of taste, combined with much sensible utility' (1851: 133). They are rendered valuable because of the expensive materials they are made from, and because of their uniqueness and beauty. Pearce's records pay no attention to the appearance, value or aesthetic quality of any of the found items, reducing them to a mass of unremarkable items.

These unremarkable items can, nevertheless, provide remarkable insights into the experience of the average visitor to the Crystal Palace. While the Catalogue shows us what was held up as special and valuable, the lost property records reveal what was ordinary and quotidian. These reveal that while visitors to the Great Exhibition of the World's Industry came to look at displays of objects, they also brought a huge number of objects with them. Some of these items – like keys, thimbles and gloves – are small and slip easily from pockets and fingers. Others – like bustles and petticoats – seem rather more difficult to mislay and raise questions, and eyebrows, about the ways women were using the new, flushing, toilet facilities at the Exhibition. The lost items give us some sense of how people engaged with the Exhibition: they brought opera glasses and eye glasses so they could inspect the exhibits more closely, they brought in baskets of food to avoid paying the extortionate prices for refreshments and carried camp-stools so they could sit down when they got tired. When the heat inside the building became unbearable, they stripped off overcoats and capes, gloves and shawls. Faced, entranced, with the marvellous objects on display – tiny silk flowers and enormous blocks of coal, wine jars and stuffed animals, a model of the human body that expanded from dwarf to colossus at the touch of a button, a tiny steam engine that fit inside a walnut shell – ordinary possessions, it seems, could be easily forgotten.

Pearce's lost property records also bear the imprint of people who have been forgotten and overlooked in discussions of the Great Exhibition and its impact on Victorian culture. Specifically, Pearce's records reveal the presence of children within the Palace. Among the hundreds of items that remained unclaimed were two children's bonnets, and Pearce's records also include letters concerning children who found items and who wanted to claim them for themselves. On 22 May 1851, twelve-year-old William Dixon of Cumberland Street in Brompton found a music holder and a silver and brass part of a French horn. On 27 January 1852, his father, William Dixon, wrote to the commissioner of the Great

Exhibition to ask for the articles. These were dutifully sent to him (Dixon 1852). A little flurry of correspondence documents the experience of Johnnie Taylor who found a little bundle of 'gold trinkets', which included a bundle of small seals, a gold ring and a pencil case. He handed the bundle in to the police. On 5 June 1852, his father John Taylor writes to the police to ask if Johnnie could have the trinkets, if they had not been claimed. A note in Pearce's own writing confirms that the articles mentioned 'have been given up to the mother of the little boy who found them in the Exhibition Building and a receipt taken for the same' (Taylor 1852). Though there is no record of the Police Office at the Prince's Gate taking care of lost children, popular accounts of the Exhibition claim that Pearce and his officers did in fact deal with lost children. The myth that there was 'a police desk for lost children and umbrellas' (Picard 2009) within the Palace itself has proved persistent, fuelled perhaps by contemporary accounts such as this one that declares:

> Of all the stray property found at the exhibition and handed over to the police, the most remarkable and perplexing items come under the head of children; some eighty or ninety boys and girls having lost their friends in the building. (Newcombe 1852: 57)

While there is no evidence to support this claim, that such a claim could be made at all reveals something about contemporary attitudes towards children and anxieties about the place of the child visitor within the Great Exhibition. To describe children as 'remarkable and perplexing items' indicates the strange position children held within Victorian material culture. At the Great Exhibition and elsewhere, they occupy a liminal space between people and things. They are treated at once as consumers and as commodities, as users of items and as items in their own right.

As 'remarkable and perplexing items', children presented the organizers of the Exhibition with some remarkable and perplexing problems. The minute books from the committee meetings record the lengthy discussions and disagreements about the way children were to be treated at the Exhibition: Were children to be treated in exactly the same way as the other patrons? Should they pay the same entrance fees? Were children expected to behave as other patrons did? Should allowances be made for them and, if so, what would these allowances be? The fact that children are only mentioned in the minutes of the Royal Commission meetings after the Exhibition had already opened suggests that the Commissioners had not anticipated a significant child audience for the event. Their subsequent dithering suggests a degree of uncertainty about the position of children as spectators. The minutes of the 41st meeting of the Commissioners on Saturday, 10 May 1851, note that 'the Report finally recommended that Children [sic] under 13 years should be admitted to the Exhibition at half-price if satisfactory arrangements can be made by the executive committee' (Commissioners of the Great Exhibition, Unpublished Minutes, 1851). The nature of the 'satisfactory arrangements' required to accommodate child visitors was not described. At the next meeting of the Commissioners, held, somewhat bizarrely, later that same day, they decided to postpone making a final decision about this recommendation. However, at the following meeting on 12 May 1851, the Commissioners decided to introduce '1 shilling' days and the proposal for half-price children's tickets is not mentioned again in the minutes, perhaps because the new lower price was deemed acceptable for all patrons.

As a result, there is no accurate record of how many children passed through the doors of the Crystal Palace between May and October 1851. While there were separate ticket prices for men and women and so the accounts of the Exhibition rigorously record the number of male and female visitors, it is not clear what percentage of those visitors were children. Considering that meticulous records were kept about every aspect of the Exhibition by the Commissioners for the Great Exhibition – from the temperature inside the hall (*First Report of the Commissioners for the Exhibition of 1851* (1852), Appendix X: 67–8), to the amount of bread and cake consumed (Appendix XXIX: 150), to the number of timber boards used (Appendix XI: 70–1) – it is remarkable that there is such silence around the question of children. Yet it is clear that children did visit the Palace, and in large numbers. Children are a constant presence in the visual records of the Palace, appearing in works as diverse as H. Sharles's 'Royal Procession with Queen Victoria at the Great Exhibition' (1851), which shows the royal family standing in the middle of the transept surrounded by applauding crowds, as well as in the cartoons published in *Punch* and other periodicals. While children are often only depicted as minor figures in the background of these images, John Leech's cartoon series, 'Memorials of the Great Exhibition', foregrounds children's experiences of the Exhibition, often to comic effect (Leech 1886: 228–40). He depicts children in all parts and at all stages of their visits to the Exhibition: crammed into lodging houses with their parents, preparing for the visit by being dressed in their best clothes, dragged by the hands around exhibits, eating picnics in the transept. Leech's cartoons suggest that even babes-in-arms were brought to the Exhibition (it is not clear whether the infant would have been charged a shilling or not) and that some children found the experience delightful whereas others were bored rigid (Figure 1.1).

Figure 1.1 Bored and hungry children at the Great Exhibition. *Source*: John Leech's *Pictures of Life and Character from the Collection of 'Mr. Punch' Vol. 1* (Leech 1886: 236), illustration by J. Leech, 'Dinner-Time at the Crystal Palace', memorials of the Great Exhibition 1851 No. xxv.

While the number of children who may have entered with their families, or in smaller groups, is not recorded, the records do show that over 35,000 children visited with school groups and charity groups. Accurate accounts of the school visits only begin on 9 July. Before that date, over 4,000 children attended the Exhibition from organizations including the Foundling Hospital at Spitalfields

(80 pupils), Mr Jay's School Argyll, Bath and Bristol (150 pupils) and the Royal Navy school at Greenwich (457 pupils), although no exact dates are recorded for their visits (*First Report of the Commissioners for the Exhibition of 1851 to Parliament* (1852), Appendix XVIII: 92). The lack of precise records makes it difficult to get at the experience of the child visitors to the Exhibition. As a result, the children at the Exhibition appear even further removed than their elders from our ability to acknowledge their existence. Our views of children at the Exhibition are second-hand, at a remove. We catch glimpses of them in the catalogue and in the minute books of the Commission. We peep at them through the eyes of letter writers and diarists and spy on them in the paintings and sketches made by artists. These glimpses allow us to puzzle out what children's experiences of the Exhibition were really like and to discover how these 'remarkable and perplexing' people engaged with and understood the objects on display.

Learning to look

The Great Exhibition ushered in a new kind of material culture, one that combined the massing of vast quantities of items with a kind of passive consumerism in which people gazed upon goods but did not necessarily seek to possess them. The innovations of the Exhibition were twofold: it changed how objects were displayed and changed how people engaged with them. Thomas Richards argues that the exhibits in the Crystal Palace constituted a new kind of display – perfectly lit, perfectly ordered and arranged just out of reach. The glass walls and the high, narrow columns of iron that supported the roof allowed for excellent visibility and very little stood in the way of the visitors and the objects on display. Richards points out that 'the organizers of the Exhibition had done their best to bring people as close as possible to things without actually allowing them to touch what they saw; some barrier, a counter or a rope or a policeman, always intervened to assert the inviolability of the object' (1990: 32). The objects on display were physically out of reach and also figuratively unattainable because none of the objects were for sale. At least, not formally. Items could be sold by exhibitors once the Exhibition had closed. These objects were, therefore, not like ordinary commodities and could not be treated in the same way as quotidian goods. Andrew Miller argues that the way these objects were organized and displayed affected the way people behaved and responded to them: 'Both department stores and exhibition halls created spectacles before which people adopted an attitude of solitary and passive observation' (1995: 57). The result was 'a more disengaged, solitary and reflective practice' than what had gone before (57). Contemporary accounts of the Exhibition attest to the impact of these innovations on the visitors. In a letter to her father on 7 June 1851, Charlotte Brontë describes the visitors to the Palace as being in a sort of trance, moving like sleepwalkers around the exhibits:

> The multitude filling the great aisles seem ruled and subdued by some invisible influence. Amongst the thirty thousand souls that peopled it the day I was there not one loud noise was to be heard, not one irregular movement seen; the living tide rolls on quietly, with a deep hum like the sea heard from the distance. (Brontë [1851c] 1908: 215–16)

In Brontë's description, the Crystal Palace takes on the air of a sacred space where an 'invisible influence' controls and subdues the public. Their hushed voices indicate a sort of reverence for the objects on display and so the Palace is endowed with the properties of a sacred space, a space of order, regularized movement and reflection. In commanding new levels of reverence and respect, the objects on display in the Crystal Palace, like the objects on display in the vitrines of the new department stores, were 'set apart from everyday things' (Bowlby 1985: 2). The fact that the objects in the Crystal Palace were displayed without price tags and were not available to buy further enhanced their unobtainability. These objects were not true commodities, they were removed from exchange value just as they were removed from use value: the clothes on display had never been worn, the chairs never been sat on, the machines never actually used in factories. These were not ordinary objects but rarefied examples of the very best that the world could produce: the finest printed fabrics from India, the most beautiful lace from Belgium, the most impressive furs from Canada, the very best steelwork from Sheffield. These were not commonplace objects to be used but exceptional things to be celebrated and revered.

The correct way to appreciate these objects was by simply looking at them. The items on display were commodities in appearance only – they could not be bought or used – and so the only appropriate way to engage with them was through superficial glances and disinterested and reflective looking. This sort of detached gazing was on the rise in mid-nineteenth century. Rachel Bowlby explains that the experience of the nineteenth-century consumer, whether in the Crystal Palace or in one of the new department stores, was primarily visual. She argues that 'modern consumption is a matter not of basic things bought for definite needs, but of visual fascination and remarkable sights' (1985: 1). Just like the window shoppers, then, the visitor to the Exhibition was, truly, a spectator. They experienced the wonders of the Palace through the gaze. While some visitors felt this purely visual experience was somewhat lacking – Brontë wrote to her friend, Miss Wooler, on 14 July to complain that '[the Exhibition's] wonders appeal too exclusively to the eye, and rarely touch the heart or head' (Brontë [1851d] 1908: 224) – others revelled in the spectacle. John Tallis argued that the event 'was first and foremost ... a panorama' (1852: 51–5) and contemporary accounts of the Exhibition in newspapers and periodicals emphasize the value of simply looking at things – the accounts are full of imperatives to 'look', 'glance' and 'gaze' at the objects. The actual usefulness or commercial value of the objects on display did not really matter. As with the window shoppers in the early department stores, for these visitors to the Exhibition 'the pleasure of looking, *just* looking, [was] itself the commodity for which the money [was] paid' (Bowlby 1985: 6).

But while adult visitors to the Crystal Palace seemed to be attuned to the unspoken rules of '*just* looking' and quite at ease with the passive, disinterested sort of browsing that the Palace inspired, the child visitors neither knew about these rules nor respected the inviolability of the objects they saw. On 11 July 1851, Charles Dickens, who had sat briefly on one of the subcommittees for the Exhibition,[1] wrote to a friend, Lavinia Watson, describing the antics of a group of one hundred schoolchildren who were taken to visit the Crystal Palace. He notes the children's urge to make physical contact with the objects on display. He writes that they 'went tottering and staring all over the place – the greater part wetting their forefingers, and drawing a wavy pattern over every accessible object' (Dickens [1851] 2012: 234). The children feel the need to touch the displays, to reach out to and mark every surface within reach. Similarly, in the visual records children are shown as active participants at the Exhibition rather than passive spectators. John Nash's painting of the Chinese Court shows two little girls – one leaning against a dais, facing the viewer directly and the other standing gazing intently at the display, her hands just touching the edge of the platform on which a collection of vases and ceramics stand. Her intense focus on the objects is accompanied by a light physical touch, indicating that she enjoys the Exhibition by both looking at and handling it. Looking, for this child, is as much a tactile, sensual, bodily act as an abstract, intellectual one (Figure 1.2).

In John Absolon's watercolour painting 'Part of the Chine Court' (1851), featuring the same part of the Exhibition, a little boy reaches out a hand to brush the base of a statue as he passes by. His passing glance is accompanied

Figure 1.2 A child engaging with the exhibits in the Chinese Court by both looking and touching. *Source: Dickinsons' Comprehensive Pictures of the Great Exhibition of 1851: From the Originals Painted for H.R.H. Prince Albert,* Vol. 1. (1854: pl. 24), illustration by J. Nash, 'China'.

by a glancing touch. Like the children in Dickens's letter and the girl in Nash's painting, this boy has an urge to physically touch the objects on display and to experience the Exhibition not just visually, but bodily too (Figure 1.3).

These accounts reveal that child visitors to the Exhibition engaged with the material goods on display in a way different from the adult visitors around them. Their urge to touch, taste and press up against the objects around them indicates that the special rules concerning goods on display had not filtered down to all members of Victorian society. They demanded, and indulged in, their own form of consumption which privileged the tactile over the visual, and the bodily experience over the intellectual one. They did not adhere to the rules of 'just looking' as older consumers did and so they cannot be said to have the same understanding of, or appreciation for, the spectacle. As a result, the child visitors to the Palace could not be guaranteed to interpret the objects in the same way as their parents. The intended audience of the

Figure 1.3 A young visitor to the Great Exhibition reaches out to touch a display. *Source*: John Absolon, 'Part of the Chine Court (from the Crystal Palace)' (1851) © V&A Museum E.9-2007.

Exhibition, the experienced, adult audience, who knew how to observe objects in the correct fashion, could readily appreciate the symbolic value and cultural significance of the Crystal Palace – as a space to promote world peace, industry and harmonious trade relationships, and the importance of labour and production. The intended visitor was a practiced and knowledgeable reader of objects who could confidently interpret the meanings of the things they saw. These informed visitors could be relied on to know, for example, that the statue of the lion in the centre court signified power and majesty and was an emblem of the British Empire, and that the infant holding a bow and arrow on the ornamental fountain in the North Transept was in fact Cupid and to recall the relevant mythology ('List of Statuary', 1851: 8–9). Much of the symbolic power of the Exhibition rested on the visitors' ability to read and interpret the displays correctly. As inexperienced readers of material culture and naïve consumers, child visitors to the Exhibition risked misinterpreting the nature and function of the Exhibition. The objects on display did not signify to child visitors as they did to adults and so the children who came to the Great Exhibition were in danger of misunderstanding what they saw.

Getting lost

It was not easy to make sense of the Great Exhibition, even for adults. Joseph Paxton's Palace was a bewildering place and visitors found it difficult to navigate the displays. There were more than 100,000 objects on display and over 10 miles of exhibits arranged across the transepts and nave of the Crystal Palace. Richard Weston argues that the structure of the building itself contributed to the confusion; the space itself was 'almost entirely devoid of the familiar cues from which people were accustomed to make sense of architectural space. It was too vast, too mind-numbingly repetitive and too transparent and diffusely lit to comprehend in traditional terms' (2001: 30). An article in *The Spectator*, 'Visits to the Great Exhibition of Industry' on 10 May 1851, declared that 'the eye is at first astonished by the enormous extent of the central vista' (Strassavuso The Prevalent, 1851: 445). The enormity of the space was enhanced by the regular placement of statues along the length of the central passage and the harmonized colours of the columns and ironwork so that the impression was of an immense pattern, repeating endlessly, as far as the eye could see. The result was an almost overwhelming sense of disorientation. Contemporary accounts attest to the confusion that accompanied trips to the Exhibition. In his letter to Lavinia Watson, Dickens confesses to feeling 'used up' by the Exhibition. He writes:

> I don't say 'there's nothing in it' – there's too much. I have only been twice. So many things bewildered me. I have a natural horror of sights, and the fusion of so many sights in one has not decreased it. (Dickens [1851] 2012: 234)

Charlotte Brontë visited five times and on 2 June 1851 wrote to tell Ellen Nussey that it was 'a marvellous, stirring, bewildering sight, a mixture of genii palace and a mighty bazaar' (Brontë [1851b] 1908: 214). Her letters to friends and family indicate an uncertainty about the experience – she vacillates between praise and dismissal, between enthusiasm and ennui. In a letter to her father on 30 May 1851 she writes:

> The interior is like a mighty Vanity Fair. The brightest colours blaze on all sides; and wares of all kinds, from diamonds to spinning jennies and printing presses, are there to be seen. It was very fine, gorgeous, animated, bewildering. ([1851a] 1908: 213)

When Brontë refers to 'Vanity Fair' she is surely thinking of a scene in Bunyan's *The Pilgrim's Progress* (1678) rather than W. M. Thackeray's recent novel.[2] In Bunyan's book, the streets of Vanity Fair are divided into 'the Britain Row, the French Row, the Italian Row, the Spanish Row, the German Row' ([1678] 1996: 72–3) and so on and the areas of the Exhibition were similarly divided according to country. This subdivision of the Palace did not lead to greater coherence, however. Rather than making 'one complete whole' as claimed in the *Illustrated London News*, the Exhibition was a fractured and disorderly institution (Richards 1990: 30). Richards comments that 'there was not even a pretence of order on the east side' and that the foreign part of the Exhibition 'looked like a dishevelled cabinet of curiosities' (25). An article in *Household Words* suggested that there were in fact two exhibitions – the 'great exhibition' and 'the little one' – and that the British part of the displays was different in quality and tone from the foreign portions of the Exhibition. However, even to argue that there were two distinct halves to the Exhibition imparts a sense of order and organization that the event did not really have. The Exhibition took place at the beginning of the first great age of curatorship, before the professionalization of curatorship and display and, though there was an organizing committee, there was no one person with organizational oversight of the way the items in each part of the Exhibition would be arranged or displayed. The accumulation of vast numbers of artefacts from across the globe, the large and relatively disparate audience and the sheer scale of the Exhibition venue meant that it was difficult, if not impossible, to render the material as a digestible whole.

In such a bewildering space there was a very real danger of becoming literally and figuratively lost, especially for small children. The literary accounts of the Exhibition reveal that child visitors were expected to feel disorientated and confused. In *Mamma's Visit with Her Little Ones to the Great Exhibition* (1852) Mamma warns her children to stay by her side, worried that 'you will perhaps lose yourselves, and I shall never be able to find you amongst so many people' (1852: 11). It seems that becoming lost was a real danger. In his letter to Lavinia Watson, Dickens recounts an anecdote about a child who went missing while on a trip to the Crystal Palace with his school:

> One Infant strayed. He was not missed. Ninety and nine were taken home, supposed to be the whole collection, but this particular Infant went to Hammersmith. He was found by the Police at night, going round and round the Turnpike – which he still supposed to be a part of the Exhibition. He had the same opinion of the police. Also of Hammersmith Workhouse, where he passed the night. When his mother came for him in the morning he asked when it would be over? It was a Great Exhibition, he said, but he thought it long. (Dickens [1851] 2012: 234–5)

This little boy was doubly lost: he was lost because he wandered off and lost because he was utterly bewildered. He simply couldn't tell the difference between the Exhibition and the outside world, between the things on display and the things in everyday life. Other contemporary accounts suggest that child visitors struggled to separate the important from the unimportant and the great and noble aims of the Exhibition were lost on them. We see the effect of these misunderstandings in fictional accounts too. In one of John Leech's cartoons, a young boy is promised sixpence if he can tell his uncle what he 'most admired' at the Crystal Palace to which he 'unhesitatingly' replies 'the veal and 'am pies and the ginger beer' (Leech 1886: 127). His concern is entirely for the corporeal and his appetite as a consumer is limited to what he can literally consume and absorb into his body. In Samuel Prout Newcombe's book *Little Henry's Holiday* (1851a), Rose seems to struggle to tell the real from the unreal. The moment she walks through the door, Rose exclaims, 'Ah! Here is the *Queen*!' Her Papa patiently responds, 'No it is only her majesty's portrait – but it is a very pretty painting' (Newcombe 1851a: 49, emphasis in original). Considering that Queen Victoria's image – on postage stamps and coins and prints – would be far more familiar to Rose than the woman herself, Papa's correction seems overbearingly patronizing. Whether or not Rose is really unable to tell the difference between the Queen herself and a representation of her in oils, it suits Papa's purposes to interpret her words as confirmation of her ignorance. He decides that she is such an inexperienced reader of material culture that she cannot fully distinguish living people from inanimate objects. These examples raise questions about how children understood and related to the material objects on display and support contemporary fears that, unaided, child visitors may not make sense of the Exhibition at all.

The fears that the true significance of the Great Exhibition would be lost on child visitors prompted many people to write to the Commissioners begging them to organize talks or lectures for child visitors to help them understand the function and the content of the Exhibition. On 9 May 1851, Joseph Soul, the secretary of the Orphans Working School, wrote to Prince Albert to ask, not only for free tickets for the orphans but also that as

> they [the orphans] are necessarily stuck out from the World and see little except by an occasional holiday ... so that the useful and beautiful are very much lost to them. ... Perhaps a sermon or lecture could be given to them in the transept on the nature and objects of the Exhibition by some one competent to impart

the useful information – this would greatly add to their pleasure and profit. (Soul 1851)

Though his letter mentions both pleasure and profit, and focuses on the material elements of the Exhibition, Soul's letter also draws, consciously or otherwise, on religious imagery. The 'sermon' to be delivered in the transept lends the Crystal Palace the air of a cathedral and it is clear that, for Soul, the 'objects of the Exhibition' are its moral and spiritual aims rather than mundane stuff on display. Soul's letter indicates a belief that, unlike adult visitors, children who visited the Exhibition needed to be guided. They needed to be inducted into material culture and shown how to read and understand the objects around them. Soul's plea was ignored. There is no record of a response from the Commissioners to Soul's letter and the Commissioners did not grant the orphans, or anyone else, free tickets. Nor did the Commissioners organize any lectures or talks for young visitors. While the Commissioners were eager that the Exhibition would have an educational and morally didactic function, their intended audience was exclusively adult. An article in *The Spectator* establishes that lectures and classes for adults were held in the building and, the very next day after Joseph Soul wrote his letter, that 'Professor Cowper, of King's College, has commenced a series of lectures to his class on the building and its contents and Professor Ansted is said to be now busily making arrangements for the formation of classes in mineralogy and chemistry, to whom he will deliver practical lectures in the building itself' (Strassavuso The Prevalent, 1851: 446). Furthermore, the article notes that 'the Executive Committee are stated to be desirous of giving all possible facilities to the great Metropolitan schools for carrying out such excellent purposes' (446). Yet there is no evidence that any lectures or sermons for children took place in the building. For the Commissioners, child visitors were 'remarkable and perplexing items' that presented a puzzle they were not interested in solving.

Guiding children

Children proved to be an unexpectedly large and potentially lucrative audience for the Exhibition and the Commissioners' lack of interest in the unprecedented number of child visitors left a gap in the market. In the absence of any official material or guidebooks aimed at child readers, a large number of writers, publishers and toy manufacturers sought to capitalize on this new opportunity.

Among 'the crowding masses of men and things' (Horne and Dickens 1851: 357) children could easily become lost and so number of texts which sought to guide the child visitor, to interest them in the Palace of Industry, to instil in them the ideological values of the Exhibition, and to induct them into the proper ways of looking at and appreciating material objects, were published in 1851. Alongside the souvenir handkerchiefs and gloves and snuff boxes marketed to the adult visitors, a number of children's souvenirs of the Exhibition survive. There are delicate die-cut paper roses that unfold to reveal a series of images of the Exhibition and little paper fans printed with the façade of the Palace and a puzzle-book *The Crystal Labyrinth* by John Eyre, a maze game for children in which the centre is represented as the interior of the Exhibition building. There were also a number of coloured perspective 'views', concertina-folded paper dioramas which, when opened out and viewed from the correct angle, recreated a view of the great hall of the Exhibition. While we cannot be sure if these items were marketed exclusively to children, they bear a striking resemblance to the perspective 'peep-show' views, sometimes called tunnel-books, that were popular with children at the time. These flimsy, mass-produced souvenirs accentuate the uniqueness and significance of the Exhibition, yet on the other hand, while the Exhibition would be short-lived, these souvenirs seemed to promise the young consumer the chance to remember and revisit the Exhibition forever. Susan Stewart argues that souvenirs offer the possibility of 'perpetual consumption' (1993: 135) and notes that children are the main market for this kind of mass-produced souvenir object. She writes:

> We must distinguish between souvenirs of exterior sights ... which most often are representations and are purchasable, and souvenirs of individual experiences, which most often are samples and are not available as general consumer goods. ... Children are the major consumers of mass-produced souvenirs because they, unlike adults, have few souvenirs of the second type and thus must be able to instantly purchase a sign of their own life histories. (138–9)

The makers and sellers of souvenirs of the Great Exhibition obviously understood the preferences of these young consumers, and deliberately targeted the child visitors with an array of commodities designed just for them. These paper souvenirs often appealed to the child visitor's desire to touch: little hands could unfold the die-cut scenes, adjust the dioramas, move little pieces around the game board or trace the outlines of the maze with a finger. These souvenirs memorialized the Exhibition but also afforded the child consumer a new sensual intimacy with the materials on display.

In addition to brightly coloured paper ephemera, child consumers were also addressed through pamphlets and chapbooks printed to celebrate and commemorate the Exhibition, and through books which sought to guide the child reader through the Exhibition space and help them make sense of the chaotic assemblage of material goods inside the Crystal Palace. For the most part, these texts have been overlooked by critics and historians but though they do not always have the highest literary quality, they provide significant insight into children's experiences of the Great Exhibition and so enable us to understand children's place within Victorian material culture more generally. Some of these souvenir books, like *The Fine Crystal Palace the Prince Built* (n.d.), focus exclusively on the 'lions' of the Exhibition, and make use of highly coloured images of the Palace and variations of the prints that were already in circulation to take advantage of public interest in the event. These texts highlight the main attractions of the Exhibition and draw the reader's attention directly towards the most important items on display. Some of the texts work hard to address their intended audience and to introduce the young reader to unfamiliar concepts through a familiar format. For example, *The Fine Crystal Palace the Prince Built* positions itself as a children's text by using the nursery rhyme 'The House That Jack Built' as the basis for the text. While the rhyme had been used before as the basis of political satire (George Cruikshank had published a very unflattering 'The Political House That Jack Built' in 1819), the rhyme was primarily associated with the nursery and was often bound for publication with other nursery rhymes and fairy tales including an anonymous, *The House That Jack Built: Also, The History of Mrs. Williams. And Her Plumb Cake, Which She Mathematically Divided among Her Pupils, according to Their Merit: The Story of Little Red Riding Hood* (1790) and William Byrd's *Cock Robin, The House That Jack Built, History of an Apple Pye, and Other Entertainments* (1800). The rhyme remained popular in the nineteenth century: Randolph Caldecott illustrated a version in 1878 and Walter Crane illustrated a version in 1886. *The Fine Crystal Palace the Prince Built* bridges the gap between printed ephemera and proper books: it is primarily a vehicle for illustrations and, because the cumulative rhyme is largely repetitive, it does not offer much by way of literary content or narrative. However, it is instructive and the repetition has the effect of making the central messages insistent and memorable. The child reader is left in no doubt who built the Crystal Palace and for what purpose. The reader is also told which are the most important exhibits and where they came from. Moreover, the reader is reassured of the value of the Exhibition – it is held in a 'fine' palace and the things on display are 'exquisite', 'beautiful', 'fair' and 'rich'. The reader is reminded that 'it is well worth the money/we paid to come in, and see just what we please' (*The Fine Crystal Palace the Prince Built*, n.d.: n.p.). This book places emphasis squarely on the visual aspects of the Exhibition and encourages the child reader to participate in passive enjoyment of the spectacle. For example, the narrator refers to the 'beautiful teas' from China and gives no sense as to how these teas taste or smell: they, like everything else in the Exhibition, are valued primarily for their visual properties. Viewed in this light, *The Fine Crystal Palace the Prince Built* becomes didactic rather than simply entertaining. The book acts as a guide to the Exhibition that shows the child reader both what was on display and how they should appreciate it. The repetitive verses have a mnemonic as well as explanatory function: as the reader repeats the verses, the narrator's message is reiterated again and again until it is, presumably, internalized.

Other souvenir texts focused on celebrating and memorializing a particular item or collection of items on display and highlighted exhibits that child visitors were most likely to be keen on. Examples of this sort of souvenir include *The Comical Creatures from Wurtemberg* [sic] (1851) which, while it is presented as 'a clever and a pleasant memento of the Great Exhibition' (n.p.), also offers a series of unique stories based on Herrmann Ploucquet's groups of taxidermy animals. Ploucquet's stuffed animals were considered 'one of the most remarkable features of the exhibition' ('The Comical Creatures from Wurtemberg', 12 August 1851: 6). The preface to *The Comical Creatures* declares that 'everyone, from her Majesty the Queen down to the least of the charity-boys, hastens to see the Stuffed animals from the Zollverein; everyone lingers over them and laughs at them as long as the crowd will allow; and everyone talks of them afterwards with a smile and a pleasing recollection' (n.p.). Indeed, Queen Victoria recorded in her diary that his work was 'really marvellous' (16 May 1851). The text is positioned as a memento of the Exhibition, which aims to 'perpetuate' (*The Comical Creatures*, 1851: n.p.) the images of the stuffed animals so that readers can continue to enjoy looking at the daguerreotypes long after the Exhibition has closed. Ploucquet's stuffed animals, and the folktales they represented, were also the subject of some of the souvenir books in George Routledge & Co.'s *Aunt Mavor's Picture Books for Little Children* series. *The Comical Creatures* records and also innovates, offering humorous stories about the scenes to entertain and engage the reader who may or may not have been able to see Ploucquet's animals for themselves.

While *The Comical Creatures*, much like Ploucquet's stuffed animals, appealed to a broad audience, the *Aunt Mavor's* series was aimed exclusively at young readers. These books exemplify the way publishers monetized the young visitors' experience of the Great Exhibition. The books were sold at two different price points – sixpence for the version printed on paper and one shilling for the 'everlasting' version printed on cloth. The 'everlasting' book encourages the buyer to connect the material object with a sense of enduring memories, promising the chance of 'perpetual consumption'. The more expensive the product, it suggests, the more likely the child reader was to remember their experiences of the Crystal Palace forever. There are indications, however, that even the 'everlasting' books were rather cheaply produced. The illustrations were cannily recycled so that, for instance, the image of 'the beautiful doll's house all made by a young lady' in *Dolls and Sights of the Great Exhibition* (n.d.) is identical to the image of the house where the young protagonist Polly and her family live in *Little Polly's Doll's House* (n.d.).

While *Dolls and Sights of the Great Exhibition*, like the other texts in *Aunt Mavor's* series, claims to act as an aide-memoire, the implied reader is one who has no first-hand experience of the Crystal Palace. The narrator's tone is one of nostalgia, looking back over the exhibits:

> I am going to tell you something about the dolls at the Great Exhibition. You cannot think how beautiful they were, and how like life. But you shall hear, and if you are good girls, I dare say mama will one of these days take you to buy you one like them. They were not common dolls, made of great clumsy blocks of wood, with a nail run through their heads to keep the hair on. They had wax faces, as soft as velvet, beautiful hair curled and plaited like your own, and their clothes were all properly made and put on neatly. (*Dolls and Sights*, n.d.: 1)

Here, the Exhibition is described as something that has passed into memory for the narrator but which cannot even be summoned in the imagination of the child readers. While the narrator has an enduring memory of the Exhibition, the child reader must rely on a material object – the book – and an adult authority – the implicitly adult narrator – to mediate between them and the actual event. The child cannot experience the Exhibition unaided. The narrator suggests that the child reader does not have the faculties to think independently about the Exhibition, and so they must trust the narrator to guide them through the objects on display. The readers are told that they 'cannot think' how lovely these dolls were and the narrator takes great pains to contrast the lovely and 'properly made' dolls that were on display with the 'clumsy' ones that are ordinarily available and so establishes the Exhibition as a space outside of quotidian material culture. The readers, however, are assured that if they are good girls, they will be rewarded with a doll 'like' one of the ones in the Exhibition. By promising material rewards for good behaviour, the narrator establishes a direct correlation between objects and moral lessons and, in so doing, sets up a correlation between moral goodness and the goods within the Crystal Palace.

The most sort of common souvenir books are those in which the child reader experiences, or re-experiences, the Exhibition vicariously through the experiences of a young character who is guided through the Exhibition by an older and more experienced character. In *Uncle Nimrod's First Visit to the Exhibition*, a book in the *Aunt Mavor's* series, four children Jack, Harry, Jane and Fanny are taken to see the Exhibition by their Uncle Nimrod. The children are uninitiated in the art of looking. When they arrive at the Palace, 'they knew not what to look at; it was so full of fine things' (*Uncle Nimrod's First Visit*, n.d.: 1). Happily, Uncle Nimrod is an informed consumer and can confidently interpret the significance of the displays for his young charges. He 'has read a great deal and knew a great deal about most things' (2). Nimrod begins his tour of the Palace by inculcating the correct sort of behaviour in his young wards:

> He did not let them run up and down like silly little boys and girls, but he took them to see one thing at a time and made them look at everything in a proper manner, and told them all about it. (2)

Here, a clear distinction is made between the correct and incorrect sorts of behaviour at the Exhibition. The 'silly' children who run up and down are contrasted with the 'wise' Uncle Nimrod who examines items one by one. The child characters, and by extension the child readers, are inducted into the proper social codes and the correct methods for looking at the objects on display. *Uncle Nimrod's First Visit* (n.d.) and its sequels, *Uncle Nimrod's Second Visit to the Exhibition* (n.d.) and *Uncle Nimrod's Third Visit to the Exhibition* (n.d.), focus on particular groups of objects too – which emphasizes the organizational system underlying the Exhibition. The first book concentrates on natural objects, the second on models of buildings and figures, and the third on the different countries that supplied materials for the foreign part of the Exhibition. In each of the descriptions of objects, the narrator emphasizes the visual. The child's gaze is continually directed towards the objects: 'Look at the Diving Dress made of India-rubber cloth' (*Uncle Nimrod's First Visit*, n.d.: 2), 'Look at the great clumsy elephant, with the richly gilt Howdah on his back' (6), 'Here is a very pretty model of the Crystal Palace made of lead and glass. If you look inside, you will see the long range of galleries, and the stairs reaching to each' (*Uncle Nimrod's Second Visit*, n.d.: 1). The value of things is entirely predicated on their appearance. The Koh-i-noor, for example, 'does not look well at all' because it is not properly cut (*Uncle Nimrod's First Visit*, n.d.: 6). The child visitor/reader is encouraged only to imagine engaging the other senses. For example, the narrator invites the visitor/reader to 'look at this case of French horns, trumpets, and trombones, and think what a noise they will make' (*Uncle Nimrod's Third Visit*, n.d.: 6). The instruments are meant to be played and heard but, here, the act of looking is sufficient to enable the visitor/reader to appreciate the other properties of the instruments and there is no indication that any of the other senses should be employed at all. The three *Uncle Nimrod* books do not merely describe the Exhibition for the child audience but also introduce this audience to the correct methods of reading and interpreting these objects. The child visitor/reader is encouraged to move in an orderly manner, to look quietly from an appropriate distance, to think carefully about the other properties the objects might hold and to be content with just looking.

Similarly, *Mamma's Visit with Her Little Ones to the Great Exhibition* (1852) places strict emphasis on the value of looking at the objects on display in the Crystal Palace. The children are directed to 'look' and 'see' the displays and though Mamma patiently explains the significance of many of the objects, the children's engagement with them is limited to regarding from a distance. Indeed, the main attraction of the Exhibition is the chance to see things.

> They next visited the machinery rooms, where they saw steam-engines at work, and printing, weaving, and many other wonders going on, of which they had heard, but only *heard* before. (*Mamma's Visit*, 1852: 20, emphasis in original)

On the one hand, hearing is presented as inferior to seeing as it puts the children at a further remove from the objects. On the other hand, hearing is presented as a source of irritation – the narrator notes that the children are 'glad to leave that noisy part of the building' (21). Noise and listening to it is not a good way to engage with material objects. On the contrary, seeing is conflated with understanding throughout the text. When Mamma asks, 'Do you not see, Mary?' she merges sight with insight (22). The relationship between looking and learning was a key factor in the success of the Great Exhibition (and in later world trade fairs for which it was the exemplar). For Paul Bourget, writing about the Columbian Exposition, the stare of the exhibition-goer was something like the concentrated gaze of the attentive student. Bourget notes their 'blank avidity, as if they were walking in the midst of a colossal lesson in things' (Bourget 1895: 231). The Exhibition offered the opportunity to learn about the world – its geography, its natural resources, its cultures – through the objects on display.

Although the child visitors to the Exhibition seemed unable to learn simply by looking, they could nevertheless be taught to engage in object lessons.

Head, hand and heart

In the nineteenth century, the standard way to introduce a child to material culture was through an object lesson. An object – such as a candle or a pen – was used as a discussion piece or as the basis for a lesson on abstract ideas or principles. These object lessons were derived from the new educational system developed by the Swiss educationalist Johann Heinrich Pestalozzi (1746–1827), which emphasized learning through observation and deductive reasoning. Pestalozzi's approach, outlined in his book *How Gertrude Teaches Her Children* (1801), promoted an educational practice which was dialogic, child-directed and spontaneous. Children would not be supplied with the answers to questions by their teachers, but would be encouraged to discover solutions through the use of deduction. Pestalozzi advocated an educational practice that engaged the head, hand and heart and prioritized learning through looking, handling and using material objects within the classroom (Murché 1895: v–vi). The object lesson became the centrepiece of Victorian education. Texts designed for use in schools, such as *Model Lessons for Infant School Teachers and Nursery Governesses* (1838) or *Information on Common Objects for the Use of Infant and Juvenile Schools and Nursery Governesses* (1845), show how versatile this particular form of pedagogy could be. Familiar objects could be used as the foundation for lessons on anything and everything from geology to Genesis. Teachers were encouraged to bring objects into classrooms and to let the students touch, smell and taste things, to learn through trial and error, and to learn through play. These texts promote a surprisingly child-centred pedagogy, enabling children to learn through tactile engagement with the objects, observation and enquiry. By using a question-and-answer model, these texts encourage dialogic learning rather than monologic teaching, thereby fostering critical thinking rather than rote learning.

Perhaps the most significant of the 'object lesson' texts for child readers that emerged from the Great Exhibition were those produced by Samuel Prout Newcombe. Newcombe had an unusual career: he appears on various census forms as a schoolmaster and as a photographer and he once donated a collection of 21,000 natural history items to the London Centre for Communications, and the Samuel Prout Newcombe collection of taxidermy forms a small part of the Horniman Museum and Garden collections ('A Natural History Reading Room',

1899: 10). He also wrote at least four books about the Great Exhibition for children between 1851 and 1860: *Little Henry's Holiday* (1851a), *The Royal Road to Reading through the Great Exhibition in Which Those Who Were Too Young to Visit the Exhibition May Learn to Read about It* (1851b), *Fireside Facts from the Great Exhibition* (1851c) and *A Book about All Kinds of Things Which We Eat, Drink and Wear: Being a Series of Object Lessons, Formally Entitled Fireside Facts from the Great Exhibition* (1860). This last text expands on the earlier *Fireside Facts* which was published shortly after the Exhibition closed. Newcombe also refers to the Exhibition in *Little Henry's Records of His Lifetime* (1852) and in his ambitious, and bizarrely eclectic, six-volume serial *Pleasant Pages* (1850–3], aimed at home educators. These texts reveal Newcombe's ambition and his commercial shrewdness. Each of his texts shamelessly advertises the others, both in the end papers and within the narrative itself. Newcombe had an eye on a market opportunity and worked quickly to capitalize upon it. Some of these texts show child characters preparing for a trip to Crystal Palace, and were probably published when the Exhibition was still open and available to visit. The texts seem to have been produced quickly and efficiently: they normally take the form of a dialogue between child characters and a parent-figure with little or no narrative in between the dialogue, and generally the names of the characters are replaced with initials after the first page or so. Newcombe even seems sometimes to forget the names of his characters in the middle of a text. For example, in *Little Henry's Holiday*, Rose is referred to as 'L.' between pages 115 and 119. His work often contains large chunks of quotation from other texts like Dickens's *Household Words* or the *Official Catalogue of the Great Exhibition*. He even calls attention to the recycled passages in the books, noting in the preface to *Fireside Facts of the Great Exhibition* that the opening sections are identical to the first part of *Little Henry's Holiday at the Great Exhibition* which had been published shortly before 'as the Author did not deem it necessary to rewrite the same particulars in a different style for this volume' (Newcombe 1851c: iv). He reuses the same illustrations by E. Whimper in several of his texts, even when they are not relevant to the material under discussion.[3] While it may be tempting to see Newcombe as a cynical businessman with no real interest in child readers, closer examination of his books reveals not only a warm understanding of children but also a keen interest in teaching them about contemporary material culture in an accessible way that respects their instinctive desire to touch and feel objects as well as to look at them from a distance.

Newcombe uses the dialogic object lesson in his educational series, *Pleasant Pages*. His work differs from other object lesson books available at the time in that *Pleasant Pages* was not aimed at professional teachers, but at home educators and parents, and at children themselves. Unlike many other contemporary object lessons, these books are not just designed to instruct but also to entertain and attempt to combine the didactic aspects of the texts with warm humour. Take, for example, *The Royal Road to Reading through the Great Exhibition* (1851). Like many of Newcombe's texts, it takes the form of an educational dialogue. In this case, the conversation is between two children – Tetty, who is judged to be too small to visit the Exhibition, and his older sister, Ada, who has recently been to see the Crystal Palace. Even though the text contains a lot of dry facts and figures, the dialogue is warm and surprisingly humorous. In one exchange, Tetty asks Ada to explain the meaning of the word 'transparent':

Ada. When we can see through anything it is called *transparent*.
Tetty. Then glass is transparent.
Ada. Tell me something else that is transparent.
Tetty. WATER is transparent.
Ada. And AIR is transparent.
Tetty. And FINGERS are transparent. I can see through my fingers.
Ada. No, you see *between* your fingers. You see through the air. Ask mamma to explain that. (Newcombe 1851b: 10, emphasis in original)

In this manner, Newcombe's texts often blur the line between pedagogy and play. Newcombe structures his texts as a series of dialogues – between a parent and child or among children – which seek to draw child characters and readers into conversation, encouraging dialogic and playful learning. These object lessons offer up a sort of script or a framework for conversation which the audience can engage with, question and speak to.

Newcombe's texts about the Great Exhibition emphasize the importance of learning through physical and sensory contact with the material world and show how learning through 'head, hand and heart' can be incorporated into everyday activities. While many of the other books about the Exhibition highlighted the importance of 'just looking', Newcombe actively encourages his child readers to employ all of their senses as they moved through the Crystal Palace. In fact, at times he actively discourages looking. In *Fireside Facts of the Great Exhibition*, he cautions the reader:

Mind that you don't look at the silk trophy! Keep off your eyes from the horse and the dragon, or the timber trophy behind it! Don't look up or down! Don't begin to look at the people! Don't look at anything, until you have made haste into the Indian Department. (1851c: 29–30)

The wonders and sights of the Exhibition are a distraction; the displays threaten to dazzle and astonish the visitor and Newcombe attempts to counter this by advocating deliberate, direct and focused looking rather than passive and disinterested glancing encouraged by contemporary consumer culture. Newcombe treats sight as just one of a number of senses that are needed to help the child visitor connect with and understand the Exhibition. In *Little Henry's Holiday*, Harry and Rose are encouraged to engage kinaesthetically with the Exhibition as well as by just looking. As the characters move through the Exhibition, the text appeals to the full spectrum of learning experiences from the visual and the aural to the intensely tactile. Papa encourages the children to touch the displays of fur (1851a: 108–9) and even to lick the block of alum (99). In this way, Newcombe endorses, more fully than other authors, the kinds of consumer experience that nineteenth-century children engaged with instinctively. Newcombe's decision to move away from 'just looking' towards a more bodily experience of the goods on display may indicate a greater sensitivity to the need for young children to participate in kinaesthetic learning and play.

What makes Newcombe's work unique is his specialism in embedding object lessons within stories and conversations. Newcombe had a particular talent for explaining the material world, for connecting complicated ideas to concrete and tangible examples, to the things that one could point at with an index finger. In his texts about the Great Exhibition, he makes a particular effort to explain the value of the Exhibition in terms that the child reader can easily understand and so initiates children into contemporary material culture. In *The Royal Road to Reading*, Ada attempts to describe the Koh-i-noor diamond to her brother and to explain why it is remarkable:

Ada. A small diamond is worth as much as a house. When a diamond is as big as the top of your finger it is called a large diamond. A large diamond would buy six houses.
Tetty. How large is the Koh-i-noor?
Ada. It is as large as the egg of a pigeon. It is worth more than six houses; it is worth more than six hundred houses. (Newcombe 1851b: 11–12)

Here, the fabulous Koh-i-noor and its equally fabulous price are related to things Tetty can readily understand – the top of his finger, a pigeon's egg, a house. The abstract is made understandable through association with the tangible and the material. We move from the finger, the thing that does the touching and the pointing, to the things that the fingers touch and point at. Thus, we move from the small to the large, from the person to the world. In this text, the author, ventriloquizing through Papa, continually draws the child characters' and the child readers' attention towards objects of practical function. When Rose gets distracted by the ornamental flowers from France, Papa directs her attention back towards a real flower, the *Victoria Regia*, and uses it as an opportunity to tell her about Sir Richard Schomburgh's discovery of the species and its subsequent cultivation by Paxton in a glasshouse which, ultimately, led to Paxton being able to design the Crystal Palace itself (1851a: 81–6). The flower becomes a vehicle for teaching Rose about botany, about the problems of growing tropical plants in rainy England and about the architecture of the Crystal Palace itself. Thus, Newcombe demonstrates how the objects in the Exhibition can be used as the basis of a series of object lessons. *Little Henry's Holiday, Fireside Facts about the Great Exhibition* and *The Royal Road to Reading* all make inventive use of the object lesson, showing the reader how a perfectly ordinary piece of cloth or a lump of coal can become the basis of a series of lessons about geography, history, geology, economy and trade.

Newcombe uses similar techniques in his other texts about the Exhibition, and once the child has engaged appropriately and sufficiently with the tangible and the immediate then they can be directed towards the intangible and the abstract. In order to facilitate this, Newcombe often uses familiar household objects, and even the house itself, as ways to explain new experiences. In *Little Henry's Holiday*, Papa helps Henry and Rose to understand the things they see in the Exhibition by comparing them to familiar household objects: the cylinder of a printing machine, for example, is compared to a garden roller (1851a: 118). The Crystal Palace itself is compared to a house and Henry and Rose are encouraged to imagine the size and scale of the Palace in relation to their own street. When Papa tells the children that the Crystal Palace is 1,851 feet long, Henry is initially puzzled:

H.   I cannot understand exactly how much that is.
P.   You can if you try. Do you know the street where your aunt lives, and where each house contains eight rooms?
Rose.   I know it papa, there are 50 houses on each side of the road.
P.   Then just imagine that, instead of 50 there were 116 houses – then you get an idea of the length of the Crystal Palace. It is as long as 116 eight-roomed houses placed in a row! (1851b: 16)

Papa's description may not initially appear to help the child reader much. Even if Rose does know the street where her aunt lives, the reader certainly does not and the unit of measurement is not clearly defined. It is not clear how large the eight rooms are, or whether the eight rooms are all on the ground floor or are arranged over two or more storeys. It seems just as difficult to visualize 116 imaginary houses in a row as it is to visualize 1,851 feet. However, considering how many contemporary texts for children merely relate the Palace to a 'great fairy palace' (*Old Mother Bunch*, n.d.: 6) or something equally fantastic, this fragment of dialogue shows Newcombe's remarkable focus in the material and the mundane. Newcombe's technique is to find a measurement that the child already knows, an object she is already familiar with and can relate the new experiences back to it. The aim of the object lesson, Newcombe notes in *Fireside Facts*, is to 'to cultivate in the reader the powers of observation, comparison, induction, and memory, by the exercise of which the mind is trained to investigate and acquire knowledge for itself' (iii). Newcombe's object lessons teach the child reader to find strategies to enable them to understand seemingly impossible figures: rather than teaching a child about one particular measurement, he teaches the reader how to understand and to calculate measurements in a practical and, above all, material way.

The world of goods

These object lessons not only helped the child readers to orientate themselves within the Crystal Palace but also helped readers to orientate themselves within the wider world. The Exhibition, though vast, acted as a microcosm of a wider and more complicated system of objects. When visitors passed through 'the Britain Row, the French Row, the Italian Row, the Spanish Row, the German Row' they were able to see what items were made in what part of the world and even which parts of the world had been colonized by which European power. Many of the books aimed at young readers about the Exhibition describe the production of objects and the movement of goods from one part of the world to another and ask the young reader to call to mind the provenance of these items and, therefore, the many processes of cultivation, trade and manufacture that are bound up in the object. In this way, the child visitor – and by extension the child reader – is made aware of the existence of a global economy. In *Fireside Facts*, Newcombe's narrator presents the reader with an account of the scale and diversity of textile manufacture in Britain, and connects the material goods with the places in which they are produced in order to give a sense of a vast web of manufacture and consumption:

> How [the foreign visitor] would open his eyes at the fleets of merchant-ships, and the immense bales of cotton with which they were laden! Lead him to Warrington, on the Mersey, and show him the hundreds of families who live by making pins. Lead him to Yorkshire, and show him thousands more machines, and tens of thousands of families which get their living by making woollen dress. Lead him to Hull, that he may see the eastern port; show him vessels bringing flax from Holland, others with wool from Germany, and others from Russia laden with hemp. Then tell him to count the merchants, the clerks, the porters, and the sailors, who depend upon the clothing market for their bread. Lead him southward to Birmingham, where men and women make buttons, and show him the thousands of people whose living depends on the button trade. Or take him up, northward, to Macclesfield and Derby, where silken dress is made. Then travel southward again, to Newcastle-under-Lyne, to see the manufacture of hats. Take him to Coventry; here are more tens of thousands employed in making ribbons and watches. Lead him northward to Nottingham, where the people are making cotton stockings, and net, and lace. Lead him down to Leicester, where woollen stockings and gloves are made. (199)

In addition to calling the young reader's attention to the geographical origins of objects, Newcombe is also at pains to explain how objects are made and, crucially, who made them. He also takes special care to remind his young readers that objects do not simply appear but are made by people: each object is the end product of a labour process. In *Little Henry's Holiday*, Papa reminds Harry and Rose that the enormous wooden 'trophy' from Canada represents not just the bountiful forests of that country but also the thousands of men employed in the timber trade (1851a: 123–6). The cotton and sugar sent by America should not be viewed without recalling the slave labour that made such production possible (Newcombe 1851c: 66). Despite this, Newcombe's attitude towards slavery is problematic. Although he refers to the slave trade as a 'wicked business' (1851a: 78) and seems to support abolition, he also espouses the idea that enslaved Africans were by nature more suited to hard labour than white Europeans and even goes so far as to suggest that 'although they undergo the most severe labour they have a plump and sleek appearance ... the very air they breathe seems to nourish them' (1851c: 66). Newcombe's dismissal of the realities of slavery undermines the value of his arguments about labour and the human effort involved in the production of goods. While his arguments are limited and clumsy, he does attempt to make the child character and the child reader aware that commodities reveal not just material relations but social relations too. The material objects on display are really only the outward and visible signs of a complex network of social, political, economic and geographical links.

Newcombe was not alone in these concerns. The Great Exhibition took place at a time of increased awareness of and concern for the labour cost of many everyday items. The abolition of slavery in the British Empire in 1838 and the widespread European revolutions of 1848 increased public sensitivity towards how products were made and by whom. In advance of the opening of the Exhibition, a cartoon in *Punch* interrogated the ethics behind the 'specimens' on display – showing tired, sick and old workers in bell jars, watched over by a rotund Mr Punch and a pensive, and passive, Prince Albert.

Though the cartoon in *Punch* seemed fanciful, visitors to the Exhibition could, in fact, look at workers in action. An article in *The Spectator* enthused:

> And if you just emerge hence for a moment to the nearest point of the central nave, you may see a crowd of spectators agape at the facility with which a little boy, aided by De la Rue's envelope-machine, converts pieces of paper into

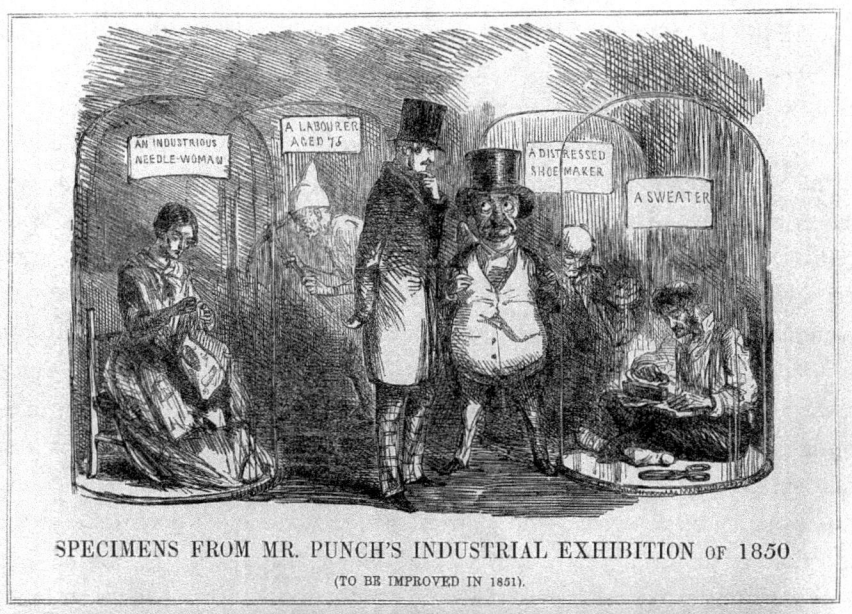

Figure 1.4 Making the unseen labour behind commodities visible. *Source*: John Leech, 'Specimens from Mr Punch's Industrial Exhibition of 1850 (to be improved in 1851)', *Punch* 18 (1850: 145).

ready-made envelopes at the rate of about one hundred per minute. (Strassavuso The Prevalent, 1851: 446)

This little boy was one of several child workers who were displayed alongside new industrial technologies. In another area of the Exhibition, a small girl demonstrated a new kind of sewing machine, turning out over a hundred tiny stitches a minute. These machines, the exhibitors seemed to say, were so simple to operate that they could be safely worked by children. What was less explicit was the fact that children were commonly employed in factories and workshops across Britain and many of the machines they worked with were not at all safe. Some children's books about the Exhibition make an effort to educate the child reader about the labour cost of the items on display. Newcombe's *Fireside Facts* draws attention to the labour value congealed within commonplace objects, mentioning in particular 'a lace dress which cost five years' labour in making' (201). Some of the texts in the *Aunt Mavor's* series highlight the poverty of the working classes. *The Victoria Alphabet* notes that 'N is for Nan-cy, a semp-stress by trade,/Who works day and night, but is ve-ry ill paid' (*The Victoria Alphabet*, n.d.: 5). The item Nancy has made is not mentioned at all; the focus of this piece is not the work itself, but how we value and reward that work. Another book in the *Aunt Mavor's* series, *Uncle Nimrod's First Visit to the Exhibition*, is even more explicit. Uncle Nimrod shows the children a huge piece of coal and explains:

> Here is a monstrous lump of coal, half as big as a small room, and raised from pits several thousand feet below the earth. In these the poor miners are compelled to work, in order that we may have a comfortable fire to sit by in the cold winter evenings. How grateful we ought to be for those who toil so hard for our benefit. (7)

Here, Uncle Nimrod juxtaposes the misery of the mines with the cosy comfort of home. Not only is the child reader told where coal comes from but is also urged to be grateful to the workers who work in the mines. Indeed, there was much to be grateful for: coal was a key commodity of the age, providing not just the fuel for the engines that drove the Industrial Revolution but also fuel to heat homes, prepare meals and boil water. Judith Flanders suggests that even a modest mid-century London household could burn through a ton of coal every month (2003: 71). Clara L. Matéaux's *Wonderland of Work* (1884) tried to put this consumption into perspective, calculating that 'every three tons of coals is the ... equivalent of one man's life-long muscular activity. ... A block some twelve feet high, the base of which is only a yard square, has more "work" in it than many a man's life labour' (1884: 21). However, neither Matéaux nor the author of *Uncle Nimrod's First Visit* makes any explicit connection between the demand for coal and the misery of the miners. Indeed, the fact that the author of *Uncle Nimrod's First Visit* cast coal as 'monstrous' rather than as an inanimate object seems to apportion blame to the material, to make it somehow culpable in the process. As I will show in Chapter 4, it was not uncommon to ascribe will to inanimate objects and to treat them as things within a complex actor-network in this period.

Although the majority of the lessons taught to child audiences through the objects on display in the Great Exhibition centred on worldly affairs – geography, geology, economics, trade and so on – other lessons about the spiritual and moral matters – supposedly connected to the objects on display – were also provided for child consumers. As the Duchess in Lewis Carroll's *Alice's Adventures in Wonderland* (1865) reminds us 'everything has got a moral, if only you look for it' ([1865] 1971: 120) and the objects on display in the Crystal Palace – and even the Crystal Palace itself – proved an easy place for Victorian writers to seek out moral lessons. An article in *Household Words*, published on 3 May just two days after the Exhibition opened, made bold claims for the spiritual qualities of the event:

> 'And what,' say some, 'is to be a benefit to the visitors of the Exhibition, who are neither artisans nor merchants – who are neither buyers nor sellers ...?' We answer – the enlargement of your minds, and of all minds – that practical education which may teach men to comprehend rightly the past and the present. ... These are the works of the heroes of this age. ... Do homage to the promoters of it, in all love and loyalty. ... In this goodly work there is hope beyond performance – hope of 'Peace on earth, good-will towards men.' ('Three May Days in London [iii]: The May Palace, 1851': 124)

The piece echoes a religious sermon, full of references to reverence and homage, peace and goodwill. The educational aspects of the Exhibition – 'the enlargement of all minds' – are overshadowed by the moral force of the works. Andrew Miller confirms the power of this moral force, arguing that the objects on display 'gained their significance not, primarily, by their contiguous relations to each other, but by gesturing towards a series of abstract codes constructed through them' (1995: 51). Contemporary children's authors were also quick to exploit the moral possibilities of the Exhibition and to use the objects as a way to induct child readers into these 'abstract codes'. One text, *The Crystal Palace: A Little Book for Little Boys, for 1851* (1851), informs the young reader that they can, and should, strive to 'become a living Crystal Palace'. By this, the narrator encourages the child reader to emulate the character Frank who wishes to be 'transparent, pure, and strong, and have the light of Goodness shining through [him]' (*The Crystal Palace*, 1851: 23). By way of contrast, the reader is presented with the story of a bad boy who sneaks into the Great Exhibition but then falls from a scaffold, breaks his collarbone and ribs (64). Frank reflects that the bad boy is 'not a crystal palace' (67). Though Frank's understanding of the Crystal Palace is explicitly termed an 'object lesson' (21) the book moves far beyond the normal scope of object lessons, drawing moral and religious properties instead (virtue, temperance, fortitude) from Frank's observations of the physical properties of crystal (hardness, transparency, clarity). By making the discussion less about material objects and more about abstract objectives, this text and many others like it diverge from the original aims of Pestalozzi's educational system.

As well as religious values, the items from the Exhibition were used to teach other kinds of value judgements. In *Little Henry's Holiday* Newcombe remarks that 'there came grand thoughts of teaching other things to men by means of the Great Exhibition' (1851a: 10) and Newcombe himself was not above manipulating the object lesson into lessons about 'other things'. While his focus may seem to lie squarely with the object, his discussion is not merely material but ideological too. Gillian Lathey argues that 'in both *Little Henry's Holiday at the Great Exhibition* (1851) and *Fireside Facts from the Great Exhibition* ([1851]), ... Newcombe draws on ill-digested contemporary theories to indulge in anthropological instruction' (2017: 79). In *Little Henry's Holiday*, Papa points out a group of four dolls and explains that 'each doll represents the character of the race it belongs to' (Newcombe 1851a: 80). The fair, blue-eyed doll represents the Germanic family. The dark-complexioned doll with dark hair and eyes represents the Celtic family. Following the 'object lesson' model, the narrator cannot be content with treating objects as they are – these items must signify something. The object must be made to resonate with cultural and social significance. As Lathey explains, 'the result is a value-laden distinction between solid and reliable Germanic Europeans and the frivolous, if imaginative, Celts' (2017: 80). As Papa leads Henry and Rose through a discussion of the dolls on display, Rose jumps to the conclusion that 'their different kinds of minds will think different thoughts, then of course they will make different things' (Newcombe 1851a: 135). Because he presents these ideas within the framework of one of Pestalozzi's object lessons, Newcombe effects a sleight of hand; he presents these ideas as though they are concrete facts that emerge from the careful observation of the items within the Exhibition. In fact, many of the words used to describe the objects – 'lumpy', 'beautiful', 'tasteful', 'savage', 'ugly' and so on. – are value judgements and rest on cultural considerations of beauty and skill and have precious little to do with the innate properties of the object the child reader is faced with.

The practice of using objects as the basis and justification of all sorts of cultural stereotypes is rife in children's books about the Exhibition. *The World's Fair: Or, Children's Prize Gift Book of the Great Exhibition of 1851* uses the exhibits as the basis of 'pretty stories about the people who have made and sent them and how they live at home'. These 'pretty stories', however, expose some pretty dark stereotypes. For the most part, the author glosses over the objects in the Exhibition and moves straight into discussions about the countries and the supposed characteristics of different nations. For instance, of the Spanish, the author writes, 'The Spaniards are not either a very active or a very cleanly people, but they are exceedingly proud, honest, and hospitable' (*The World's Fair*, 1851: n.p.). He goes on to say:

> I don't think you would find the Spanish cookery much to your taste; for the Spaniards are very fond of rancid butter in their meals, and of oil that has a very strong smell and flavour; indeed, when they are going to cook anything that requires fat, they lift down the lamp from the ceiling, and take out what oil they want. (n.p.)

Here the sense of taste is used to impart lessons on cultural taste; the author dissuades the reader from ingesting Spanish food and, by extension, from imbibing Spanish habits and morals. The child is made, not merely into a consumer, but into a discerning consumer through an imagined object lesson. The primary value of this lesson, however, is not material, but moral.

In order to make these lessons work, the authors disregard many of the items on display in favour of making remarks about commodities that the child reader is assumed to be more familiar with. The author of *The Children's Prize Book of the Great Exhibition*, for example, does not bother to discuss any of the metalwork, lacework or carvings sent to the Exhibition from Ireland, but instead explains that 'some of the nice butter you eat on your bread and rolls comes from Ireland' (n.p.). Just as Newcombe relates the Palace to the ordinary house, this text continually relates the objects in the Exhibition to the child reader's everyday experience. The foreign space – Ireland – is rendered comprehensible through the image of butter on the breakfast table. Thus, the foreign is linked to the domestic, the product to the consumer and, through invoking images of eating and orality, the text positions the child reader as a consumer. This text is addressed directly and intimately to the child reader and the child is given a sense of privileged insight into the exhibits, a sense of being led by the hand around the Crystal Palace and reassured that everything on display, the 100,000 items from all the corners of the world, only matter insofar as they touch on that child's own life. From being an outsider to the Exhibition, not even acknowledged as a possible visitor, the child is suddenly brought into the very centre of the action. The child is inducted into contemporary material culture, given a private tour of the best that the world can offer. This text, like Newcombe's, inducts the child into material culture, and assures the child that she holds a key position in the world of trade and commerce. The child reader is encouraged to position herself as a consumer at the very heart of the British Empire, at the centre of the world of goods.

Conclusion

The Great Exhibition marks a sea change in the way material goods were displayed, thought about, talked about, consumed and understood. Richards describes the Crystal Palace as both 'a museum and a market' (1990: 19) but in truth, in its first incarnation at Hyde Park between May and October 1851, the Palace was neither. The things on display were not for sale and though cartoons showed people returning with all sorts of fanciful purchases, there were strict limitations of the sale of items during the period of the Exhibition. But that does not mean there was nothing to consume. The Palace was full of food – the records of the Commission note the vast quantities of bread, tea, lemonade and so on consumed within the Crystal Palace. Moreover, the spectacle of the Crystal Palace was a commodity in its own right, a brand new kind of product that the Victorian public consumed most eagerly. As well as representing a new kind of product, the Great Exhibition also stimulated consumption and trade. While the public could not actually buy any of the items on display, they could order items from the exhibitors and buy their products elsewhere. Peter Gurney notes that the role of the Crystal Palace in driving commercialization was realized most perfectly in its later incarnation at Sydenham where exhibitors could sell their wares and where 'the Palace played an important role in shaping bourgeois shopping habits and taste in the widest sense and no doubt stimulated demand for a plethora of commodities' (2007: 143). In shaping shopping habits and in creating new appetites for material goods, the Exhibition was the forerunner of the department store, inducting the Victorian consumer into the pleasures of the spectacle of commodities.

In bringing together goods and exhibitors from around the world the Exhibition brought about both conceptual and concrete changes in the relations between people and objects. Ideologically, it was 'a new starting-point from which all nations will be able to direct their future exertions' (Newcombe 1852: 111). Although there were clear demarcations between the different areas of the building, the overall aim was for a sense of unity and clarity. This unity was facilitated by the architectural space provided by Paxton's glasshouse with its rows of transparent windows and 'delicate network' of iron tracery that visually connected one side of the Palace to the other (Weston 2001: 27). While John Ruskin declared that the Crystal Palace 'possess[ed] no more sublimity than a cucumber frame between two chimneys' ([1885] 2012: 31), others were enchanted by it. Lother Bucher, a German émigré living in London, hailed it as 'a revolution in architecture from which a new style will date' (Weston 2001: 27). In addition to a new kind of architecture, the Great Exhibition marked the beginnings of a new kind of material culture which affected the ways objects were experienced, understood and discussed for many years. Several critics including Thomas Richards, Peter Gurney and Susan Buck-Morss have argued that the Exhibition and the development of modern consumerism were concomitant. Richards argues that the Exhibition

> prescribed the rituals by which consumers venerated the commodity for the rest of the century. It was the first world's fair, the first department store, the first shopping mall. The Exhibition rooted the commodity in the sense of being near to the heart of things, of being caught up in the progress of people and institutions that dominated Victorian society. Until the Exhibition the commodity had not for a moment occupied center stage in English public life; during and after the Exhibition the commodity became and remained the still center of the turning earth, the focal point of all gazing and the end point of all pilgrimages. (1990: 17–18)

As the end point of pilgrimage, the Exhibition takes on a quasi-religious role, and ushers in a new world in which commodities become objects of worship – a place where objects were 'enshrined' (Buzard et al. 2007: 1). The veneration of objects in the Great Exhibition echoes and gives form to the commodity fetishism that concerned Marx in *Capital*. While the English-language edition of *Capital* did not appear until 1887, much of the research for the book was conducted in London during the 1850s and 1860s and Marx discusses the Exhibition of 1851 and the later exhibition of 1862 as emblematic of the fetishism of commodities in nineteenth-century London. Since 1851 was a census year, it becomes a marker against which Marx measures the increases and decreases in British population, manufacture and exports. Consequently, 1851 and its most notable event, the Great Exhibition, become an origin point of the development of nineteenth-century capitalism and consumer culture.

Yet not all consumers were equally ready to be inducted into this new world of consumption. As I have shown, children posed a problem to the organizers of the Exhibition. The Commissioners' dilemma over whether to charge children a special entrance fee indicates that children were not among the anticipated audience for the Exhibition and suggests that children were customarily excluded from contemporary material practices. As a result, while the adult visitors to the Palace were sufficiently familiar with cultural codes to appreciate the spectacle, the child visitors did not really understand what they were looking at. The child visitors needed to be taught how to value the goods on display and, thereby, to be inducted into commodity culture. The authors of texts like *The Fine Crystal Palace the Prince Built* and the *Aunt Mavor's* series guided the naïve reader through the Exhibition, highlighting the most culturally and materially important aspects of the spectacle. Newcombe takes these object lessons a step further, helping the child reader to understand how and where the objects were made and so helps the reader to understand the Exhibition's – and by extension Britain's – place within a global economy. Newcombe enables the child reader to become an informed and discerning consumer. His books chart the progress of the child visitor through the Exhibition and map on to this physical journey a metaphorical movement from ignorance to knowledge. Newcombe's books, like others about the Exhibition, reveal that the Great Exhibition marked a turning point in children's material culture. In May 1851 it was inconceivable that children could even attend the Exhibition, but by October 1851 there were toys, books, keepsakes, pamphlets and all kinds of souvenirs of the Exhibition aimed directly and exclusively at child consumers. These items – along with the celebratory tone of many of the children's texts – not only educated children about the items on display but also helped to stimulate new appetites for commodities for these new consumers. The recognition that children were a distinct and lucrative audience for exhibitions and events of this scale impacted the way later exhibitions were organized in Britain. Children were not 'remarkable and perplexing objects' but consumers in their own right who must be accommodated alongside adult patrons. For example, the *Art Treasures of the United Kingdom* exhibition held at Old Trafford in Manchester in 1857 made a special fund available to enable Sunday School children to attend (Haskell 2000: 88). The Great Exhibition of 1851, therefore, brought about a reimagining of the child, not as a remarkable and perplexing object but as a consumer at the centre of a world of objects.

2

'The wonders of common things': Worldly goods in the nineteenth century

In the Christmas holidays of 1888–9, a group of children crowded into a lecture theatre at the London Institution building on Finsbury Circus in London to hear a lecture by Dr Charles Meymott Tidy titled 'The Story of a Tinder-Box'. It was a strange space for children to occupy. A watercolour sketch of the theatre by Robert Blemmel Schnebbelie shows the lecture hall as it was in the early part of the nineteenth century: it was an imposing space, with pilasters, a deep pit and a wide semicircle of tiered benches arranged to face the speaker's podium at the bottom. The room could accommodate 750 people and 'in the winter time when the lectures are delivered by leading men of science, the theatre [was] as full as can well be imagined' (Thornbury 1878: 208). The space was lit by the soft glow of wall-lights, and by a circular window set into the ceiling. But when Charles Tidy began his lecture, the room was almost dark. His lecture made use of light projections and slide lanterns and he needed his young audience to see these clearly.

Tidy was a professor of chemistry and an accomplished public speaker, most famous for his work as a coroner with specialisms in poisons and medical jurisprudence, and for his service as an expert witness in several high-profile criminal cases. By late 1888, he had attended over 1,000 post-mortems and had written one of the first books of forensic pathology, *A Handy Book of Forensic Medicine and Toxicology*, as well as a two-volume study of legal medicine. Most notably, Tidy was the expert witness at Florence Maybrick's trial in 1889. She was convicted of murdering her husband, James Maybrick, though Tidy had argued that the traces of arsenic found in his body were not enough to be fatal. Given his grave occupation, Tidy seemed an unusual choice of speaker for the Christmas lecture. The tradition of holding scientific lectures for children during the Christmas holidays began in 1825 with a lecture by Michael Faraday organized by the Royal Institution. The tradition continues today with the BBC broadcasting a series of 'Christmas lectures' on science, technology and engineering for young viewers during the holiday period every year. The BBC lecture series evolved out of the Royal Institute lectures. Tidy's lecture was not part of the popular Royal Institution series, but one of a rival series of lectures organized by the Society for Promoting Christian Knowledge. That both organizations could hold lectures in the same city at the same time suggests that there was a sizable audience of children prepared to attend such lectures. The fact that both organizations engaged leading scientists and engineers for their lecture series suggests that this young audience was held in high esteem and that these lectures were intended both to entertain and instruct.

Tidy was more than up for the challenge. He appears keenly aware of the needs of his young audience and enlivens the lecture with practical demonstrations, holding up objects for the children to inspect and projecting images and diagrams on a large screen to help the children at the back of the hall to see precisely what was taking place at the front of the lecture theatre. He seeks to amuse them by using bisulphide of carbon to freeze a beaker to the top of a stool, showing them how he can lift the stool up just by holding on to the top of the beaker. As an extra piece of showmanship, he sets fire to a mixture of chlorate of potash and sulphur so that it will explode, presumably to the surprise and delight of the young audience. Throughout his lecture, Tidy leads his audience from raw materials to finished products, all the while keeping up a lively chatter, balancing the scientific information he imparts with light and whimsical pieces of storytelling and anecdotes. When he introduces the old tinderbox, the subject of his lecture, he tells his audience:

> I have no doubt this very old tinder-box that you see here was once upon a time kept on the mantel-piece of the kitchen well polished and bright, and I do not doubt but that it has lit hundreds and thousands of fires, and, what is more, has very often been spoken to very disrespectfully when the servant wanted to light the fire, and her master was waiting for his breakfast. (Tidy 1897: 9)

His description suggests that the tinderbox is not simply something to be spoken *about*, but also something to be spoken *to*. A little later in the lecture, the tinderbox becomes an item that can speak for itself. Tidy says:

> I cannot help thinking that the old tinder-box, which I have placed on the table … before you to-night, feels a certain pleasure in listening to our story. Envious perhaps a little of its successor, it nevertheless fully recognizes that its own reign had been a thousand times longer than that of the lucifer match. If we could only hear that tinder-box talk, I think we should find it saying … to the lucifer

match – 'I gave way to you, because my time was over; but mind, your turn will come next, and you will then have to give way to something else.' (1897: 23)

In this moment, Tidy slips outside of the role of the scientist and into the role of the coroner. The tinderbox is placed, like a kind of courtroom exhibit, before the audience. And, like a courtroom exhibit, the tinderbox becomes an object that tells a narrative. He speaks not as a rational scientist but as a passionate man of law and as a teacher, and accords the tinderbox unscientific subjectivity. Under Tidy's direction, the audience is encouraged to see the tinderbox as capable of feeling pride and pleasure, and envy – perhaps even murderous envy. In his imagination, even familiar household objects are possessed with dangerous emotions and destructive impulses. Most importantly, they are endowed with subjectivity and voices of their own.

Tidy's decision to include this moment of imaginative fiction within his scientific lecture indicates his awareness of the 'it-narrative', a literary genre where ordinary commodities take on the role of narrators. Tidy recognized, as did many of his contemporaries, the particular value of this kind of narrative for engaging and educating young audiences. While the topics he covers in the lecture are complex, he knows that using practical demonstrations and narratives will make these ideas clear and tangible. Tidy ends his lecture by advising the prospective scientists in the lecture hall 'to listen to the familiar stories told you by the commonest of common things' (68). The stories told by 'the commonest of common things' are the subject of this chapter; I examine here a selection of texts in which objects, like Tidy's tinderbox, tell their own stories. These objects are 'common' in the sense that there were manufactured in enormous quantities, and in the sense that they were part of the everyday, collective experience of the majority of middle-class child readers at the time. The object-autobiographies or it-narratives discussed here are 'prose fictions that take inanimate objects ... as their central characters, sometimes endowing them with a subjectivity – and thus a narrative perspective – of their own' (Blackwell 2012: vii). These speaking items assert their individuality, even personality, while at the same time reminding the audience of their status as commodities which are made, used, consumed, exchanged, gifted, lost, stolen and dumped. The it-narrative had first appeared in the eighteenth century as a genre for adult readers, but was reinvented in the latter part of the nineteenth century as a genre of children's literature. While critical opinion about children's it-narratives is low, and many critics including Bill Brown and Leah Price view them as inferior to the adult it-narratives of the eighteenth century,

I argue that these books are misunderstood: far from being sanitized stories cut down to size from adult books, nineteenth-century children's it-narratives were intrinsically linked to modern developments in science and manufacture, and sought to use everyday objects to instruct and induct young readers into a world of goods (Brown 2016: 221; Price 2009: 124).

The history of the it-narrative

The typical eighteenth-century it-narrative traces the biography of an ordinary object from its first appearance in the world to its eventual demise. The item is often lost or given away or traded and so moves from person to person. Unlike the human narrators of Bildungsromane, who start in a low position and move towards a high one, these items generally move from a high social position to a low one. The it-narrative often begins when the object is newly made and sold for the first time. The brand new object has a high position – it is new and lovely and desirable – but, through use and experience, the object is worn out or broken and, by design or accident, passes from the hands of the original owner into the hands of someone further down the social ladder. From there, the object often descends further and further down the chain until it is put beyond use, either because it is irrecoverably damaged or because it no longer serves its intended function. The it-narrative typically involves a small item – a coin, a pocket watch, a button – that can be easily overlooked, mislaid or lost. These little items can also be easily concealed; they may hide in pockets where they can eavesdrop on their owners, or secrete themselves at the back of cupboards where they might observe without being seen. As they circulate among users, the objects gain privileged insight into the social and material relationships between people and commodities. I consider these objects as 'worldly goods' in the sense that they are mundane, but also in the sense that they are very knowing. Unlike the objects on display discussed in Chapter 1, the objects at the centre of the it-narrative are not wholly passive: though they are seldom endowed with the power to move, or to act of their own volition, they nevertheless narrate the stories of their own experiences and, in having biographies to narrate, blur the line between objects and subjects (Bellamy 2007: 121). As they record their autobiographies, these narrative objects reflect on the people around them and on the lives they intersect. Blackwell argues that 'in most it-narratives, the role of things and animals as characters, or objects of narrative attention, is displaced by their function as attractors and collectors of narrative as means of narrative focalization' (2012: xi). In becoming collectors of stories, and in a sense archivers of narrative, these objects trace the social and material relations between people and commodities.

While the origins of the it-narrative have been traced back to classical texts like Ovid's *Metamorphoses* and to Anglo-Saxon texts like the tenth-century *The Dream of the Rood*, the it-narrative properly emerges as a distinct literary genre in the eighteenth century. Jonathan Lamb, Mark Blackwell, Aileen Douglas and others identify Charles Johnstone's *Chrysal: The Adventures of a Guinea* (1760) as the forerunner of the modern genre, and in the wake of its publication there was a surge of it-narratives published in the eighteenth century. For many critics, the rise of the it-narrative is closely connected to the rise of consumer culture: the fresh abundance of commodities arriving in Britain from across the globe sparked a new interest in buying, collecting, gathering and displaying worldly goods. For Aileen Douglas, it-narratives are 'emblematic of a burgeoning consumer culture' (2007: 148), and there is a deep symbiosis between wanting to possess objects and wanting to possess the stories about these objects. As Christa Knellwolf King summarizes:

> The proliferation of 'it-narratives' in the eighteenth century testifies to a preoccupation with the role played by things in a world that came to be cluttered with an ever-increasing amount of material goods. The emergence of a new taste for stories about things, told by the things themselves, was founded on a new fascination for the minute, insignificant, and trivial. (2014: 452)

For King and for many other critics, there is a close connection between the emergence of the 'taste for stories about things' and the emergence of new appetites of commodity consumption.

Though eighteenth-century it-narratives have been the subject of 'increased scholarly scrutiny in the last decade' (Lake 2013: 183), nineteenth- and early-twentieth-century it-narratives have been critically overlooked. This may be because it-narratives are not always considered worthy of critical attention. Even at the height of the it-narrative craze, the genre fell in for criticism. A 1781 review of *The Adventures of a Hackney-Coach* published that year complained that the narrative was 'nothing but a heap of uninteresting, ill-written adventures, in a pompous and turgid style' (Smollett 1781: 651) and Linda Rodriguez McRobbie notes that even into the twentieth century, 'it-narratives, for most of the adult literary establishment, were too clunky, too obvious, not real enough'; she quotes Blackwell's description of the it-narrative as a kind of 'junk fiction' (McRobbie 2016: n.p.). Like junk food, these fictions are appealing and readily consumed but lack any long-term value or substance. Nevertheless, this peculiar genre of junk fiction proved remarkably resilient and survived into the nineteenth century, albeit in much altered forms. Even though the it-narrative for adults had supposedly fallen out of fashion by this time, there are numerous examples of the genre in the popular press – appearing in periodicals and in advertisements. *Household Words*, the periodical 'conducted' by Charles Dickens, is full of 'biographies' of objects and stories where household items are capable of expression, such as Sidney Laman Blanchard's 'Biography of a Bad Shilling' (1851) and the dubiously titled 'My Mahogany Friend' (1851) by Mary Louisa Boyle and Dickens. In this latter story, the narrator conducts a series of conversations with a hatstand and discusses 'the habit I have contracted of conversing with what we commonly call inanimate objects, or, at least, of listening to their long stories' (1851: 558).

This 'habit … of conversing with what we commonly call inanimate objects' became widespread in the latter part of the nineteenth century. Speaking commodities appeared regularly in nineteenth-century advertisements: objects address potential customers directly through the words emblazoned on the sides of omnibuses, on the posters pasted to hoardings, on the signs carried as sandwich boards. These commodities extol their virtues and their value as consumables. Within the world of advertising, commodities would talk to one another too. In an 1897 advert for Eyebright Polish, a spoon carrying a cane says to another: 'Hello Chappie, you're looking well – been re-plated?', to which the other spoon responds: 'No, dear boy. Just had a dose of "Eyebright". It's made a new spooney of me! Try it, you're looking dull' (Figure 2.1). The appeal of the advert lies in its humorous juxtaposition of the human and the material. Even as they are personified, the two spoons assert their status as commodities. Though the spoons in the Eyebright commercial have arms and legs, and even carry miniature eye glasses and walking sticks, there is no doubt that these are speaking objects rather than people.

The 'Eyebright' advertisement is clearly aimed at adult consumers, those who are concerned with such niceties as the polishing of silver-plated cutlery or the advantages of one brand of cleaning product over another. For the discerning consumer, engaging in conspicuous consumption, the commodity *must* speak – not only of the buyer's economic power but also of their good taste (Veblen [1899] 2007 44). The kinds of 'conspicuous consumption' identified by Thorstein Veblen depended on the efficacy with which consumer goods communicate their qualities – economic or otherwise – to potential purchasers and to envious shoppers. While it may seem strange to draw connections between economic

Figure 2.1 Talkative commodities appear in advertisements as well as fiction. *Source*: 'Eyebright' metal polish advertisement, 1897 © National Archives, COPY 1/134 f.107.

theory and lively objects, we should remember that there are moments of this sort of animation in Karl Marx's economic writings. He speculates about what commodities might say if they could speak and muses on the way a table might 'evolve[e] out of its wooden brain grotesque ideas' ([1887] 1990: 163). For Marx, the commodity is 'a very strange thing' (163) and one that speaks not only of its own manufacture but also comments on the social relations between commodities, and the material relations between people.

In the wake of the Great Exhibition, as children emerged as a distinct consumer group with their own social and material relations, they also emerged as a distinct audience for these kinds of it-narratives. While the eighteenth-century it-narrative was aimed at an adult readership, nineteenth-century it-narratives began to address child audiences too and to seek out registers and formulas that enabled them to engage child audiences in new ways. If we accept Douglas's argument that the it-narrative is symbiotically linked to the rise of consumer culture, it follows that children's it-narratives could not properly emerge until children developed as a distinct consumer group in their own right. As the power and potential of children as consumers was established in the mid-nineteenth century, there was a corresponding resurgence of the it-narrative, and a reimagining of the genre as children's literature. Blackwell observes: 'By the final decades of the eighteenth century, … it-narratives were metamorphosing into a popular children's genre still familiar today in the myriad picture books, films and chapter books stocked with voluble animals and animate things' (2012: vii).

In spite of this reinvention of the genre, critical opinion about nineteenth-century children's it-narratives is low, as indicated above. The general consensus is that these are derivative, dull, overbearingly didactic texts focused on moral and spiritual improvement, containing little to charm the sophisticated reader or interest the serious researcher. There are some pockets of interest, and it-narratives concerning dolls and toys have fared better than those concerned with ordinary household objects. However, just as the plaything is separated from other household goods because its function links it to play and, by extension, to the fantastic rather than the quotidian, the texts that focus on the adventures of dolls and other playthings are not like the majority of it-narratives from this period. Indeed, these children's it-narratives are dismissed as dull, moral and uninteresting. Brown, borrowing from George Eliot, describes them as 'a chalky mixture meant to pass for milk' (2016: 221), suggesting that even if these narratives appear wholesome, they are nothing more than a nauseating imitation of the real thing. John Plotz, though somewhat more positive in his appraisal, characterizes these texts as 'sweetly' sentimental (2008: 30). Blackwell describes these children's it-narratives as 'moral-didactic works' and connects their continued success to the charity-school movement, the Sunday School movement and various religious organizations such as the Religious Tract Society (2012: vii–viii). However, Blackwell is mistaken in assuming that works published for young readers by Christian publishing houses such as the Religious Tract Society were merely vehicles for trite morality. In much the same way that the Society for Promoting Christian Knowledge organized a lecture for young children delivered by Britain's leading coroner, Charles Tidy, these Christian publishers were not averse to publishing it-narratives that did not have an overtly religious theme. In fact, just like Tidy's lecture, many of these children's it-narratives were used to frame and present complex information about science, manufacture and trade for a young audience.

Children's it-narratives

The nineteenth-century children's it-narrative is distinct from their eighteenth-century counterparts in several important ways. Though these narratives retain many key elements of the genre – 'circulation, the absence of volition, the confrontation with a series of otherwise unrelated characters' (Brown 2009: 634) – there are several crucial points of deviation.

First, these are narratives intended for young readers. These narratives are tailored to their implied audience in a number of ways. The majority of the human characters that the object encounters are children rather than adults. The narratives, like many children's texts of the time, concentrate on the kinds of dilemmas that could affect children and on the experiences that a nineteenth-century authorship would suppose are appropriate for a young reader. Moreover, the object at the centre of the children's it-narrative rarely travels as widely or as circuitously as the objects in texts aimed at a more mature audience. In contrast to the commodity characters of eighteenth-century texts that move across continents, across oceans and pass through numerous hands as they tell their tale, the it-narrators in these children's texts are relatively static and move in more restricted circles. Frequently, there is a simple three-part movement from a place of manufacture, to a place of sale and then to use by a single or at most a handful of human characters. Very often, the object at the centre of these narratives does not leave the possession of its first owner or pass outside of the immediate family. If the object does leave their first owner, it is almost always returned to this original owner by the end of the narrative. Lynn Festa notes:

> If ... the eighteenth-century tales end either with the annihilation of the object or the anticipation of its unremitting circulation in the market, the Victorian tales reunite objects with their most virtuous owner, or otherwise carry them into sentimental retirement. What once was lost will eventually be found. The restoration of property to its 'rightful' owner constitutes a happy ending. (Festa 2007: 234)

So, unlike their eighteenth-century counterparts, these stories are not so much narratives of circulation but circular narratives. The limited topographical and narrative scope of these stories reflects the more limited social circles within which their child audiences moved.

Second, and perhaps most importantly, children's it-narratives differ from their eighteenth-century forerunners in that they are not merely concerned with how objects circulate within society, but also with educating the reader about how these mass-produced commodities are made and, by extension, about the social codes implicit in the cycles of production and consumption. Many of these narratives embed lessons on metallurgy, geography, geology, in addition to their commentary on the sale and circulation of goods. While eighteenth-century it-narratives are principally concerned with society and social interaction, children's it-narratives are primarily scientific stories that combine elements from the object lesson with the qualities of the narrative of circulation to produce a new, hybrid genre that seeks to educate as well as to entertain. For example, 'The Adventures of a Gold-Ring' published in 1783 begins thus: 'After having gone through the usual process and received my proper shape, stamp &c. I found myself in the show-glass of an eminent goldsmith and jeweller in Cornhill' (1783: 84–7). Here, the reader is expected to know exactly what the 'usual' way of making rings entails and to have a fair sense as to what the narrator means by the euphemistic '&c'. This narrative assumes a knowledgeable reader, who already understands much about the manufacture and circulation of commodities. By contrast, the it-narratives aimed at young readers cannot assume an experienced, knowledgeable reader and one of the ways that we can identify the author's assumptions about the reader lies in what they choose to explain – or feel obliged to explain – to the implied reader. While there were discussions of the history and manufacture of household goods aimed at adult readers too (for instance, Harriet Martineau's article 'What There Is in a Button' in *Household Words* (1852)), these are not framed as fictional narratives and are not part of this genre. In the texts discussed in this chapter, the object narrators offer explanations of the manufacturing process that are clearly intended to educate and to impart this knowledge to a young reader, and to instil in them a greater awareness of this crucial aspect of material culture.

By involving child characters, by narrowing the range of the narrative to reflect the more limited social scope of children and by using the narrative as a vehicle to inform young readers about the origins and manufacture of goods in addition to their circulation, children's it-narratives can be seen to coincide with, reflect and further the rise of the child consumer in the nineteenth century. Far from being substandard imitations of an old-fashioned and outmoded genre, children's it-narratives offer something new and innovative. The old genre is endowed with new relevance and energy when it is directed towards this new audience. These are often lively, funny texts where authors use humour to induct child readers into contemporary material culture. As children's it-narratives are tightly focused on the interconnections between human characters and objects, this neglected genre can tell us much about the material practices of contemporary child consumers or, at the very least, what adult authors assumed were, or proposed should be, the material practices of contemporary children.

Although many children's it-narratives follow the lives of remarkable and special objects, such as Julie Gourard's *The Adventures of a Watch* (1864) and the anonymous *Grandpapa's Walking Stick* (1873), these special objects do not follow the usual trajectory of the genre. These objects are, rather, very static. The true worth of these unique objects is not connected to their market value as commodities. For example, in Gourard's *The Adventures of a Watch*, when the watchmaker, Nugald, is asked to name his price for the exquisite pocket watch he replies cryptically: 'To an Englishman, I should not say less than £20; to a German, £16; but to a Frenchwoman, who would promise to wear it suspended from her left side, £13' (6). The price of the watch varies according to Nugald's personal and cultural values rather than to any market value. The more he values the buyer, the lower the price of the goods. The lady who buys the watch, Louise Sorris, also cherishes this watch in a way that surpasses the normal relationship between people and commodities. She calls the watch '*Schätzele*' (treasure) and, in giving it a name, she ensures that the watch becomes less of a commodity and more like a member of the family. Schätzele is symbolically and literally connected by the watch chain to Louise and this physical closeness fosters a deep attachment between person and object. Schätzele's life is bound up with the life of the Sorris family. An early indication of this is when Louise's son Oliver has an accident and falls unconscious, and the watch's 'life stopped suddenly' (20). In her distress, Louise neglects to wind the watch and both watch and child share a temporary moment of lifelessness. The sympathetic bond between the family and the watch continues for many years, elevating this watch beyond the status of an ordinary consumable commodity.

A similar sympathy is found between a clock and a person in the music-hall song 'Grandfather's Clock' where the clock is bought on the day the man is born, shares 'both his grief and his pride' and 'stopped short, never to go again when the old man died' (Work 1876). My concern in this chapter is not with these unique, artisanal objects but with narratives told by 'the commonest of common things', by objects that are so ubiquitous as to be routinely overlooked. One needle is, at the moment of purchase, absolutely identical to the others made by the same manufacturer, on sale in the same shop; such objects cannot be said to be individualized in any way and they have no distinctive features. One lump of coal has the same basic properties as another. Nevertheless, the very mundanity of these items makes for interesting study. As Deborah Lutz suggests, the close study of a small number of objects may 'shift our understanding of all objects during the period' (2015: 4), and this seems to be the aim of the authors of many of these texts selected here. These it-narratives seek to show the child reader how objects are made, and the authors deliberately concentrate on items that are made on a massive industrial scale. This has the double effect of educating the young consumer about the way that everyday objects are produced, and of showcasing the mighty reach of the industrial empire. Artisanal work and handcraft have no place in these texts: these are stories about objects made by machines, and about the interface between industry and the young consumer.

The History of a Pin and the circulation of domestic goods

The interface of manufacture and consumption is a key theme of E. M. Stirling's *The History of a Pin; or, The Changes and Chances of an Eventful Life* (1861), a narrative that seeks to educate young readers about the intersecting networks of production and consumption, and to draw attention to the connections between the domestic sphere and the world of industry. Although there is a popular assumption – made increasingly popular in the twentieth century – that the Victorian home was somehow at a great remove from the world of industry, in actuality these spheres not only overlapped but were also indelibly connected. The little girls stitching quietly in parlours were an integral part of a global and industrial economy. The threads they stitched with were spun by machines, the needles that pierced their fabric were factory-made, the fabrics brought to Western Europe from India and America were dyed in vats of chemicals produced in massive factories in Birmingham, and woven on mechanized looms in Manchester. So, the material objects of needlework become, by the middle of the nineteenth century, complex symbols of both domesticity and industry, of masculine and feminine labour, of both tradition and innovation.

Among the findings associated with needlecraft, the pin is especially emblematic of the intersection of domesticity and industry. In the nineteenth century, pins were produced in such huge quantities that they were not numbered, but weighed. A single pin-making machine could produce 288,000 pins in a day (Ledbetter 2012: 97) and Asa Briggs claims that by the end of the century 500 million tons of pins were being made weekly in Britain (1993: 180). As well as being made in enormous quantities, pins were also sold in large batches – costing between 1s 3d. and 3s per pound (Ledbetter 2012: 97). In 1880, it was possible to buy two hundred lace pins for a penny (Beaudry 2006: 21, 26). While some types of pins – hat pins for instance – were used singly, they were generally used in large numbers: dozens of pins are needed to make an item of clothing, a quilt or even a short piece of bobbin lace. Pins were cheap and utterly fungible and, as a result, were considered disposable, or at the very least not worthy of much consideration. While the needle and the art created with it became, as Rosika Parker has pointed out, synonymous with women's virtue, the pin was not endowed with such significance ([1984] 2012: 7). They were too ubiquitous, too commonplace, to serve as a sign of anything other than the consumer culture of the age.

The Pin at the centre of Stirling's narrative must, therefore, be understood as both a domestic and an industrial object. Though Stirling's text opens with a frame narrative in which two little girls come across an old workbox, the Pin's own history, as she tells it, begins as a lump of metal ore 'in the bowels of the earth' ([1861] 1868: 4). Although she affects not to remember it in any detail, the Pin mentions the 'variety of horrible processes, of burning, cutting, &c.' that form her early experiences. Although the Pin suggests that these 'tortures' are 'too painful to be dwelt upon', even this casual allusion indicates a new awareness of and interest in the manufacturing processes that are almost entirely absent from the eighteenth-century texts. The anonymous *The Adventures of a Pin, Supposed to Be Related by Himself, Herself, or Itself* (c.1796) begins with the place of sale and purchase. The Pin's account of its life starts thus: 'I received my birth in a capital shop in Gracechurch-street, and was inclosed [*sic*] in a paper, with a multitude of brothers, and removed to a shop in Cheapside' (1).

Similarly, Eliza Andrews's *The History of a Pin as Related by Itself* (1798) begins when the Pin is already 'under the protection of an amiable and honourable mistress' (3). Neither of these texts pays any attention to the processes by which pins are made, and the objects arrive on the shelves of the shop or in the hands of the user complete and fully formed. Throughout her text, Stirling presents the Pin as explicitly female and emphasizes the overlaps between the domestic and the industrial spheres by drawing comparisons between the manufacture of the Pin and the education of a young lady. Both pins and ladies must be 'well-polished' before they are sent out into the world to seek their fortune. The Pin is disappointed to discover that she is not treated as an individual but is crammed unceremoniously 'into a most uncomfortable little box, with about two hundred others – at least as nearly we could calculate, for … lay our heads together as we might, we could not collect our few ideas' (Stirling [1861] 1868: 12–13). This passage wryly balances the experience of the individual character – who distinguishes herself both through her appearance and her good manners – and the fact that pins are mass-produced, fungible objects. The Pin's narrative moves through the phrases typically associated with the it-narrative but simultaneously recalls the patterns of the melodrama through the sudden shifts in fortune and circumstance. By balancing these two narrative patterns – the it-narrative and the melodrama – Stirling presents the Pin as both an object and as a heroine, a character with both delicate sensibilities and a tough, steely personality. The Pin's adventures are varied and lead to encounters with many kinds of people: she holds a young lady's sash at a ball, and fixes a bandage to the ankle of a young thief; she goes to a cottage with Auntie Caw to help save a baby's life, and fixes a corsage to the bosom of a lady, Mrs Fitznobbe, as she is presented at Court. The Pin has moments of unconsciousness when she is dropped on her head (19), and she can stab people who she takes a dislike to or when she feels ill-used. Appropriately, her defining characteristic is her big-headedness and she offers haughty commentary on the world around her. She spends a good portion of the narrative jammed into various pincushions and, as she is literally and figuratively stuck up, the reader may delight in her inevitable fall from grace.

At her lowest point, the Pin is bent over backwards for use as a fish-hook and abandoned in a horse-trough. She is eventually rescued by a Mr Scrape, a rag-and-bone man. While it is tempting to read this as a symbolic baptism and rebirth, the Pin does not progress to a higher state after this moment but rather returns to her origins as one among a number of other pins sold by the pound. Mr Scrape adds the Pin to a collection of pins he has found and, once he has amassed a pound of pins, sells them to a dealer:

And so it came about that I was passed from hand to hand as a fraction of a pound of pins, till I arrived, in course of time, at the grocer's shop, No. 110 High Street, Kirktoun, Linstshire; – which was indeed a curious coincidence for, as you may or may not remember, it was in that good old town, though in a different shop, that I first entered active life as a pin of first-rate quality. Many things had come and gone since then, and here I was again as a pound-pin! (131–2)

By having the Pin return to its point of sale, Stirling's narrative offers a commentary on the different sorts of economies that exist within nineteenth-century society. The sale of new goods is juxtaposed with the sale, a few doors away, of second-hand or used goods. For all her personality and unique adventures, the Pin becomes a fungible item once more, indistinguishable among the assortment of pins sold at No. 110 High Street. Through this narrative, the child reader gains not only a sense of how pins are made, but also of how different and competing modes of sale exist within a single town. Through this narrative, the young reader is invited to consider the means by which worldly goods circulate through the population, passing from hand to hand, from house to house, and to consider whether the items they find at home have had longer and more complex histories than they may initially have guessed. Stirling's choice of a pin as her central character is telling. Pins are made to hold surfaces together for a brief time and though the pin does not bind together (as the needle does), it creates connections and joins between things. Through this story, the child reader is asked to see the ways members of different social classes interact, and how the domestic and the industrial intersect.

The Story of a Needle: Worldly goods at home

If Stirling's *The History of a Pin* hints at an increased awareness of the intersection of domesticity and industry, A. L. O. E.'s *The Story of a Needle* (1858) makes this intersection a key feature of the narrative, with both human and object characters reflecting on topics such as metallurgy throughout the text. A. L. O. E. draws the reader's attention to the ways that people and objects may be considered to resemble one another and calls on the reader to see the domestic space, and the work carried out within it, within the context of a wider and more complex economic and social system.

The needle, and the work it does, has become almost synonymous with Victorian domestic femininity. Mary Beaudry notes that needles were deeply symbolic as well as functional items: needlework, and particularly fancy work, told of a woman's social aspirations, her taste and manners, the amount of 'leisure' time she had in which she had no other household chores to complete but could sit stitching away. There were even particularly recommended ways to hold a needle alluringly, to show off the delicate movements of hands and wrists to their best effect (Beaudry 2006: 45). The cult of the needle encouraged women to stay at home producing endless fripperies to muffle and embellish every available flat surface, including 'fire screens, footstools, piano stools, pillows, and cushions ... slippers, pen wipers, needle covers ... antimacassars, doilies, mats, and table covers ... lambrequins, lampshades, and draperies' (Logan 2001: 167–8). An illustration for George Du Maurier's *English Society* (1886) shows the elaborate extent of this obsession with drapery: the room and its occupants are swathed in layers of fabric, ruffles and cloths (Figure 2.2).

The middle-class home was thick with fabric, and needles were in high demand. This demand led to an extraordinary increase in the industrial production of needles in the mid-nineteenth century. In *The History and Description of Needlemaking*, M. T. Morrall notes that by 1854, about 50,000,000

Figure 2.2 The nineteenth-century parlour, and its occupants, swathed in fabric. *Source: English Society Sketched by George du Maurier* (Du Maurier [1886] 1897: 20), illustration by G. Du Maurier, 'Rival Small and Earlies'.

needles were made every week in Redditch alone ([1854] 1862: 21). Needles were difficult to make, requiring twenty separate processes in their manufacture and, even in the late nineteenth century, were pointed by hand. Needle pointing was an especially difficult process: needle pointers worked in the dark and shaped the needle in the light of the sparks it threw off as they ground it to a point. In his description of the manufacturing process, Morrall devotes considerable space to describing the 'pointing' process. He writes:

> We will suppose the workman to be seated in front of a grindstone revolving at a velocity of from two to three thousand times per minute, he takes up from fifty to a hundred wires, spreads them out so that they lie singly (but close together) with their ends perfectly even, and then introduces them between the palms of his hands, which are brought together so that the fingers on one side point towards the wrist on the other, the ends of the wires are then pressed upon the grindstone, and by a slight motion of the hands to and fro, each wire is made to turn on its axis at the same time, and thus they are all pointed perfectly and beautifully at once, and with incredible rapidity. But whilst we are looking on, admiring the brilliancy of the scintillations produced by the friction, lighting up the squalid face of the operative, and thinking it forms a scene worthy of a Rembrandt, we are crossed by a reflection upon the deadly character of the work, – those very sparks which give a character to the scene, carry death in their path, for fatal experience has told us that where the workmen are daily exposed to the influence of the dust produced by the grindstones, six or seven years will be sufficient to terminate their existence. (15)

An astute observer of Tidy's lecture on the tinderbox will note that the sparks of 'scintillations' that fly up in the air are really tiny pieces of metal that burn upon contact with oxygen (Tidy 1897: 42). The needle pointers, working in air that was full of tiny pieces of metal, died young as a result of inhaling these fragments of steel. In the *Hand-Book of Needlework*, Frances Lambert records that many needle pointers were 'clever children' who could 'trim the eyes of four-thousand needles per hour' (1843: 115). As a kind of compensation for the dangers associated with their work, they were paid up to three times as much as other workers in the needle-making industry. The human expense of pointing needles, and the efforts involved in drilling them – that is, boring a hole for the 'eye' of the needle – meant that they were more complicated to make than pins. Accordingly, needles were significantly more expensive than pins and, as they tend to only be used one at a time, they were sold in smaller quantities. John Timbs records that in the middle of the nineteenth century, a packet of twenty-five Whitechapel 'sharps' – that is ordinary sewing needles – sold for one penny (1855: 368).

Charlotte M. Tucker, who published under her pseudonym A. L. O. E. (A Lady of England), published *The Story of a Needle* in 1858, just four years after Morrall's *History and Description of Needlemaking*, and many of Morrall's observations about the way needles were made and sold are present in the fictional text. The Needle, who is both narrator and protagonist of the narrative, is sold in a little paper packet with about two dozen others of her kind. Like other children's it-narratives from the nineteenth century, A. L. O. E.'s text pays special attention to the industrial processes by which these objects are made, tracing the Needle from its 'low' origins as a lump of ore in Cornwall through the manufacturing process by which it becomes steel. As with many of these narratives, A. L. O. E. positions her object characters as gendered. The Needle begins her account:

> I was once part of a rough mass of iron ore, that had lain for ages in a dark mine in Cornwall; that I was dug out, and put into a huge furnace, and heated till I became red-hot, and melted; that I was made into part of an iron bar, and when in a fiery glow was suddenly plunged into cold water, which changed my whole constitution and name, for iron was thenceforth called steel. I can just fancy how the water fizzed and hissed, and how my fiery flush faded suddenly away, and I became again quite black in the face! I can fancy all this, as I said, but I really remember nothing about it. (1858: 9)

Though she does not remember these experiences, nor the experience of being 'forced to push myself through little holes, smaller and smaller, till I was long enough, and slim enough, for the purpose for which the manufacturer designed me' (10), the Needle nevertheless describes these stages of the manufacturing process in great detail, and her descriptions accord closely with Morrall's account of the process. A. L. O. E., like Stirling and many other contemporary authors, balances moments of anthropomorphism with carefully researched details about the industrialized manufacture of needles. The reader is presented with sentences such as 'My very earliest remembrance is of finding myself lying on an anvil, along with thousands others of my species' (10), which finely balances the personal memoir with the technical account. In this moment, the Needle is both an inanimate object (on the anvil), and a living subject (a member of a species). Moments like this allow A. L. O. E. to move smoothly between the Bildungsroman and the it-narrative, encouraging the reader to engage in this sort of double awareness and to see both the personal history and the manufacturing history in one moment.

Tucker was a Christian missionary and this narrative, like all those in her corpus, has a strong moral dimension. The Needle believes herself to be 'an instrument of good' (24) and throughout the book we see comparisons drawn between the sewing needle and the needle of a compass. This comparison becomes most obvious – and most heavy-handed – in the story George, a young boy who returned home for the school holidays, tells his younger siblings to entertain them. In this story, a pair of idle siblings is punished by a fairy for their laziness and selfishness. The fairy decides:

> As you have never, with your wills, done any service to mankind, it is your doom to do service without them. Your eyes, your ears, your hands, your tongues, have been given you to no purpose; their powers shall now be taken quite away; for seven long years you shall toil in humble estate, till you have learned how great is the value of time, and opportunity to do some good to others! (86–7)

The boy is turned into the needle of a compass, and the girl into a sewing needle. For seven years they remain in their transformed states, the compass needle guiding lost sailors to safety and the sewing needle performing 'good deeds ... in its quiet little home'. While A. L. O. E. adheres to conservative notions about the gendered division of labour, even in the fantastical story-within-a-story, she nevertheless draws comparisons between the labour performed by the compass and that performed by the sewing needle. This sewing needle is given a set of tasks by the fairy: 'What is marred, make right;/What is severed, unite;/And leave where'er you pass a golden thread of light!' (91). And so the Needle does not merely serve to repair and create clothes, but also to mend moral and conceptual rents too. Like the compass needle, this sewing needle points the way: she is the needle of a moral compass. While the scissors are made to divide and separate, the needle is a tool that can join things together, can repair the damage done – not only to fabrics but to relationships too – and mend these rents so that they become all but invisible.

This moral interlude reflects the strong religious aspect of A. L. O. E.'s work but the frame narrative more closely adheres to the narratological and thematic principles of the nineteenth-century it-narrative. Although the story is almost entirely set within the domestic space familiar to middle-class child readers, it draws attention to the object's interactions with a child, and includes technical and scientific information intended to inform the child reader about the manufacture of familiar and apparently insignificant household objects.

Throughout the text, moral knowledge is continually paralleled with scientific knowledge, and snippets of technical and scientific information are delivered by both human and object characters. When the narrative focus shifts to the human characters, Lily (who owns the workbox), her siblings George and Eddy, and their parents, the fine balance between moral learning and scientific learning is maintained. Significantly, George is not just a good boy; he is also an educated boy, who regales his siblings with stories of metallurgy as well as fairy tales. Like Tidy, he uses fiction as a means to engage his young audience and embeds scientific information within easily understood anecdotes. When Lily dismisses the book George is reading as uninteresting, he corrects her, saying:

> 'Well, I've been reading a little in the train, and I did not find it stupid at all. It tells one so much that is curious and new. Did you ever hear, Eddy, of metal spoons that would melt in hot tea like sugar?'
>
> Eddy opened his eyes very wide.
>
> 'Well, men really make such spoons; I mean that they would, if they thought that any one would buy them, – of a mixture of bismuth, lead, and tin!' (70)

George goes on to describe bismuth and the properties of other metals including lead and brass. This discussion echoes an earlier discussion held among the items in Lily's workbox on the various properties of common and precious metals. The Thimble informs the Needle:

> 'Gold is what is called a perfect metal', replied the Thimble; 'it is injured by neither fire nor water, and it is reckoned of great value in the world. It is found chiefly in South America, California, and lately in the immense island of Australia.'
>
> 'And has it to submit to the hammer as well as we?' I inquired.
>
> 'It has much more wonderful power of enduring it than either silver or steel', replied the Thimble. 'It never breaks beneath the heaviest stroke, but it spreads itself out beneath it, and that to such an amazing extent that I have heard that a bit of gold not so large as a half-penny can be beaten out into a wire a thousand miles long.' (34–5)

Both objects and people are interested in metallurgy and this information is presented as equally useful to the Needle and to her owner, Lily.

The slippage between human and object, rendered obvious in the story of the two naughty siblings who are transformed into needles, affects this whole narrative. Material and human characters are closely connected throughout. The Needle describes how she is raised up from her humble beginnings in an iron mine through effort, and how she is refined by hard work (though the Needle does not mention the fact that the hard work is all done by factory workers rather than by herself). As with Stirling's pin, the Needle compares the processes of her manufacture to the education of a child and reassures the reader that anything is possible with hard work. Like a young lady, she must obtain a degree of 'polish' before she is sent out into the world. Once out in the world – or, more accurately, in the Ellerslie's drawing room – the young Needle reveals herself to be 'sharp' and 'bright': she is clever and quick to draw conclusions from her observations. The Needle's chief feature is her smooth eye with which she gazes around her. She is intensely curious, longing for opportunities to be taken from the workbox so she can look around. She is 'sharp' in another way too – and is liable to prick people who do not behave as she wishes. As well as ascribing human characteristics to objects, A. L. O. E also uses objects as a means to understand human behaviour. The younger boy, Eddy, is compared to quicksilver, while his older brother, George, is as good as gold. In this way A. L. O. E. draws connections between the human characters and the object characters, and encourages the reader to see the properties ascribed to the objects – sharp, dull, useful, beautiful, poisonous, yielding or steady – as applying equally to the human characters. So, there is a playful correspondence between the world of objects and the world of people; they share characteristics and personalities, they have shared interests and information, and they can help one another. A. L. O. E.'s story is as much a family drama as an it-narrative. The social and economic relations between people are mapped onto and made legible through the relationships among the objects in Lily's workbox.

Various values in 'A China Cup'

The close connection between people and objects comes to the forefront in Felix Volkhovsky's 'A China Cup' (1898). Volkhovsky was a somewhat unlikely children's author. A Ukrainian revolutionary and journalist who came to London after escaping detention in Siberia, Volkhovsky remained politically active – lecturing the Morris Society, producing political pamphlets and editing the periodical *Free Russia* (1853–70). His collection of short stories aimed at young readers, *A China Cup and Other Stories for Children* (1898), blends the plot of the it-narrative with both scientific and political elements. Perhaps more than any of the other texts examined here, Volkhovsky's Cup has a clear sense of its role as a commodity, and of the shifting ideas of value and worth that surround it.

Following Marx's definition of a commodity as 'an external object, a thing which through its qualities satisfies human needs of whatever kind' ([1887] 1990 125), it must be noted that the commodity is not merely a physical item bought and sold, but the confluence of items and the feelings of desire and satisfaction that these objects provoke among consumers. Georg Simmel, writing only a few decades after Marx, goes even further, arguing that 'economic objects ... exist in the space between pure desire and immediate enjoyment' (see Appadurai 1986: 3). Thus far, the worldly goods examined in this chapter have been rather aloof observers of human activity and human emotion. While their experiences are managed by metaphors of human growth and even human qualities, neither Stirling's Pin nor A. L. O. E.'s Needle – nor indeed most of the other object narrators of the nineteenth century – are endowed with any human sensibilities. They are never really emotional and, while the manufacturing processes cause them physical pain, they do not feel emotional anguish. So, even though the object may play the role of subject in these stories, they are not especially subjective. Volkhovsky's work is different because it foregrounds the emotional aspects of nineteenth-century commodity culture.

The title story in Volkhovsky's collection follows the experiences of a little lump of clay, who is transformed into a beautiful china cup. Like so many children's it-narratives, 'A China Cup' begins with a detailed description of the processes of manufacture, after which the Cup is sold and taken home by a new owner. However, rather than being used and then passing from person to person, the Cup never fulfils her intended function at all but is broken the very first time her new owner tries to use her. The little girl who has bought the Cup scalds herself on hot tea and throws the Cup to the ground in a temper. The broken pieces are then dumped. The Cup exists only briefly as a commodity whose 'beauty is ... openly acknowledged' (12) before being thrown out on the rubbish heap 'with the bits of old leather, broken glass, rusty pieces of tin, and a pair of decaying cucumbers' (14). An old woman retrieves the fragments of the Cup and, after gluing them back together, gives the Cup to her granddaughter. This poor girl is delighted with the Cup and the Cup grudgingly allows herself to share in the poor girl's happiness, recognizing that 'no one had loved her so deeply' (32) and that she has some value at last. Although she imagines herself to be a remarkable and exceptionally beautiful object, the Cup's potential is only recognized by the people at the very bottom of the economic chain – the ones who do not buy new commodities but who make do with the commodities dumped or passed on by their original owners. This narrative plays on ideas of desire and satisfaction, and foregrounds the sense that the satisfaction we gain from commodities can only be short-lived.

While the plot follows the typical trajectory of the it-narrative, Volkhovsky complicates his story by introducing an affective element – a pattern of alternating scenes of pride and despair: as the Cup is admired or scorned, she is, by turns, excessively joyful or utterly miserable. The Cup's subjectivity comes, not through metaphorical alignment between the Cup's experiences and those of a young lady in education, but through her deep, and melodramatic, emotional experiences. Like many nineteenth-century children's it-narratives, 'A China Cup' includes an account of the manufacturing processes by which the Cup is transformed from clay to vessel. While many of these narratives suggest that the manufacturing process is physically gruelling for the commodities at the heart of these stories, Volkhovsky dwells on the agonies of the manufacturing process and describes the process as a kind of physical and emotional torture:

> Our Lump no longer existed but all its little particles which before formed it were now like clay-jelly, and kept close together. Ah how they suffered! The awful millstone pressed upon them with its whole weight – squeezed, flattened, ground them. They shrivelled, groaned, cried from pain and said: 'Oh-o-o! what a torture! it is all over with us!' (5–6)

In spite of these agonies, the Lump is later, briefly, satisfied with her finished appearance. After she is painted, and transformed into a cup, she is, for a moment, happy, declaring: 'Ah how happy I am! … it was worth while to suffer all that I suffered. I am the most beautiful here, and there is and will be no one happier' (8). However, her brief happiness is destroyed once she is taken to the china shop where 'she was forced not only to acknowledge that there were more beautiful ones, but to listen to the mocking words and endure the most offensive looks' (11). The Cup imagines herself to be superior to all others but her narcissism is cruelly undercut when she sees the other commodities on display. The Cup switches from pride to jealousy:

> Envy, vexation, shame, tormented her, and she would fain run away somewhere, yet she could not move from the stop. This helplessness added still to her pain and anger. She would like to have sunk into the earth. 'Ah', thought she, 'why did I not die before! Why does death not come now!' (11)

But when she is chosen by a little girl, the Cup becomes 'bright with happiness, and slightly trembled when the shopman took her from the counter to wrap her in paper' (12). In comparison to the manufacturing process which is painful, the experience of being sold is presented as delightful. Her vacillations between despair and joy are comic and highlight both the emotional aspects of commodity culture and the absurdity of these emotions. This emotional quality is the key to understanding Volkhovsky's narrative as bringing something entirely new to the it-narrative, and the key to understanding this it-narrative as a work that pokes fun at the commodity culture of late-nineteenth-century England.

Many nineteenth-century children's it-narratives, including Stirling's *The History of a Pin*, or the anonymous *Adventures of a Tract* (1852), include observations about social class in the way in which they chart the object's progress from the top of the economic ladder to the bottom. This is a sort of inverse Bildungsroman, where the central character moves from a high position to a low one, from desirable commodity to trash. Volkhovsky's narrative condenses this charting, making the object's journey one with very few steps. While Stirling's Pin travels all around the countryside and passes through many hands, the Cup only has two owners – both of them young girls. By creating this condensed narrative, Volkhovsky sets up a clear juxtaposition between the two child consumers. It would be easy to read this as a moral text and to see the two girls as representing gratitude and ingratitude but, given Volkhovsky's political leanings, it makes more sense to read this as a story about power and economics.

The two girls in the story live close to one another, yet they are worlds apart in terms of their economic and material situations, representing the extreme ends of a broader spectrum of commodity culture in nineteenth-century England. Their attitudes towards commodities are similarly distinct. For the rich girl, the commodity is something to buy and to replace once it has been damaged; for the poor girl, the commodity is something that must be carefully repaired and used over and over again, regardless of its appearance. For the rich girl, the commodity is primarily valued for its appearance; for the poor girl, it is valued for its function. The function of this it-narrative is not just to inform the child reader about the way cups are manufactured (though certainly this information is present in the text), but also to open a discussion about the ways that cups are used. The vainglorious Cup may be the focus of our derision in the narrative, but the rich girl also comes in for criticism. She only cares about the outward appearance of the objects and does not show any proper regard for their purposes; the result is that the Cup is destroyed and thrown away before it ever fulfils its proper function. The poor girl values the Cup for its ability to function as a vessel. Its aesthetic qualities are of lesser importance to her. In juxtaposing these two characters, Volkhovsky allows his narrative to function as a social satire.

Many of the eighteenth-century it-narratives aimed at adult readers have satirical dimensions – particularly those involving commodities that end up in the possession of prominent political figures – and Volkhovsky's narrative continues in this tradition but does not aim to satirize or mock particular individuals. Volkhovsky's target is, rather, a whole social group, the consumers with large amounts of disposable income who discard commodities – and with it disregard the effort and labour that goes into producing such items – and who are only interested in new and perfect items. The rich child is not interested in objects, only in commodities; that is, she has no particular interest in or attachment to the object once it has been purchased, and only shows interest in the object when it is, briefly, a commodity at the point of sale. In the brief time between seeing the Cup, buying it and taking that first mouthful of scalding tea – the temporal space 'between pure desire and immediate enjoyment' (Appadurai 1986: 3) – the Cup exists as a commodity and is desirable. Once the Cup disappoints, the girl rejects it and breaks it. While it may seem that the Cup only ceases to be a commodity once it is broken and unusable, I argue that it actually ceases to be a commodity the moment it no longer satisfies the girl's desire. The shift from commodity to useless junk is a matter of emotional investment, rather than of economic value or practical function. In contrast to the rich girl's disregard for the Cup, Volkhovsky presents the poor girl who has no spending power but has to make do with the items retrieved from the rubbish heap. Nevertheless, the poor girl loves the Cup – or at least the Cup feels that 'no one had loved her so deeply' – and the value she places on the object endows the object with a sense of worth. This is a purely emotional value, though, absolutely separate from the economic value the Cup holds for the shopkeeper. While the 'pure desire' of the commodity consumer is brief and lasts only until the object satisfies a desire, the 'love' the poor girl feels for the Cup is implied to be something deeper and more permanent. In this way, Volkhovsky suggests that there is more than one value system in operation, and draws the child reader's attention to the ways these systems of values intersect and overlap – even if the social circles these characters move in are apparently distinct.

'The wonders of common things'

The close connections between people and commodities, and the slippages between subject and object are the central focus of Annie Carey's *The Wonders of Common Things* (1880). Carey's book, like Tidy's lecture, consciously engages with the structures of the it-narrative to impart scientific information and frames her educational text through fiction. *The Wonders of Common Things* is an odd text because it is really a clumsy amalgamation of two of Carey's earlier works, *Autobiographies of a Piece of Coal, a Grain of Salt, a Drop of Water and a Piece of Old Iron and a Piece of Flint* (1870) and *Threads of Knowledge Drawn from a Cambric Handkerchief, a Brussels Carpet, a Print Dress, a Kid Glove, a Sheet of Paper* (1872). Although both of these earlier books focus on objects, the two halves of *The Wonders of Common Things* belong to two distinct genres – the latter to the object lesson, the former to the it-narrative. In *Threads of Knowledge*, the children's mother, much like Papa in Samuel Prout Newcombe's *Little Henry's Holiday* discussed in Chapter 1, acts as guide for the child characters and uses the objects as the basis of a series of object lessons, during which she dispenses moral advice along with the lessons in manufactory. *Threads of Knowledge* examines objects that are the end product of complex and lengthy manufacturing processes, often involving several raw materials, and the information given to the children is mediated through the voice of an adult character. My focus here is on the first half of *The Wonders of Common Things*, which, apart from the omission of the chapter about the piece of flint, is a faithful reproduction of *Autobiographies*, in which the objects directly engage the child characters in dialogue and explain their technical and material origins in their own voices. These chapters are especially interesting because many of the speaking objects are, in fact, natural substances – salt, wood, iron – which have become commodities. They undergo long and often quite complicated processes of transformation as the natural substances are refined, shaped and sold. In showing readers how raw materials are transformed into commodities, Carey demonstrates the connections between nature and culture, and clearly illustrates where many everyday items come from.

Carey uses the it-narrative as a way of giving shape to a series of scientific and technical topics including geology, chemistry, geography and metallurgy. Nevertheless, *The Wonders of Common Things* is full of playful anthropomorphism and, perhaps most remarkably, in this text the objects speak directly with the child characters. Rather than occupying a separate sphere and serving as unnoticed spies or private commentators on human activity, these objects speak to and are heard by the people around them. This introduces a new sense of equity between the material goods and the human characters – a new confluence of object and subject. Carey's anthropomorphism enables her to endow these objects with peculiarly human characteristics: the Bit of Old Iron speaks with a 'rough and rusty voice' (1880: 89) and the Salt responds 'dryly' to questions. The

Lump of Coal – who is particularly pompous – presents his life story as a sort of tragedy, as a tale of a great family brought low by hard times:

> The ancient name of my family was Wood, and ... by degrees, like many another great family we decayed, mouldered away, as it were, and that, under the pressure of circumstances and of forces that we were unable to resist, our fortunes, modes of life, places of abode, even our very characters, altered and altered again and again, till at last we sank into a sleepy state, and remained for ages and ages, unknown and uncared for, out of sight and out of mind. (12)

The account of how a piece of wood rots within the earth and becomes coal as a result of geological pressure is overlaid with the story of a genteel family in decline, a narrative pattern familiar to nineteenth-century readers of domestic fiction and family sagas. The Lump of Coal narrates this story while burning on the fire, on his deathbed as it were, and his tale comes to an end when the children finally beat him to death with the poker (22).

Like many it-narratives, the anthropomorphism of the object is managed through metaphor and analogy. While most of the object narrators in Carey's text take the form of raw materials and do not frame their manufacture in terms of education, they consistently draw on human activities to give shape to their own experiences of the world. The Lump of Coal returns often to images of family, estate and heritage in order to explain its qualities to the child characters:

> If you were to pay a visit to any of our subterranean estates, you would find that there is a great deal of order and plan to be noticed in them. Except in cases where some of your race have roughly disturbed us, we should never be seen lying about, helter skelter, here a heap and there a heap ... in our territorial possessions we occupy successive *layers* or 'strata' as you term them, in the most orderly manner. Of course there are exceptions to the general rule, and breaks and disturbances in the order of succession, some dispositions being more 'conformable' to a certain arrangement than are others; but such things are by no means uncommon, I understand, in the settlement of your own estates above-ground. (20–1)

The image of the stratified beds of rock and mineral is mapped neatly on to the image of the well-managed estate. Interference by humans creates disturbances in the natural order, and upsets the tidy order of succession, just as colonial incursion disrupts human kingdoms and dynasties. Similarly, the Bit of Old Iron speaks in terms of a career history, and of the various jobs it had had over the centuries. It presents itself as an aging veteran, having served as the sword for

'Gustavus Ericson Vasa, the deliverer of Sweden and founder of her liberties, glory, and religion' (94), and as now wearing a 'rusty great-coat' (97). Though the Iron is old and tired, he cheerfully reminds the children that he still retains a good deal of his former energy and power, saying: 'You look surprised at my warmth, but you need not; for although not used to the melting mood, I yet possess a good amount of latent heat, which certain circumstances can excite' (94). By drawing on images of family and friendship, in making heat and emotion analogous, the objects in Carey's text gain social as well as material value.

Like Tidy, Carey's primary interest is scientific and so she must negotiate a fine line between fiction and fact, allowing her narrative both to entertain and instruct. The Drop of Water merrily chats to the children about the amazing things he has witnessed on his travels around the world in the hydrologic cycle, and the Lump of Coal weaves up-to-date information about Charles Lyell's works on geology (Lyell 1830–3) into his pathetic narrative about his family's fortunes and sadly reduced circumstances. Lars Bernaerts, Marco Caracciolo, Luc Herman and Bart Vervaeck argue that Carey aims for an 'ideological … reconciliation of subject and object' (2014: 88). While there are moments of tension between Carey's attempts to make the objects entertaining and anthropomorphic and her desire to keep the scientific focus of the text clear, such as when the Lump of Coal announces, seemingly at random, that his 'specific gravity is only one and one-quarter' (16), or when the Grain of Salt rattles on about the various kinds of salt that are formed by different rates of evaporation (33), the overall effect is a text that is able to instruct and entertain simultaneously. Bernearts et al. highlight the 'perfect harmony [that] is created between nature, things, and humans' (87) in Carey's text. Here, we see a powerful example of the ways that the nineteenth-century children's it-narrative is distinct from its eighteenth-century forerunners: by placing far greater emphasis on the educational quality of the narratives, and weaving scientific information into the narratives, children's it-narratives merge entertainment and instruction and move the genre beyond the status of 'junk fiction' (McRobbie 2016: n.p.).

Although many it-narratives make much of the ways the objects pass from consumer to consumer, they generally make very little of the actual financial transactions that take place or of the market value of any of the objects. Carey's work is unusual because it contains details about the price of objects, which suggests that she aims to educate the child reader not only about the ways objects are made but also how they are sold at the present time. In the 'Autobiography of a Grain of Salt', the children's nurse reminds them:

'Salt was none so cheap in my young days ... salt was uncommon dear then, sure enough, when we paid *fivepence for a pound* and can now get five pounds for a penny.'

'I wonder why', said Edith; 'I should have thought there had always been plenty of salt.'

'I think I know how it was', said Adelaide; 'papa was telling me the other day that in order to help pay the cost of the French war, the duty on salt was raised from £10 to £30 a ton; so it is no wonder that people were obliged to be careful with it.' (1880: 25, emphasis in original)

Similarly, in 'A Print Dress' in *Threads of Knowledge* (1872), which begins immediately after the Piece of Iron finishes its account of its life, Mrs Norton reminds her children: 'It was not until 1831 that the duty of threepence on every square yard [of calico] was repealed' (211). In this way, Carey embeds information about the ways commodities are sold and valued, reminding her young reader that, while the material properties of objects – such as the specific gravity of coal – are fixed, the economic worth of objects is inconstant. The reader is encouraged to think about objects in terms of their place within a wider system of exchange, one that is affected by human and social factors, international conflicts and changes in domestic policy. Furthermore, by discussing the different parts of the world where salt is produced or where iron may be mined, these speaking objects impart a sense of a global market to both the child characters and the child reader. The objects in Carey's text may be domestic and familiar objects but they are also worldly goods: they are mundane objects, deeply endowed with a sense of their own physical and material nature, and a profound awareness of a global economy and networks of production, exchange and consumption.

Conclusion

While the majority of it-narratives tell the story of a single object – an autobiographical account of the object's life that moves from the raw materials, through the manufacturing process, to the experience of being sold, and then use by a series of different consumers – Carey's text is unusual in gathering together many objects and stories. Carey's text exemplifies many of the qualities of the nineteenth-century children's it-narrative: it has a clear focus on child characters; the objects do not circulate as widely as they do in earlier it-narratives – and the text is a vehicle for scientific and social knowledge rather than a space for satire. As Tidy used the formula of the it-narrative to enliven a scientific lecture and to foster among his young audience a fresh awareness of and appreciation for the complexities of ordinary and familiar objects, the child consumers reading these it-narratives are given insight into the way these ordinary objects are made, sold and circulated through society. The it-narrators here are not merely objects but commodities, mass produced and fungible, and their stories are as much about the networks that the manufacture and sale of these goods create among people as they are about the intersections of material goods. While the eighteenth-century it-narratives that served as models for this genre primarily functioned as social satire, these children's texts are a complex mix of social commentary and scientific lesson. They serve to educate young readers about the everyday objects that they encounter in their daily lives. The focus of these texts is on the commonest of common things, on commodities that are so ubiquitous as to be overlooked by the average consumer. These narratives recentre the child reader's – and the child consumer's – attention on these objects, promoting new interest in and awareness of the origins and production of these commodities, and encouraging the reader to consider the role these commodities play within their lives.

The objects that speak in the narratives examined in this chapter are worldly, both in the sense that they are very mundane and in the sense that they are very knowledgeable and have experience of the world beyond the reach of the implied child reader. Chapter 3 discusses objects that are 'other-worldly', everyday objects that are transformed through contact with the supernatural.

3

'A hailstorm of knitting needles': Other-worldly goods and domestic fantasy

In early December 1847 in a small house in Rochester, upstate New York, two young girls and their parents were kept awake by some strange noises. Margaretta (Margaret) Fox, who was either fourteen or fifteen at the time, and her sister Catherine (Katie), who was between ten and twelve, were disturbed by a series of strange thumps and rattles. At first, the family dismissed the noises as being made by rats. Some of their accounts of the sounds describe them as being heavy thuds; others suggest that the sounds were more like that of a chair being dragged across the floor. The account given by their father, John Fox, makes it clear that while the family initially suspected vermin, it was soon obvious that there was something more fantastic at work in the house:

> It sounded like some one knocking in the east bedroom, on the floor. Sometimes it sounded as if a chair moved on the floor; we could hardly tell where it was. This was in the evening, just after we had gone to bed. The whole family slept in the room together, and all heard the noise. ... It was not very loud, yet it produced a jar of the bedsteads and chairs, that could be felt by placing our hands on the chairs, or while we were in bed. It was a feeling of tremulous motion, more than a sudden jar. It seemed if we could hear it jar while we were standing on the floor. It continued this night until we went to sleep. I did not go to sleep until nearly twelve o'clock. The noise continued to be heard every night. (Capron [1855] 1976: 39)

The noises were uncanny; while they were disturbingly inexplicable, the noises were also mundane in the sense that they were made tangible through their impact on the furniture – the sounds rattled the house as much as they disturbed the people living within it. Over the following weeks and months, from being a general cacophony, the noises resolved into a series of distinct clicks and taps.

By March 1848, the girls' mother, Margaret Fox, decided the sounds were a sign that someone – or something – was trying to communicate with the family, and that the taps were a sort of primitive telegraph or Morse code. It is not recorded who first suggested that the sounds originated with a spirit, but soon the girls discovered that by snapping their fingers and asking the spirit to imitate them, they could put questions to the spirit, asking it to respond with a single tap for 'yes' or with a silence for 'no'. The Fox sisters were 'mediums' or 'media' for the voices of the dead. They were, as Kenneth Pimple explains, 'a conduit for communication between this world and the other side' (1995: 79). The idea that there were two worlds – a mundane, everyday world and a hidden, supernatural one – that closely adjoined one another, and that people or objects could slip from one world to another or communicate across that void, captured the public imagination.

Just as the sounds of the knocking spirits reverberated through the Fox's house, the impact of the Fox sisters' sensational demonstrations spread like a ripple across America and Europe. Soon, the world was gripped by a Spiritualist craze. The weird knocking and tapping created echoes that were felt in the most unlikely places – in busy stores and private parlours, in toyshops and nurseries. This chapter traces these echoes and explores the ways in which nineteenth-century consumer culture embraced the connections between the mundane and the supernatural and, specifically, how contemporary consumer culture readily accepted the notion that ordinary household objects could become other-worldly goods. In some cases, this aura of other-worldliness was temporary and superficial, a mere illusion created by advertisers and retailers that clung briefly to the fetishized commodity; in other cases, the object was endowed with – or possessed by – magical powers that extended far beyond the 'commodity phase' (Appadurai 1986: 13) of the object's life and continued to affect the consumers who brought these items into their homes. Spiritualism did not only affect advertising and retail but also had an important impact on contemporary British children's literature, leading to a surge in domestic fantasy narratives – narratives in which characters move between worlds, passing from the mundane 'primary' world of a narrative's consensual reality into a fantastic 'secondary' world. The transitions between these worlds, as this chapter demonstrates, are framed by domestic spaces and facilitated by household goods, by commodities that were simultaneously ordinary and other-worldly.

The latter part of the nineteenth century saw both an exponential increase in commodity culture and a rise in fantasy narratives for children. To date, these have been examined as separate movements, and the close links between the ways that commodities appealed in almost 'mystical' ways to Victorian shoppers and the ways that many of these fantasy texts foregrounded ordinary objects endowed with supernatural powers have been virtually overlooked. This chapter examines the rise of the magical object and interrogates the ways in which ordinary household objects were transmuted – in both literary texts for children and in popular culture – into other-worldly goods.

Spiritualism arrived in Britain in 1852 along with Maria B. Hayden, an American woman who 'took up residence in Portman Square and advertised her services and "Spiritual Phenomena" in *The Times*' (Melechi 2008: 163). Although Hayden stayed in London for only one year and, arguably, was not commercially successful, she nevertheless had a profound impact on the way séances were conducted in London and beyond. More importantly, her performances indelibly affected the way that the supernatural was conceived of and represented in British popular culture. Although the people attending these séances were divided between those (like Michael Faraday) who sought scientific explanations for the events and those (like Elizabeth Barrett Browning) who were wholly convinced of the presence of the spirits, Hayden's impact on the public imagination cannot be underestimated. As with the Fox sisters' séances, the spirits communicated with Hayden through sounds that were distinctly material and mundane. However, the spirits with which Hayden communicated did not inconvenience her with night-time shenanigans but were politely punctual, turning up regularly from '12 to 3 and 4 to 6', like proper Victorian ladies and gentlemen who were 'at home' to visitors. With Hayden, the spirits had entered the respectable middle-class domestic space, and Spiritualism became an acceptable pursuit for middle-class Victorians.

Like any genteel visitors, Hayden's spirits were appropriately confined to the parlour. Thad Logan identifies the parlour as the centre of Victorian home life, a space intimately connected with both 'the emergent culture of consumerism and the ideology of domesticity' (2001: 23). The parlour – sometimes called a saloon or a drawing room, the terms are effectively interchangeable – was 'reserved for social interaction' (12), a room dedicated to receiving and entertaining guests. Hayden's parlour at Portman Square admitted both worldly clients and other-worldly guests. It also became a space in which ordinary household goods – and specifically the goods one might commonly find in any parlour – became mediums of the supernatural. At Hayden's sessions, 'a noise similar to that of knitting needle dropping on to marble indicated each letter of a given message' (Melechi 2008:165) and, in some sessions, 'a hailstorm of knitting needles was heard, crowded into certainly less than two seconds' (A. De Morgan 1863: xli) when a whole host of spirits tried to communicate all at once. While the needles and pins I discussed in Chapter 2 were curiously reluctant to speak to human characters, the unseen knitting needles that surrounded Hayden were not so shy. Moreover, while it-narrators are usually disempowered and passive objects, the commodities that spoke with Hayden embodied a kind of eerie power: the image of the 'hailstorm' of needles suggests a weird confluence between the commodity and the forces of nature, hinting that the power of these items was only just barely held in check by the medium.

In addition to rapping, Hayden introduced an exciting new dimension to the Spiritualist demonstration or séance: moving furniture. While the spirits that chatted to the Fox sisters limited themselves to raps and knocks, and only ever 'sounded' like they moved chairs about, the spirits that communicated with Hayden were altogether more rambunctious. They shoved tables and chairs about the room, tilting and lifting the furniture, even sometimes pushing chairs around while people were sitting in them. John Townsend Trowbridge, writing in 1908, recalled one session that took place in Boston in the early 1850s with Hayden in the company of her husband, the journalist William R. Hayden:

> Only he and his wife were present with me at ... a heavy centre table. The doctor and I were on opposite sides of it, the medium at my right hand. I have quite forgotten what had been going on, when the raps became so unusually loud that the doctor said, jokingly, 'Can't you knock any louder than that?' Instantly there came so tremendous a blow in the massive mahogany that I cried out, excitedly, 'Hayden, you kicked it!' 'Did I?' he said, at the same time moving his chair back two or three feet towards the wall. Immediately another resounding blow followed, and the table, as if impelled by it, rolled towards him on its casters and tilted over upon him, the leaf resting on his knees. 'Who kicked it that time?' he retorted, while Mrs. Hayden also moved her seat back, as if to get out of the way of such antics. I followed their example, so that the table had a wide space for its uncanny performances. After resting on his knees for a few seconds, it righted itself (his hands were held up in full view over it), glided back across the floor, gently at the start, then with increasing momentum, and tipped over again lightly as a feather, this time on my knees. Both the doctor and Mrs. Hayden were several feet away from it, and I remained passive, holding up my hands until it once more righted itself and rolled to its original position in the centre of the room. All this was in broad daylight. (1908: 526–38)

The passivity of the human spectators stands in stark contrast to the activity of the inhuman spectres. However, the actions of the spirits are only made tangible through the movements of the table, that most common and familiar of household objects. The table's movements render it 'uncanny' to Trowbridge because although this table has castors, and is therefore designed to move, the movements it makes during the séance – its gliding and tilting and rolling – were not under the proper control of the people in the room. Indeed, the table seems to manifest a will of its own, an other-worldly power that burst forth in a flurry of unpredictable and unsettling movements. Although the term 'uncanny' was common in eighteenth- and nineteenth-century literature, as Annaleen Masschelein observes, it was not fully theorized until the twentieth century: 'Indeed, the one thing that nearly all critics agree on is that Freud's text "The 'Uncanny' ("Das Unheimliche") provides the starting point for the twentieth-century conceptualization of the uncanny – even if Freud himself does point out some earlier sources on the uncanny' (2002: 54). In Freud's discussion of the term, the 'uncanny' connects the homely to the unhomely, the safe to the strange. I therefore understand the uncanny not as 'the imperceptible sliding of cosiness into dread' (Vidler 1987: 22), but as a slippage between the familiar and the unfamiliar, the domestic and the other-worldly. While this other-worldly aspect may, in some instances, provoke a sense of horror or creeping unease, in the examples I deal with in this chapter, it brings a sense of excitement and wonder. In Trowbridge's account, the moving table acquires an almost ludic quality, which effectively removes any sense of terror or dread from his encounter with the supernatural. This ludic quality is also apparent in the nineteenth-century children's fantasy texts which feature animated commodities.

Considering Spiritualism concerned itself with the other-worldly and the ethereal, it is perhaps surprising that it was simultaneously bound up with the quotidian and the material: the spirits only made their unearthly presence known through knocks and raps on domestic furniture or by rearranging the furniture. Indeed, once Hayden's fame had spread, spirits across Britain seemed to become inordinately fond of moving domestic items around. While the spirits had a preference for tables – 'table-rapping' or 'table-turning' was by far the most common way for the spirits to manifest their presence – other common household commodities could be possessed or haunted by the spirits. Eliza Lynn Linton's article 'Modern Magic' in the 28 July 1860 edition of *All the Year Round* recounts that at séances 'tables are made to rear up in the air, paw the ground like horses, and rub themselves against you like dogs; ... sofas and chairs run of themselves about the room, and cushions and footstools are flung about by unseen hands' and, during one séance, 'a small bell was then set running about the room – they said it was running through the air – and ringing as it went'

(372–3). In 1867, William Lloyd Garrison wrote to a friend describing a séance where he had witnessed

> bells ringing over the heads of the circle, floating in the air, and dropping upon the table; ... pocket books taken out of pockets, the money abstracted, and then returned; watches removed in the same manner; the contents of one table conveyed by an invisible power from one end of the parlor to another; the bosoms of ladies partially unbuttoned, and articles thrust therein and taken therefrom; powerful rappings on the table and floor; ... a basket, containing artificial oranges and lemons, emptied, and its contents distributed around the circle, and the basket successfully put upon the head of every one present in a grotesque manner; striking and tickling of persons by spirit hands – etc., etc. (Moore 1972: 483)

Garrison's account does not mention whether the spirit hands themselves were visible, or whether the presence of hands was inferred or assumed because of the apparently dexterous ways that small objects were manipulated during this session. It is the commodities that take centre stage. In this séance, and in many others over the following decades, 'ordinary, everyday objects, things that were supposed to fulfil routine functions, were suddenly endowed with supernatural capacities' (Briefel 2017: 212). While mediums might speak in the voices of the spirits or pass messages from the spirit world to clients, these animated commodities added a thrilling dynamism to the proceedings. Clients came to expect table-turning and haunted objects roaming about the parlours at séances; they expected to see uncanny forces embodied and made visible by mundane commodities. And the spirits were only too happy to oblige.

By 1858, *The Westminster Review* suggested that the haunted commodities had become a sort of bizarre epidemic, remarking that 'there is hardly a piece of domestic furniture that does not perform the most extraordinary and equally well-attested feats' ('Spirits and Spirit-Rapping', 1858: 43). *Punch* ran a series of cartoons about the phenomena of lively furniture: significantly, most of these cartoons do not depict actual séances but show household objects moving about quite independently of any spiritualist or medium. This suggests that the phenomenon was so widespread as to be immediately recognizable to the average reader. Often in these cartoons, the animate objects have some human attributes – hands or eyes or other recognizable features. At other times, the objects are shown to be moved about by the disembodied – though demurely gloved – hands of the spirits. In this example by John Leech, a housemaid is startled by the liveliness of the furniture (Figure 3.1). She drops her dustpan and

Figure 3.1 Ordinary furniture endowed with new life in the aftermath of a séance. *Source*: John Leech, 'Things Have Come to a Pretty Pass Indeed…', *Punch*, 11 August 1860: 60.

brush (items which are inanimate) when confronted with the sight of a round drawing-room table that stretches out one gloved hand on a wiry, jointed arm towards her. The table has winking eyes, and its attitude is benign, even friendly. The caption informs us that it has just 'played a tune on the accordion', a trick performed 'without any of the gammon of putting lights out and darkening the room'.

By 1860, then, the spectacle of moving furniture at séances was so common that *Punch*'s readers were presumed to know exactly what was meant by the 'gammon of putting lights out' and to recognize the friendly, musical table as a leftover from a Spiritualist session in the house. We can understand this scene as an encounter between the maid, who enters the drawing room the next morning to tidy up after the séance, and the table that had been the centrepiece of the previous evening's entertainments. This highlights the juxtaposition of the uncanny forces at play in the Spiritualist séance with the ordinary routines of domestic life. Most significantly, Leech's cartoon presents the supernatural forces not as something that invade or threaten the house from the outside, but as being latent within the domestic space – ready to make their presence felt through the manipulation of ordinary objects. The supernatural is both contained within the domestic space, and is something that threatens the stability and normalcy of that space. As Aviva Briefel observes, these animated commodities 'are doubly destructive to domestic regulation: their erratic energy prevents persons and things from performing the work expected of them. ... Things could thwart the rules and logic of domestic spaces' (2017: 216). In Leech's cartoon, the domestic space is freshly disordered, the familiar space and the housemaid's routine forever altered by the encounter with the otherworldly. The table, the centrepiece of normal domestic life, is newly invigorated: it becomes something more than a background piece of furniture, it becomes a fetishized commodity.

Commodity fetishism

Briefel argues that the extraordinary energy of these objects is inextricably connected to the rise in consumer anxieties about the influence domestic items may have over them, and anxieties about the 'residue of anonymous labour found in commodities' (2017: 211). Briefel is not the only critic to draw connections between Spiritualism and Marxist ideas of labour, capital and commodity culture. J. Hillis Miller suggests that 'spiritualism is a feature of a certain stage in industrialized capitalism and commodity fetishism' (2009: 19). He supports this through reference to an enigmatic passage in which Marx considers the commodity as a being under capitalism:

> It is as clear as noon-day, that man, by his industry, changes the forms of the materials furnished by Nature, in such a way as to make them useful to him. The form of wood, for instance, is altered, by making a table out of it. Yet, for all that, the table continues to be that common, every-day thing, wood. But, so soon as it steps forth as a commodity, it is changed into something transcendent. It not only stands with its feet on the ground, but, in relation to all other commodities, it stands on its head, and evolves out of its wooden brain grotesque ideas, far more wonderful than 'table-turning' ever was. The mystical character of commodities does not originate, therefore, in their use value. Just as little does it proceed from the nature of the determining factors of value. (Marx [1887] 2015: 47)[1]

As with Leech's cartoon, which relies upon the audience's familiarity with the tropes and stereotypes of the séance, Briefel argues that 'Marx's reference to the fantastic effects of table-turning, in which objects take on a life of their own separate from their use value, relies on Victorian readers' knowledge of Spiritualist rituals. Both the possessed table and the commodity are haunted by something intangible and intractable that imparts new identities to them' (Briefel 2017: 220). Some contemporary writers made light of the fact that some objects were much more favourable – and amenable – to mediums than others: an article in *The Launceston Examiner* observed: 'And so the carpenter takes a plank, and cuts it in two, and with one half he makes a table, capable of the most wonderful intelligence and animation, and with the other he makes a kitchen dresser, which cannot speak a word, which knows nothing, and is as inanimate as any other log' ('Table-Turning and Table-Talking', 1854: 2). On the other hand, Marx argues that all commodities are haunted by external forces. In *Capital*, Marx makes it clear that it is not just a handful of items that are endowed with ethereal power by the presence of a medium, but that *all* commodities are always already imbued with, and haunted by, these transcendental forces by the way in which they are manufactured, sold and fetishized.

The idea of the fetish, which has its origins in certain West African religious practices wherein objects were venerated as having inherent magical power, was popularized in Europe from the eighteenth century through the work of Charles de Brosses (Pietz 2003: 306–7). Although William Pietz notes that '"fetish" has always been a word of sinister pedigree' (1985: 5), the missionary John Leighton Wilson, writing in 1856, reminded his European readers that fetishes – or 'fetiches', as he terms them – could have both positive or negative effects and could be the focus of joy or dread accordingly. He explained:

> Where a person has experienced a series of good luck, through the agency of a fetich, he contracts a feeling of attachment and gratitude to it; begins to imagine that its efficiency proceeds from some kind of intelligence in the fetich itself, and ultimately regards it with idolatrous veneration. Hence it becomes a common practice to talk familiarly with it as a dear and faithful friend, pour rum over it as a kind of oblation, and in times of danger call loudly and earnestly upon it, as if to wake up its spirit and energy. (212)

The fetish, then, combines 'irreducible materiality' (Pietz 1985: 7) with an energetic spirit or force that either lies latent within, or clings to, the object. In this manner, the fetish 'both mystified the physical world ... and reified the social world' (308), bringing a frisson of the magical to everyday commodities.

By the time Marx was researching and writing *Capital*, the term 'fetish' was in common circulation, providing a term that, by being at once familiar and exotic, echoed the familiar and uncanny aspects of the objects it described. The word 'fetish' occurs for example, in George Eliot's *The Mill on the Floss*. Maggie keeps an old doll as a 'Fetish' that she abuses as a means of exorcising her various rages and disappointments (Eliot 1860: 26). Marx connects the idea of fetishism to contemporary consumer culture, using the term 'commodity fetishism' to encapsulate both the material properties of human labour and the impalpable social qualities of commodities. In this way, Marx draws parallels between the religious veneration of fetishes in West African cultures and the quasi-religious fervour surrounding commodities in capitalist societies. Pietz summarizes the connection between fetishism and commodity fetishism, writing: 'If primitives irrationally overvalued the desire-gratifying powers of mistakenly divinized material objects, so moderns falsely looked to capitalized economic objects as the magical sources of wealth and value' (2003: 310). Slavoj Žižek explains commodity fetishism more succinctly as 'our belief that commodities are magic objects, endowed with an inherent metaphysical power' (2018: n.p.). This magical, metaphysical power, a 'mystical character' hung around common objects like an aura or a veil that simultaneously made the commodity more alluring to consumers and concealed its true properties (Marx [1887] 2015: 47). Crucially, this aura was not a permanent quality of the object, but rather an ephemeral quality that possessed, and perhaps haunted, that object for a brief moment during the commodity phase of its life (Appadurai 1986: 13). The commodity, thus, becomes something like a will-o'-the-wisp, entrancing and bamboozling the consumer, projecting an other-worldly mirage that veils the actual, mundane item from view and shielding it from scrutiny.

In the latter part of the nineteenth century, shopkeepers, advertisers and commercial artists developed new ways to enhance and exploit the mystical aura which surrounded all commodities in order to 'beguile' (Lambert 2020c: 108) and bewitch buyers. Once the potential customer was lured as far as the shopfront, further strategies were used to deepen this sense of fascination. In his popular book *The Art of Decorating Dry Goods Windows and Interiors: A Complete Manual of Window Trimming, Designed as an Educator in All the Details of the Art, according to the Best Accepted Methods, and Treating Fully Every Important Subject* (1900), L. Frank Baum, who worked in commercial display, advocated using mechanical and automated displays to draw shoppers' attention. By making inert objects appear to move of their own accord, Baum, like other commercial artists of the period, could blur the lines between mundane and wonderful objects. In this way, the shop window and the shop floor became stages for marvellous displays that encouraged shoppers to focus, not on the commodities themselves but on the seemingly magical properties that clung to these items. Baum played with these ideas on the page as well as in the storefront, allowing ordinary commodities to coexist with special objects imbued with magical powers. In *The Wonderful Wizard of Oz* (1900) the Silver Shoes that Dorothy takes from the Witch of the East hold a 'powerful charm', and other Oz books feature a magical fan that summons the wind, and a magic dinner-bell that summons an enslaved genie. Perhaps most significantly, there is a magic belt belonging to the Nome King that enables the wearer to transform anyone into a new (usually inanimate) form. While my focus is on British texts, I feel it important to mention Baum's work as it highlights one of the many intersections between children's literature and the world of commercial display. In this manner, commerce became ever more closely interwoven with fantasy, with commodities appearing to sate desires, while simultaneously generating new fantasies. As Lori Anne Loeb observes, even disappointing purchases fuelled the desire for more purchases, as the consumer becomes increasingly 'determined to satisfy the longing generated by day-dreams and fantasies' (1994: 4). Retailers and advertisers carefully cultivated consumers' fantasies, creating displays and adverts that presented commodities as wonderful rather than merely useful. When presented in the right manner, commodities could momentarily captivate shoppers, becoming alluring, enchanting objects. While the haunted objects in Spiritualist séances spoke only to and through the medium, commodities in shop displays and adverts seemed to 'speak' directly to the buyer. And, just like the spirit hands that lifted the pocketbooks out of people's pockets in Garrison's account of the séance, these enchanted commodities also aimed to separate consumers from their money.

British high streets and department stores embraced the fantastic in their displays of commodities, luring shoppers with the promise that the commodities on show were something more extraordinary than everyday items. Indeed, even the most ordinary objects could seem alluring when displayed in the right way. Rachel Bowlby argues that

> glass and lighting ... created a spectacular effect, a sense of theatrical excess coexisting with the simple availability of individual items for purchase. Commodities were put on show in an attractive guise, becoming unreal in that they were images set apart from everyday things, and real in that they were there to be bought and taken home to enhance the ordinary environment. (1985: 1)

The promise offered by the new department stores of London such as Harrods (from 1849), Liberty (from 1874), Morris & Co. (from 1875), Fenwick (from

1882), Whiteley's (1889) and by other retailers, was that the objects on display could retain their enchanting power when they were removed from the shop and placed within the home. In this manner, just as the store became something like a 'second home' (Bowlby 1985: 2), so too the private home became a secondary display space, where the newly purchased wares could be arranged to their best effect. While the department store offered 'the fantasy world of escape from dull domesticity' (2), they also presented customers with the possibility of transforming their home lives into something remarkable, a place imbued with an air of fantasy, of luxury and of exotic splendour.

One way to access this sense of the fantastic was to draw on imperialist and stereotyped ideas of the Orient. European colonial expansion enabled an influx of new consumer goods from all corners of the world. Indeed, as Edward Said notes, 'the period of immense advance in the institutions and content of Orientalism coincides exactly with the period of unparalleled European expansion; from 1815 to 1914' (2003: 41). This same period was also marked by an enormous surge in consumerism. While there was nominally a reciprocal trade among the various parts of the British Empire, in truth, the majority of the products flowed in only one direction: towards Britain. Catherine Pagani observes that while the British public had 'acquired [a taste] for Chinese products', 'the Chinese ... had little use for English goods' (1998: 29). Some British retailers capitalized on the public's growing desire for commodities from the East by playing upon an imagined idea of the East as an exotic and fantastic space. In contrast to the supposedly rational, logical and orderly West, Oriental countries and their products were routinely fetishized as sensual, emotional, mysterious and mystical (Said 2003: 46–9). For example, Liberty's made much of the global commodities they sold, advertising themselves as 'Persia, India, China and Japan Merchants' ('Eastern Carpets', 1897), exhibiting Japanese and Chinese fans (*Fans, Ancient and Modern, Eastern and Western*, 1894), and cramming the shop floor and their catalogues with goods that spoke to a sense of luxury and the marvellous. In this manner, both Eastern countries and their products became commodities (Pagani 1998: 37). Liberty's further enhanced this effect by commissioning testimonials that depicted the shop as a fantastic and foreign space. One testimonial describes entering the shop as entering a kind of dream, where the ordinary world is stripped away:

> The moment we step inside the door the olfactory organs are regaled with that unmistakable aroma which appertains to all things coming from the countries east of Egypt and the Levant; and as we go farther into the interior, and up the

dimly-lighted, cashmere-hung staircase, the sounds in the busy street become deadened and hushed, and we have little difficulty in imagining ourselves far away, in Damascus or Bagdad, in one of those dreamy interminable bazaars we read of in the charming sketches of Eastern travel. ('A Visit to Messrs Liberty's', 1897: 16)

A shopping trip in London is presented as a way to access the exotic, to enter not into an ordinary store but a dream-like bazaar. The act of shopping becomes a way to access the magical and the mysterious.

While some retailers relied on shop-dressing to conjure a sense of the fantastic, many manufacturers tried to connect their goods to a sense of the other-worldly through advertising and drew inspiration not from the Empire, but from the spiritual. Julie Codell notes the incongruous nature of some of the contemporary advertisements in which 'goddesses in classical drapery extolled the virtues of Aspinall's Enamel, Fry's Cocoa, Beecham's Pills, and Vogeler's Curative Compound' (2018: 222). Victorian advertisements transformed the ordinary female body into a kind of goddess, draped in diaphanous gowns, crowned with flowers, and transformed the domestic space into a space for fantasy. In much the same way that Spiritualism introduced the supernatural into the Victorian parlour and enlivened ordinary furniture, advertising promised that, for the right price, the right commodities could transform the home into a space of exotic, even mythic, delight. The ordinary commodity thus became an other-worldly object, an uncanny item wrapped in its own mystical aura, enchanting the consumer and changing the home into a space of fantastic potential.

Spiritualism and fiction

While Spiritualism infected the popular consciousness and influenced everything from Marx's economic theories to advertisements for common commodities in the popular press, it also had an enormous impact on contemporary literature. While Briefel insists that 'the alleged uselessness of table-rapping offers one explanation for the minimal role it plays in the fiction of the period – very few Victorian ghost stories describe the repetitive rituals of the séance' (2017: 212) and it is true that very few séances, either authentic or fraudulent, appear in the popular fiction of the period, Spiritualism nevertheless flourished within distinctly literary contexts. There was a veritable boom in autobiographical accounts of séances, memoirs written by mediums, as well as written confessions and testimonials by mediums who had either been publically discredited or who had turned their backs on the profession including titles such as Catherine Crowe's *The Night Side of Nature, or, Ghosts and Ghost-Seers* (1850), Sophia De Morgan's *From Matter to Spirit: Ten Years' Experience of Spirit Manifestations, Intended as a Guide to Enquirers* (1863) and Catherine Berry's *Experiences in Spiritualism* (1876). There was also a sharp rise in fiction that included some of the trappings of Spiritualism: mesmerism and trances were especially popular tropes. Alison Winter identifies Edgar Allen Poe's 'Facts in the Case of Mr Valdemar' (1845) and Margaret Oliphant's sensation novels as among the texts that feature mesmerism (1998: 121, 234–6), and Sarah Willburn argues that there are so many narratives featuring trances or trance-states as to constitute a distinct subgenre, the trance novel (2006: 115). In addition, Shane McCorristine notes that there was a large market for ghost stories in the Victorian periodical press, and that ghostly figures appear in a huge number of novels from the mid-century onwards (2010: 19). While there was a clear interest in trances and in ghostly apparitions, the other quintessential element of the séance – the animated furniture – rarely appears in Victorian novels for adult readers. The haunted furniture, which was so prominent in the British Spiritualist movement and in periodical accounts of séances, is commonly found in children's literature – specifically in children's fantasy literature of the late nineteenth century, where ordinary household objects are routinely animated and endowed with fabulous powers.

Children's literature is an appropriate place to look for the literary impact of Spiritualism because children, especially young girls, were closely linked to the Spiritualist movement: the Fox sisters were young girls when they first began their careers as mediums, and many successful mediums in North America and Britain were young children. The séance described by William Lloyd Garrison was conducted by a twelve-year-old girl (Moore 1972: 483). Contemporary British illustrations of séances show that children were often present at these events as audience members too.

In Figure 3.2, two young children join the circle around a table, while a veiled medium sits at the head of the group. Close examination shows that the boy has his hands spread on top of the table, his fingers touching the hands of the women on either side of him, completing the physical connection both with the people and the furniture required to make the table move. Child spirits were also commonly invoked at séances, with mediums sometimes coddling phantom babies swaddled in ectoplasm; other accounts noted that all spirits behaved in a peculiarly mischievous and child-like manner (Lehman 2014: 142). Alfred Russel

Figure 3.2 Children present at a séance. *Source*: 'Table Moving', *Illustrated London News*, 21 May 1853: 404.

Wallace described the way a table moved at one séance, seeming 'as if a small invisible child were by great exertions moving it and raising it up' (1875: 128). Later in the century, the connection between children and the supernatural was formalized and further commercialized through the development of the Ouija board, a 'Wonderful Talking Board' that was marketed to young buyers by toy shops (McRobbie 2013: n.p.). The Ouija provided a ready-made system for communicating with other-worldly forces, complete with a pre-made wooden planchette and a board marked with the alphabet, a sequence of numbers and the words 'yes', 'no' and 'goodbye', to speed up conversations with the spirits. An advert for the game in *The Pittsburgh Dispatch* promised to 'unit[e] the known with the unknown, the material with the immaterial' ('Danziger's "Ouija"', 1891: 12) but more than that, it permanently linked children and the supernatural.

Within children's texts about the supernatural – fiction and non-fiction alike – the parlour becomes a key topos for all encounters with the other-worldly. As Spiritualism boomed in England, there was a flurry of publications aimed at teaching child readers how to perform what was called 'parlour-magic', simple sleights of hand and illusions that were suitable for an evening's entertainment at home. These books do not promise a genuine connection with the spirit world – as, for example, the Ouija board did – but attest to the popularity of magic among young readers, and reinforce the connection between the magical and the domestic space of the parlour. Titles such as *Parlour Magic: A Manual of Amusing Experiments, Transmutations, Sleights and Subtleties, Legerdemain, &c. for the Instruction and Amusement of Youth* (1861), *The Boy's Own Conjuring Book: Being a Complete Hand-Book of Parlour Magic* (1860), John Henry Andersen's *The Fashionable Science of Parlour Magic: Being the Newest Tricks of Deception, Developed and Illustrated* (1839) and Henry Perkins's *Parlour Magic* (1838), which promised 'to furnish the ingenious youth with the means of relieving the tediousness of a long winter's or a wet summer's evening, – to enable him to provide for a party of juvenile friends, instructive as well as recreative entertainment' (1838: v), were popular on both sides of the Atlantic. These handbooks blended scientific experiments in basic chemistry and rudimentary physics with optical illusions and simple acts of legerdemain, and were often didactic rather than primarily entertaining.

Alongside these non-fiction books, there was also a growing appetite for children's fiction that capitalized on the connections between children and the other-worldly. British children's fantasy emerges from and draws upon a contemporary cultural context in which the average reader was familiar with the idea that the ordinary, familiar world sat side by side with unknown and unknowable worlds. Whether the average person believed in Spiritualism or felt the whole thing was a sham was of little importance: the trappings of Spiritualism, the mesmeric trances, the ghostly knocking, the shifting tables and capering furniture in the parlour, were familiar tropes that were easily replicated within fictional texts. While fiction for adult readers emphasizes the motif of the trance-state and the ghostly apparition, children's literature is more directly concerned with the motif of the ordinary commodity becoming a fetishized vehicle for some mystical force. In children's books, it is common objects, more often than people, that have the potential to tether the real world to a fantastic space. Given that descriptions of séances often described moving furniture in terms of 'childish' behaviours, it may be that some authors felt that the motif of the magical object was somehow too juvenile to include in a text for a serious adult audience. But in children's literature, ordinary commodities run wild: they become vehicles for the supernatural and form a distinctive element of British domestic fantasy from the mid-nineteenth century onwards. While I also touch on the phenomenon of trance-states when I discuss Mary Louisa Molesworth's *The Cuckoo Clock* (1877), my primary interest here is in other-worldly goods – in the apparently mundane commodities that become infused with magical powers. Whereas moving furniture originally signified the presence of spirits, the signification shifts in these literary texts and indicates, not the presence of ghostly spirits specifically, but the presence of the otherworldly more generally.

The rise of domestic fantasy

Objects that simultaneously fulfil both magical and mundane functions appear in many children's fantasy narratives. In some narratives, like Lewis Carroll's *Through the Looking-Glass and What Alice Found There* (1871) (hereafter, *Through the Looking-Glass*) or Christina Rossetti's *Speaking Likenesses* (1874) (which consciously echoes Carroll's work), the whole fantasy landscape is a jumble of domestic objects that behave in uncanny ways. In other texts such as Molesworth's *The Cuckoo Clock*, one magical item exists among a clutter of domestic objects and can appear perfectly innocuous when it needs to. Unlike the sentient, talkative, but motionless objects that populate the pages of children's it-narratives, the animated objects of children's fantasy are characterized by their ability to move about according to their own free will and to interact directly with human characters: these objects can move of their own accord and are far more obviously 'animate' than their counterparts in it-narratives. Most importantly, these fantasy narratives do not take household objects as their primary protagonists. While the magical objects may be crucial to the narrative action, the other-worldly goods are not the central characters of these narratives. Furthermore, unlike the it-narratives examined in Chapter 2, these fantasy texts seldom have a clear pedagogic function; the intention of these stories is not the scientific or material education of the child reader. While some of these texts may have moralizing elements, the primary function of these narratives is entertainment rather than education.

The kind of fantasy narrative that revolves around magical objects is especially common in late-nineteenth-century and early-twentieth-century British children's literature. Just as table-turning is a distinctive feature of British versions of the séance, enchanted domestic objects are characteristic of British children's fantasy. These other-worldly commodities emerge from and speak back to their particular cultural context. While it may seem that enchanted objects have long been associated with children's literature, aside from a handful of early examples such as the dish who absconds with the spoon in the nursery rhyme 'Hey Diddle Diddle' (Opie and Opie [1951] 1997: 203–4), animate magical objects only appear in significant numbers in the latter part of the nineteenth century. When Patricia Pringle attempted to trace the literary origins of the moveable and personable object, she found that

> when I turned to earlier versions of fairytales, such as the original stories collected for publication by the Brothers Grimm in 1812, I found to my surprise that the chattering cups and saucers, talking kettles, and other lively interior artifacts [*sic*] that I had expected were not there. The anthropomorphism that such tales contained was confined to other living entities like animals or plants, or elements of nature such as sun or wind, rivers or clouds. (2010: 223)

Significantly, the animate objects in nineteenth-century British children's fantasy are manufactured objects, not natural ones. They are *facticius*: they are commodities. And so this emergent literary genre is deeply connected to and dependent upon the concurrent emergence of late-nineteenth-century material culture and, particularly, the rise of commodity culture.

For the most part, the nineteenth-century children's narratives revolving around magical objects can be categorized as 'domestic fantasy', a subgenre which, as Louisa Smith puts it, integrates 'the fantastic mode in domestic life' (2004: 448). For Smith, true domestic fantasy exists on the threshold between the normal and the supernatural, the worldly and the other-worldly. She argues that domestic fantasy involves 'a touch of magic – a magic that appears in a realistic setting within a realistic family', and notes that 'in domestic fantasy … magic stays only briefly' (447). While the ordinary and the fantastic may seem like modes that could only exist in opposition, within domestic fantasy, the two are held in a delicate equilibrium –with neither one overwhelming the other. For Clayton Tarr, this balance between fantasy and the everyday is necessary because 'the wonderlands of the 1860s and 1870s – the fairytale realms where precocious children interacted with anthropomorphized objects, plants, and animals – not only represented the experience of the Victorian consumer, but also acted as guidebooks on how to resist the dangerous, addictive attractions of the market' (2018: 26). While I agree with Tarr that this genre is connected on the one hand to ideas of other-worldliness and manifestations of strange and uncanny powers and, on the other hand, bound up with quotidian commodity culture, I do not see these texts as 'guidebooks' for the child consumer as their function is not so overtly didactic.

Domestic fantasy in this period is, I argue, enmeshed with contemporary material culture. Spiritualism had created the impetus for objects to move and act and converse freely with child characters within these texts and, just as the parlour became the appropriate space for the respectable séance, the parlour or drawing room also became the topos in which the encounters between the ordinary and the magical took place in children's fiction. Children's fantasy literature is also heavily influenced by late-nineteenth-century attitudes to commodities. This newly emergent genre coincides with the rise of the department store, with the rise of shop-display strategies and visual merchandising and with an increasing awareness of the way that ordinary household objects could become alluring, exciting and outlandish when displayed in the right context. Just as the great Victorian shops were filled with exotic goods taken from the far reaches of the British Empire and beyond, in children's literature we find the fad for exotic objects – from the cabinet of Chinese ornaments kept by Aunt Tabitha and Aunt Grizzel in Molesworth's *The Cuckoo Clock* to the 'bazaar' that the children fill with items taken from Persia in E. Nesbit's *The Phoenix and the Carpet* (1904). Just as the new department stores appealed to a particular kind and class of consumer, the children's fantasy narratives that emerge from this cultural context also address a particular sort of reader. The average consumer targeted by the new department stores and their advertisements was an affluent, white, middle-class woman who, through her employment of domestic servants, was free from manual labour inside and outside the home (Loeb 1994: 3). Her leisure time and disposable income afforded her the opportunity to browse the shops, to be enchanted by the moving displays and the fabulous array of commodities available. Similarly, the child character at the heart of these narratives is typically female, white, middle class and free from labour or responsibilities. While they are considerably younger than the consumers targeted by the new department stores, these characters are enchanted by their encounters with magical commodities, and are drawn by these commodities into wonderful new worlds.

Most significantly, these narratives centre around a single object, or at most a handful of objects, that is highly valued within the narratives themselves. Unlike the object narrators of the it-narratives discussed in Chapter 2, which are always mundane, common and mass-produced commodities, the magical objects at the heart of these domestic fantasies are marked out as special within the texts. They may still be commercial rather than artisanal products, made by machines rather than by hand, but they are not so blandly ubiquitous as needles, pins and lumps of coal. For example, a person may have had hundreds of pins but likely only possessed a single chess set, and each piece within the set performs a distinct function. Significantly, the objects at the centre of domestic fantasy are simultaneously magical and mundane: while the object may be enchanted or possessed by a spirit – like the magical chair at the centre of Frances Browne's *Granny's Wonderful Chair* (1857) or the 'fairyfied' cuckoo of Molesworth's *The Cuckoo Clock* – they are also objects that fulfil the concrete, commercial and material qualities expected of them. There is seldom any clear explanation for the magic that animates the objects in these narratives. Just as the presence of spirits at séances was inferred from the ways they shoved tables about and rang invisible bells, the presence of the fantastic is inferred through the ways ordinary household items are transformed into other-worldly objects in these stories.

Lewis Carroll, Spiritualism and domestic fantasy

Lewis Carroll's *Alice* stories are sometimes credited as ushering in the first 'golden age' (Grenby 2008: 35) of children's literature but, more specifically, these texts laid the foundations for the emerging genre of domestic fantasy. The elements that Carroll includes in these texts – dream sequences, animated objects that converse with human characters, speaking animals, journeys within strange lands – are at the core of British children's fantasy from this point onwards (Hunt 1987: 11). Carroll had a keen interest in Spiritualism and his books for young readers bear the influence of the Spiritualist movement. Carroll was 'an enthusiastic member of the psychical society' (Collingwood 1898: 92) from its foundation in 1882, and was particularly interested in ghosts and thought-reading. Franziska Kohlt, tracing the evidence of Carroll's interest in the supernatural through his diaries and the records of his personal library, notes:

> Carroll owned a significant collection of works related to spiritualism including Catherine Crowe's popular *Night-Side of Nature* (1847), and the Reverend Frederick Lee's *The Other World* (1878) and *Glimpses of the World Unseen* (1878), which examine supernatural phenomena alongside their medical preconditions and equivalent religious concepts. ... He attended a dozen séances, including one in June 1876, following which he purchased Dale Owen's *Debatable Land Between this World and the Next* (1874); Carroll already owned Owen's earlier *Footfalls on the Boundaries of Another World* (1860). (2019: 190)

While Kohlt characterizes Carroll as 'hardly a spiritualist' (190), his letters point to a hesitation between rational and supernatural explanations for some of the stranger phenomena associated with séances. In a letter to James Langton Clarke

(4 December 1882) Carroll describes reading the first report of the Psychical Society and concludes:

> The evidence, which seems to have been most carefully taken ... seems to point to the existence of a natural force, allied to electricity and nerve-force, by which brain can act on brain. I think we are close on the day when this shall be classed among the known natural forces, and its laws tabulated, and when the scientific skeptics [*sic*], who always shut their eyes, till the last moment, to any evidence that seems to point beyond materialism, will have to accept it as a proven fact in nature. (Carroll [1882] 1978: 471–2)

Later in the same letter, he declares his conviction that 'trickery will *not* do as a complete explanation of all the phenomena of table rapping, thought reading etc.' (471) but then goes on to admit, 'at the same time, I see no need as yet for believing that disembodied spirits have anything to do with it' (471). While Carroll is obviously not completely convinced of the existence of spirits and of their power to influence people's minds – and furniture – he is nevertheless interested in the phenomena around séances including table-moving, trances and telepathy. It is unsurprising that this interest should influence his literary output. Between 1868 and 1876, a period in which his 'interest in psychic research escalated' (Ackerman 2008: 12), Carroll produced two significant texts, *Phantasmagoria and Other Poems* (1869) and *Through the Looking Glass*, which are both concerned with fantastic occurrences inside ordinary domestic spaces.

While the mock-epic poem 'Phantasmagoria' is largely overlooked in discussions of Carroll's corpus, it is worth discussing here because it shows Carroll engaging with Spiritualism's literary tropes. The poem concerns a spirit who turns up one night to haunt a man named Tibbs, only to discover that he is haunting the wrong house (the narrator is named Tibbets). The spirit, abashed, leaves but the narrator is lonely and calls for the friendly spirit to return. The poem playfully juxtaposes the domestic with the supernatural. At first, the narrator observes 'a strangeness in the room, / and Something white and wavy' but decides that it is only the 'carpet-broom' left by a careless housemaid (Carroll [1869] 1911: I, 6–10). This juxtaposition is continued in Arthur B. Frost's illustrations: in the first illustration, the spirit stands beside a chair, which can be seen through its semi-transparent limbs, but other elements of the room are given the same indistinct quality as the spirit. This spirit demonstrates a deep concern for domestic matters, complaining about the hassle of acquiring the 'heaps of things you want at first' (IV, 101–5) when setting oneself up for a proper domestic haunting, and grumbling that new houses do 'not suit' him (V, 31). He has a connoisseur's eye for domestic detail and criticizes the layout and appointment of Tibbets's room:

> Then, peering round with curious eyes,
> He Muttered 'Goodness gracious!'
> And so went on to criticise –
> 'Your room's an inconvenient size:
>
> It's neither snug nor spacious.
> 'That narrow window, I expect.
> Serves but to let the dusk in –'
> 'But please,' said I, 'to recollect
> 'Twas fashioned by an architect
> Who pinned his faith on Ruskin!' (III, 71–80)

Here, Carroll pokes fun at contemporary fashions in interior design and at the social pressure to acquire 'heaps of things' to decorate the home. The spirit and Tibbets are able to converse as equals because they share a mutual vocabulary and a mutual interest in domesticity. In this way, the poem uses Victorian commodity culture to yoke together the supernatural with the mundane.

This yoking of two apparent opposites comes to the forefront in *Through the Looking Glass*, which of all Carroll's texts is the most deeply embedded in contemporary commodity culture. Carroll continually draws the reader's attention to the strange assemblages of objects in the book, perhaps most memorably in the narrative poem recited by Tweedledum and Tweedledee that includes the verse 'The time has come, the Walrus said, / To talk of many things: / Of shoes – and ships – and sealing-wax – / Of cabbages – and kings – ' (Carroll [1871] 1971: 235). In this text, objects both disorientate and orientate Alice and the reader: while the objects that appear in Looking-glass Land are often bizarre and confusing, at the start of the narrative objects play an important role in Carroll's world-building, allowing him to establish a clear sense of place and time and to anchor the plot, such as it is, within a familiar and navigable space. The narrative opens with Carroll and Tenniel combining their efforts to create a sense of a realistic domestic setting for the reader: it is 4 November and Alice sits in the drawing room, 'curled up in a corner of the great armchair' (176). The drawing room, which performs the same architectural and material role as the parlour, offers a space for social interaction and for private reflection (Logan 2001: 13, 23). There is mention of a hearthrug, of snow falling gently against the window, the fireplace, worsted yarn and books. The overall mood is one of softness and warmth. Tenniel's illustrations offer greater specificity, showing Alice seated in a heavy upholstered chair with a high, curved back, and thick carved legs.

While Carroll's text only sketches the transition between the real world and Looking-glass Land – 'in another moment, Alice was through the glass' (184) – Tenniel marks the transition from England to Looking-glass Land in a pair of matched illustrations: in the first, Alice kneels on a mantelpiece that is swagged with fabric, trimmed with fussy little pompoms, flanked on either side by a carriage clock and a vase of flowers, both encased in protective glass cloches. The swathes of fabric, perhaps evocative of the image of the draped and veiled medium at the séance, hint that this is a space that can both conceal and reveal. The nature of Carroll's narrative, with its patterns of concealment and revelation, is already hinted at through this image. Tenniel makes further deft use of domestic items in the paired image in which Alice emerges into Looking-glass Land: all of the material accoutrements are still present, though reversed, and the carriage clock has acquired a lugubrious moustachioed face. The difference between the real world and the fantasy world is signalled first to the reader through the changes in the household objects. We understand immediately that this is a world of inversions and reflections, where household items are personified and animated. The textual and illustrative elements in the opening chapter work together to move the character and the reader from the familiar world of domestic reality to an uncanny and supernatural world.

As Alice moves through Looking-glass Land, she finds the objects around her less and less likely to behave as expected. The Looking-glass house stubbornly refuses to stay behind her when she tries to walk away from it, and though the chess pieces seem to obey the rules of their game, they quibble with Alice and one another as they move about. While the royal family in Wonderland comprised animate playing cards, the vast majority of the characters Alice encounters there are recognizable as living creatures, from the Cheshire Cat to the March Hare, to Bill the Lizard and the sleepy dormouse. In Looking-glass Land, the majority of characters are animated objects or else are tightly bound up with objects, such as the man on the train swathed in newspapers, or Tweedle-Dum and Tweedle-Dee, whose bodies are almost entirely obscured by the improvised armour they wear.

Through the Looking-Glass also contains two scenes that bear distinct similarities to the depiction of séances in the contemporary British press. When the Lion and the Unicorn are due to be 'drummed out of town', Tenniel's

Figure 3.3a 'Where the noise came from, she couldn't make out …'. *Source: Through the Looking-Glass* (Carroll 1871: 291), illustration by J. Tenniel, 'The Drums Began'.

illustration (Figure 3.3a) shows the drums appearing in mid-air, beaten by disembodied hands, a clear echo of the disembodied hands that moved the household furniture in *Punch*'s cartoons of the séance (Figure 3.3b), and of the way bells and drums could be played by spirits in Garrison's account of the séance. Significantly, Alice is unable to see the drums, though she can hear them: 'Where the noise came from, she couldn't make out: the air seemed full of it, and it rang through and through her head till she felt quite deafened. … She dropped to her knees, and put her hands over her ears, vainly trying to shut out the dreadful uproar' (Carroll [1871] 1971: 290–1). The noise made by the drums, like the 'hailstorm of knitting needles' or the knocks and raps heard in séances, is both real and intangible, a recognizable sound made by an unseen or unknown force. In Figure 3.3a, the reader is allowed to see something that Alice herself cannot.

Figure 3.3b Spirit hands making a racket. *Source*: 'A Spirit Drawing. By Our Own Medium', *Punch*, 25 August 1860: 74.

Later, when Alice is crowned as queen and lauded with a feast, the objects at the feast behave in very peculiar ways that make them appear to be possessed by unseen forces. A pudding appears 'in a moment, like a conjuring-trick' and

> the candles all grew up to the ceiling, looking something like a bed of rushes with fireworks at the top. As to the bottles, they each took a pair of plates, which they hastily fitted on as wings, and so, with forks for legs, went fluttering about in all directions. (335)

Like the animated furniture at contemporary séances, the furniture in Looking-glass Land becomes unruly. The flying bottles echo the *Punch* cartoon where bottles become the centrepiece of the action, shaking hands and playing on the piano (which itself remains inanimate) and so it is implied that a similar, unseen, magical force animates these objects.

The disorderly objects come again to the forefront of the narrative when Alice enters the Sheep's shop. The shop in Tenniel's illustration is a copy of a small grocery shop at 83, St Aldate's Street in Oxford, though Tenniel has cannily reversed the position of the door and the shop-counter in keeping with the mirrored Looking-glass world (252). The shop sells an odd assortment of objects: the window advertises tea at 2 shillings but also contains a toy horse, a doll, various things in glass jars, and the counter holds a basket of eggs, canned goods, a selection of toy hoops, small spades and a parasol. The initial exchange between Alice and the Sheep is a standard, polite exchange between a shopkeeper, asking the customer what they would like to buy, and a customer responding that they should prefer to look around first. This suggests that Alice is a somewhat practiced consumer: she knows the behaviour expected of a shopper and uses appropriate verbal formula in her interaction with the shopkeeper. Despite her confidence, once Alice tries to get hold of the goods in the shop, she finds herself unable to catch hold of any of the commodities:

> 'Things flow about so here!' she said at last in a plaintive tone, after she had spent a minute or so in vainly pursuing a large bright thing, that looked sometimes like a doll and sometimes like a work-box, and was always in the shelf next above the one she was looking at. 'And this one is the most provoking of all – but I'll tell you what –' she added, as a sudden thought struck her, 'I'll follow it up to the very top shelf of all. It'll puzzle it to go through the ceiling, I expect!' (253)

For Tarr, the ambiguous quality of the items in the Sheep's shop is symptomatic of all commodities in nineteenth-century capitalism, and he suggests that 'the commodities achieve such dynamism in the shop that they begin to be immaterial, impossible to grasp and difficult to even see directly. ... The unreachable objects in the sheep's shop might also suggest the fleeting, capricious, insatiable desires of the Victorian consumer' (2018: 36). The frustrating dynamism of these objects also connects this scene to Bill Brown's Thing Theory. The term 'thing', Brown argues, 'designates an amorphous characteristic or a frankly irresolvable enigma' (2001: 4). This slipperiness comes about when the object refuses to obey or refuses to behave as we expect. Brown suggests:

> You could imagine things ... as what is excessive in objects, as what exceeds their mere materialization as objects or their mere utilization as objects – their force as a sensuous presence or as a metaphysical presence, the magic by which objects become values, fetishes, idols, and totems. (5)

In 'flow[ing] about', the items in the Sheep's shop cease to be knowable, passive objects and become amorphous, wilful things. These objects become haunted, not by supernatural forces, but by the 'mystical' qualities that all commodities have. These objects are pure fetish; their practical use value is entirely surpassed by the fleeting attraction that they hold for Alice who, in the role of consumer, strives vainly after the objects she cannot quite lay hold of.

Significantly, Alice awakens from her dream-adventures only when she apprehends the objects in front of her, both physically and intellectually: she wakes from the first dream when she declares that the whole court is 'nothing but a pack of cards' (Carroll [1865] 1971: 161), and from the second when she grabs hold of the Red Queen and shakes her violently ([1871] 1971: 336–7). The act of grasping these items and naming them, forcing them to be objects rather than things, brings both dream-adventures to an end. By holding on to the commodities, Alice deprives them of their ability to move about thereby asserting her control over them. Her power wins over the unseen powers that animate the commodities and she is able to break free from their enchantment.

Speaking Likenesses and friendly furniture

Carroll's *Alice* stories sparked many imitations. Sanjay Sircar estimates that there are more than 150 books written in imitation of *Alice's Adventures in Wonderland* (1984a: 23–48, 1984b: 59–67). Perhaps the most significant of these imitations is Christina Rossetti's *Speaking Likenesses* (1874). Of the three stories nested within the frame narrative, only the first bears an obvious resemblance to Carroll's work and contains the motif of moving commodities. In this story, a girl called Flora walks away from a frustrating birthday party and comes across a door in a tree in her garden. When she reaches up to knock on the door, she 'was surprised to feel the knocker shake hands with her, and to see the bell handle twist round and open the door' (Rossetti 1874: 17). Once inside the tree, Flora finds a strange room filled with animated furniture:

> All the chairs were stuffed arm-chairs, and moved their arms and shifted their shoulders to accommodate sitters. All the sofas arranged and rearranged their pillows as convenience dictated. Footstools glided about, and rose or sank to meet every length of leg. Tables were less obliging, but ran on noiseless castors here or there when wanted. (17)

Andrea Katson argues that this scene tethers Rossetti's work firmly to Carroll's, noting that 'the idea of sentient furniture, of course, is completely fanciful and reminiscent of a number of surprisingly conscious beings that Alice encountered less than a decade before' (1998: 313). But while Carroll's work features myriad animated objects, Rossetti's decision to use only animated furniture is significant. While Alice quickly passes from the familiar, everyday space into courtly spaces – the first ruled by cards, the second by chess pieces – Flora passes from one domestic space into another. In *Speaking Likenesses*, Rossetti presents a world in which the domestic space, and more particularly the parlour, is the appropriate topos for the encounter between the ordinary and the extraordinary. While the people who occupy this magical realm are bizarre, even monstrous, parodies of ordinary children – including boys covered in hooks or quills, and girls who ooze slime or sticky fluids – the furniture is recognizably domestic. This space is perfectly uncanny; it is simultaneously mundane and magical, familiar and other-worldly.

In a text poised between fantasy and realism, the sentient furniture serves as the fulcrum on which the mundane and the magical are held in balance. As Katson has pointed out, *Speaking Likenesses* is 'a liminal work' (1998: 307), and suggests that it is finely balanced between fairy tale and didactic realism, genres which were often viewed as distinct and incompatible. She argues that 'in resisting the standard separation of imagination and reality', Rossetti's narrative breaks 'the conventions of children's fiction' (307). The generic and thematic dualism in this text generates, according to Katson, an 'uncomfortable feeling' akin to Tzvetan Todorov's idea about the 'hesitation' between the real and the imaginary that characterizes the fantastic and the uncanny, where both characters and readers vacillate between natural and supernatural explanations for the events (1975: 307–8). Yet, this sense of unease is not linked to the sentient furniture but to the 'human' characters. On the contrary, the furniture seems to go out of its way to make Flora feel at ease. This is neatly illustrated by Arthur Hughes's illustration of the encounter between Flora and a parlour chair (Figure 3.4).

Figure 3.4 The child and the object on friendly terms. *Source: Speaking Likenesses* (Rossetti 1874: 22), illustration by A. Hughes, 'A Chair Pressed Gently against Flora until She Sat Down'.

Flora and the chair are presented against a stark white space, forcing the reader to focus on the moment of their encounter. This image recalls Leech's cartoon of the encounter between the surprised maid and the convivial table (see Figure 3.1) – though in Hughes's illustration, the child is charmed rather than alarmed by the animated object. Both images suggest that the furniture is not possessed by an external spirit, but has a life of its own. While the relationships between the mundane and the fantastic characters are not always harmonious, and the monstrous children Flora meets in the enchanted parlour torment her, this illustration suggests that an encounter between the real and the fantastic can be benevolent. Flora and the chair meet as equals, both of a similar height, both reaching towards the other in greeting. Moreover, their eyes are fixed on one another, creating a sense of reciprocity between them and encouraging the reader to see the focus of the scene as shared equally between the child and the object. While Looking-glass Land is full of rude, antagonistic objects, the objects in Rossetti's magical parlour are perfectly charming; it is only the other 'human' characters that are hostile towards Flora.

Stephanie Johnson notes the recurring motifs of haunting and ghostly presences in Rossetti's poetry but cautions that, while these spectral presences may serve 'as material evidence of Rossetti's fascination with spectral presences', we should not mistake this as 'just another nineteenth-century flirtation with spiritualism – the spiritualism by which her brothers William and Gabriel were intrigued, attending séances and testing the validity of communications from the dead. Rossetti, however, clearly dismissed spiritualism as false belief and a means to sin' (2018: 381). That is not to say that the trope of the moving furniture in *Speaking Likenesses* does not bear any relationship at all to Spiritualism, but rather that we should be mindful of how the text might be connected with another mid-nineteenth-century movement: the Arts and Crafts movement. Rossetti was conscious of the movement's interest in the decoration of homes. The movement generated, and promoted, new fantasies about private domestic space, drawing inspiration from (albeit largely imagined versions of) medieval art and traditional crafts, and created new appetites for artisanal, elegant, hand-crafted pieces. Through stores like Morris & Co. and Liberty's of London, this kind of fantasy could be bought and installed in the private residence.

Rossetti's vision of a domestic space transformed into a realm where every commodity and every item of furniture bends to the consumer's whim connects her text to contemporary discussions about home decoration and consumerism. While the Arts and Crafts movement was a political and social movement, and advocated for factory reform and workers' rights, the focus of the movement was the domestic sphere and the ways that individuals could uphold the ideals of the movement within their daily lives. Many of the lectures, pamphlets and books produced by the movement were aimed at educating the tastes of private consumers. In his 1882 lecture 'On the Beauty of Life', William Morris, socialist and leading figure in the movement, describes the ideal parlour space as needing,

> first, a book-case with a great many books in it: next a table that will keep steady when you write or work at it: then several chairs that you can move, and a bench that you can sit or lie upon: next a cupboard with drawers: next, unless either the bock-case or the cupboard be very beautiful with painting or carving, you will want pictures or engravings such as you can afford, not only stop-gaps but real works of art upon the wall. (Morris 1883: 108)

In *Speaking Likenesses*, Rossetti playfully dismantles Morris's vision by providing a table that will not 'keep steady' but wanders, and chairs that do not wait to be moved around by people but move all by themselves. Like the tables that are animated by spirits in mid-century séances, these tables move in surprising ways and seem to communicate with the people who sit around them. Morris advocates stripping the domestic space of all 'troublesome superfluities' (107–8), and Rossetti provides her reader with a glimpse of an interior in which no item could be considered 'troublesome'; every object and every piece of furniture goes out of its way to be helpful and accommodating to its guests. As Hughes's illustration of the encounter between Flora and a chair makes clear, the furniture is amiable, hospitable as well as aesthetically attractive. While Rossetti's text is often dismissed as being dully derivative, it offers some interesting innovation – creating a fantasy world that is recognizably, and fashionably, domestic. Her work builds on and intersects with contemporary ideas about consumerism, particularly with the Arts and Crafts movement, and the desire to create, in the home space, a space that carries connotations of an imagined, idealized past, of sophisticated personal taste and artisanal elegance. In intersecting playfully with the ideals of the Arts and Crafts movement, Rossetti offers her readers a fantasy of the domestic space as well as a work that belongs to the genre of domestic fantasy.

The Cuckoo Clock as trance novel

Alice's ordeals with myriad recalcitrant things in Looking-glass Land, and Flora's encounter with the assortment of sentient furniture, are unusual in late-nineteenth-century fantasy texts. It is more usual for a sense of the supernatural to be attached to a single, significant object. The 'fairyfied' cuckoo in Mary Louisa Molesworth's *The Cuckoo Clock* (first published under her pseudonym Ennis Graham) is an example of one such object (Molesworth 1877: 45). Although Hugh T. Keenan describes the text as a 'typical' plot for Molesworth's stories – 'a lonely older child takes therapeutic trips to a fantasy world and returns adjusted' (1988: 409) – Molesworth innovates by connecting this standard plot to contemporary trends in commodity culture and to the broader interest in the supernatural.

The first indication that Molesworth is directly engaged with the Spiritualist trend is her characterization of Griselda. Griselda is not out of place in the fairy-worlds she visits but a liminal figure in her own right, who moves on the margins between the ordinary world and the fantastic world. I have discussed elsewhere the trope of the orphan girl with supernatural qualities and while Griselda is not, technically, an orphan, she has been effectively abandoned by her father, and so occupies much the same narrative position as orphan girl characters in contemporary children's fiction such as Heidi (Spyri's work was first translated into English in 1882) and Sara Crewe in Burnett's *A Little Princess* (first serialized in *St Nicholas Magazine* in 1887–8). Like these other figures, Griselda has something uncanny about her (Carroll 2020: 189–90). While Alice and Flora are interlopers in the fantastic worlds they enter, Griselda commutes easily between the two worlds, slipping back and forth throughout the narrative. Griselda's most remarkable other-worldly quality is that she closely resembles her dead grandmother, Sybilla. Her great-aunts Tabitha and Grizzel remark often on the physical similarities between the young girl and their dead sister. But the connection between them goes beyond superficial resemblance: Griselda can channel, and even embody, Sybilla's spirit. The narrative climax of this spiritual communion comes when Griselda falls ill and has a series of trance-like visions of Sybilla, and becomes a sort of medium for the woman's spirit. While Anita Moss identifies Griselda's visions as related to medieval dream-vision poems such as Geoffrey Chaucer's *The Parlement of Foules* (1988: 106), I argue that the scene has stronger parallels with contemporary Spiritualist practices – particularly the performance of trance-states and mesmerism during séances. Indeed, Griselda is mesmerized by the cuckoo's song, and enters not a dream-state, but a trance-state.

The trance novel, identified by Sarah Willburn as a distinct subgenre of the Victorian novel, emerges in the middle of the nineteenth century (2006: 115). Trance novels are those which, according to Willburn, prominently feature 'trance states that evoke scandal, and mediumship, mesmerism, or visions that threaten the institution of marriage [and] characters who have beyond-physical vision' (115). While Willburn's analysis focuses on novels with adult or young-adult female protagonists, such as Charlotte Brontë's *Villette* (1853) or Marie Corelli's *Romance of Two Worlds* (1886), there are also contemporary trance novels with child protagonists aimed at child readers, and the trance-states entered into by these child characters are not as socially disruptive as those of their adult counterparts. Johanna Spyri's *Heidi* (1881) may be considered one such text. Heidi's anxieties and desire to return to the mountains are manifested in a series of somnambulant excursions of which Heidi herself is completely unaware. Young female characters seem especially well placed to experience this sort of trance: in addition to women's supposedly innate 'nervous sensitivity' (Willburn 2006: 118 n.4), the '"constantly shifting" nature' (Rodgers 2016: 5) of girlhood renders these characters socially and psychically liminal, enabling them to move easily 'between the boundaries of childhood and adulthood, the real and the imaginary, the natural and the supernatural, the living and the dead' (Carroll 2020: 203). While Molesworth also makes use of the trope of the enchanted object, her decision to include a trance-sequence firmly connects *The Cuckoo Clock* to the spiritualist movement.

Significantly, Griselda is afterwards unable to 'make up her mind' (108) whether these visions are real or not, a moment of hesitation between a rational and a supernatural explanation for the events which recalls Todorov's understanding of the fantastic (1975: 26–7). Though she is the medium for Sybilla's spirit, Griselda herself remains oddly detached from the scenes she witnesses and cannot explain what she has experienced. But when she tells her great-aunts about her visions, and offers up details about Sybilla's life that she could not have learned from any living person, they understand immediately that Griselda has seen into the past and that she is a medium for her dead grandmother's spirit:

> 'Yes,' said Griselda. 'My grandmother died in the summer, when all the flowers were out; and she was buried in a pretty country place, wasn't she? ... And when she was a little girl she lived with her grandfather, the old Dutch mechanic', continued Griselda, unconsciously using the very words she had heard in her vision. 'He was a nice old man; and how clever of him to have made the cuckoo clock, and such lots of other pretty, wonderful things. I don't wonder little Sybilla loved him; he was so good to her. But, oh, Aunt Grizzel, *how* pretty she was when she was a young lady! That time that she danced with my grandfather in the great saloon. And how very nice you and Aunt Tabitha looked then, too.'

Miss Grizzel held her very breath in astonishment; and no doubt if Miss Tabitha had known she was doing so, she would have held hers too. But Griselda lay still, gazing at the fire, quite unconscious of her aunt's surprise.

… Miss Grizzel glanced at her sister. 'Tabitha, my dear', she said in a low voice, 'do you hear?'

And Miss Tabitha, who really was not very deaf when she set herself to hear, nodded in awe-struck silence.

'Tabitha', continued Miss Grizzel in the same tone, 'it is wonderful! Ah, yes, how true it is, Tabitha, that "there are more things in heaven and earth than are dreamt of in our philosophy"' (for Miss Grizzel was a well-read old lady, you see); 'and from the very first, Tabitha, we always had a feeling that the child was strangely like Sybilla.'

'Strangely like Sybilla,' echoed Miss Tabitha. (Molesworth 1877: 110–12)

I quote at length here to illustrate how this moment of mediumship works: although the cuckoo mesmerizes her with his song, Griselda is particularly receptive to the psychic visions imparted while in this trance-like state, suggesting that in addition to the cuckoo's magical powers, Griselda has some latent psychic ability of her own that the cuckoo draws out. For Griselda, the enchanted visions of the past seem perfectly natural and she remains 'unconscious 'of their true significance. By contrast, this moment greatly unsettles her aunts. They are 'awe-struck' and recognize the girl as having 'strange' qualities. She does not merely physically resemble her dead grandmother but serves as a medium for her and is, however briefly, possessed by her spirit. In this moment, Griselda becomes something like a medium, serving as a channel between the living and the dead, the ordinary and the fantastic.

Molesworth also makes use of the other-worldly qualities of household goods, particularly the cuckoo who is the main conduit between the primary world and the fantastic world: he is simultaneously a mundane – if very beautiful and intricate – piece of the household furniture and an other-worldly spirit who whisks Griselda away on adventures to strange worlds. He is not a magical object within a nexus of ordinary commodities, but an object that is always both mundane and magical: he occupies a prominent position in the parlour and so serves to show that the boundaries between the ordinary and the extraordinary are always blurred in this space. This sense of the fantastic is further enhanced by Walter Crane's illustrations. Crane was well used to presenting commodities in fantastic ways: in addition to working as an illustrator, Crane also produced commercial art, including posters for lead pencils, Pears Soap, Champange Hau as well as for 'an array of insurance companies including Economic Life and, notably, Scottish Widows, for whom he designed prospectuses and a whole series of bookmarks' (Lambert 2020b: 80–3). In keeping with the emphasis on materiality and commodities in this book, Crane uses the graphic conventions more commonly associated with posters in his illustrations for Molesworth's novel, utilizing a narrow, vertical rectangle in which a female figure is prominent but usually on either the left- or right-hand edge, framing the action and detail of the image, which are pushed to the background. With the exception of the illustration 'My Aunts Must Have Come Back' in which the girl slumps sleepily on an armchair, Griselda is usually depicted like the graceful female figures in Crane's advertisements, tall and slender, draped gracefully in her nightgown or the fabulously feathered cloak given to her by the cuckoo. For instance, when Griselda and the cuckoo enter Butterfly Land, the image of Griselda dancing nimbly on the edge of a pool, surrounded by flowers and butterflies, recalls Crane's more stylized adverts, such as his 'On Liberality' for Selfridge & Co., in which a mythic female figure holds an abundance of fruit in the gathered folds of her dress, or his cover for the 1898 issue of *Jugend* in which a girl dances against a sumptuous backdrop of flowers and foliage. In this scene in Molesworth's book, the child takes on a visual role more usually reserved for elegant adult figures in Victorian commodity culture. Crane presents Griselda as other-worldly in her own right, as a kind of goddess or spirit within the domestic space, draped in diaphanous material and poised on the threshold of the familiar and the unknown. Crane also injects a note of the uncanny into the images of the primary world. Just as Tenniel uses the physical details of the drawing room to convey the differences between England and Looking-glass Land, Crane too uses objects to mark the transition between the primary world and the fabulous secondary worlds into which Griselda is introduced by the cuckoo. The first image in the book emphasizes the texture and materiality of the primary world (see Figure 3.5), tightly framed on one side by a curtain and, along the bottom of the image, by the edge of a heavily patterned rug. Griselda's left hand holds the heavy jacquard curtain aside as she gazes at the parlour with its clutter of furnishings: in addition to the cuckoo clock, which takes the form of a wooden chalet, there is a framed picture, two circular items that might be hanging plates, a vase of tall flowers resting on a spindly console table and a 'Queen Anne' dining chair. The reader is ushered into this typical, even stereotypical, Victorian parlour space, by Griselda's pale, almost spectral figure. As a character who channels the spirits of the dead, Griselda has a supernatural quality that Crane enhances in this illustration. By presenting the protagonist as a ghostly

Figure 3.5 Griselda presented as a ghostly figure in the parlour. *Source: The Cuckoo Clock* (Molesworth 1877: opp 41), illustration by W. Crane, 'Why Won't You Speak to Me?'

figure in a domestic space, Crane deliberately evokes the image of the draped, spectral figures who appeared in parlours at the behest of mediums – furthering the sense that Griselda herself is an uncanny figure.

Despite the visual differences between the primary world and the secondary worlds of the novel, the fantastic realm begins to encroach upon and influence and even 'interlock' with the primary world (Rosenthal 1986: 190). The interlocking of the primary and secondary worlds in Molesworth's novel is, Smith argues, 'characteristic of the way in which domestic fantasy developed' (2004: 451) and, I suggest, reflects the way contemporary commercial culture treated ordinary household items as fabulous and other-worldly. This was a culture in which all domestic spaces could be fantasized and rendered fantastic. As parlours and drawing rooms around Britain became stages on which the supernatural was performed, children's fiction made increasingly sophisticated use of enchanted objects which passed easily between primary and secondary worlds and of characters who occupied the uncanny border between those worlds. Molesworth's cuckoo acts this way: his dual role allows him to act at once as a timepiece for Aunt Grizzel and Aunt Tabitha, a warden of chronological time, and as a spiritual guide for Griselda, a conduit to mythic time. He flits between these roles and these worlds, between the parlour and Griselda's dream landscapes. Significantly, the interior of the cuckoo clock also shimmers between two worlds:

> Inside there was the most charming little snuggery imaginable. It was something like a saloon railway carriage – it seemed to be all lined and carpeted and everything, with rich mossy red velvet; there was a little round table in the middle and two arm-chairs, on one of which sat the cuckoo – 'quite like other people,' thought Griselda to herself –. (Molesworth 1877: 63)

While the cuckoo clock looks like a house and the furniture inside reminds Griselda of a parlour, the space also evokes a railway carriage, a space that, Alice Jenkins argues, functions as a heterotopic space in children's fantasy, bridging the gap between the worldly and the other-worldly (2013: 23–37). Of the three adventures on which the cuckoo brings Griselda – to the Land of the Nodding Mandarins, to Butterfly Land and to the Moon – the first is the most important for my purposes here because it shows how Molesworth negotiates the intersection of fantasy and reality.

In her visit to the Land of the Nodding Mandarins, Griselda never properly leaves her aunts' house, but enters into another world through 'a marvellous Chinese cabinet, all black and gold and carving. It was made in the shape of a temple, or a palace – Griselda was not sure which' (Molesworth 1877: 14) that stands in the drawing room. Griselda is immediately drawn to the cabinet, finding it 'very delicious and wonderful' (14), a description which unites sensuous – and bodily – pleasure, with the other-worldly sense of the fantastic. Though the cabinet is described as very old, Molesworth's implied readers would also have been well aware of what the cabinet looked like and what sorts of objects it contained because of the enormous popularity of Chinese artefacts in late Victorian Britain. Sarah Cheang notes that 'from the mid to late nineteenth century onwards ... Chinese decorative objects were also available in a wide variety of shops across the country. Large drapers and ladies' outfitters sold Canton shawls and embroidered work, whilst fancy goods shops, gift shops and antique dealers supplied carvings, fans, ceramics and other curiosities' (2007: 1). When she enters the Chinese cabinet, Griselda is not transported to a totally unfamiliar secondary world, then, but to an exotic, sophisticated realm that readers would have already glimpsed through advertisements and shop displays. For Griselda, the cabinet, and by extension China, is a '*queer* place' (Molesworth 1877: 69, emphasis in original) – a place that evokes an uncanny sense of being at once strange and recognizable. Molesworth's world-building uses material description, loading the scene with details of textures and fabrics to assure the reader that Griselda experiences this secondary world through her bodily senses and not through her imagination. A typical detail is Molesworth's description of the silk cushions that are 'not "fruzzley" silk, if you know what that means; it did not make you feel as if your nails wanted cutting, or as if all the rough places on your skin were being rubbed up the wrong way; its softness was like that of a rose or pansy petal' (78). Unlike Alice's encounters with the elusive and illusive objects in the Sheep's shop which appear familiar but slip out of reach, the material objects in Griselda's fairy-worlds appear exotic but are ultimately tangible, knowable and recognizable.

Conclusion

British children's domestic fantasy emerges from a cultural milieu in which commodity fetishism reached new heights. From the mid-nineteenth century onwards, ordinary commodities were presented in increasingly fabulous ways, as advertisers and retailers reached for new and exciting ways to market familiar goods. The fantasies created by advertisers around commodities were aided by the fact that the Victorian public were increasingly willing to see the domestic space as a space in which fantastic events could occur, and where other-worldly visitors could meet with and converse with people in private parlours. Crucially, in Britain, the Spiritualist movement was indelibly connected to material objects, as the spirits made their presence felt by moving furniture and small commodities about during séances. Victorian consumers became accustomed to the idea that commodities could become emissaries for the supernatural. The trope of the moving or haunted object became an important element of British children's fantasy around this time, and many narratives featured apparently mundane commodities that then reveal their supernatural potential to the child character. As I have mentioned, the parlour or the drawing room is a key topos for these narratives; it is a space that is at once intimately associated with the domestic and a space that offers opportunities for meetings and encounters between members of the household and their visitors. These so-called domestic fantasies are, then, narratives that interlock the domestic and the other-worldly, drawing equally on Spiritualism and on commodity culture to create narratives which are absolutely of their time.

The texts by Carroll, Rossetti and Molesworth discussed here are a small sample of the domestic fantasy genre that emerged in the latter half of the nineteenth century, and became more popular and prominent in children's fiction throughout the twentieth century through the work of authors like Lucy Boston, Elizabeth Goudge and Philippa Pearce. Texts belonging to this genre have distinct characteristics: thematically, they are concerned with the uncanny, with the intersection of the strange and the familiar within the domestic setting. These texts are not concerned with educating their readers except, perhaps, covertly through the moral didacticism and the personal growth and moral development that is sometimes detected in the main characters themselves though this didacticism is not the focus of the narratives. Above all, these texts are deeply and indelibly connected to the domestic space, using this familiar setting not simply for realism but for fantasy too. In the texts discussed here, magic is connected to commodities, to permeable mirrors and bowing armchairs and chatty clocks. While they initially appear ordinary, these common items reveal themselves to be possessed with – rather than possessed *by* – otherworldly powers. The magical commodities presented by Carroll, Rossetti and Molesworth are not possessed by spirits or moved about by spectres, but have their own magical properties. Unlike the voluble commodities of it-narratives, the commodities in these domestic fantasy narratives have the power to move by themselves and to speak directly to or otherwise interact with human characters. They are haunted, not by supernatural forces, but by the 'mystical', quality that all fetishized commodities share.

While these magical objects are a source of fascination for characters and readers, other commodities that seem to have minds or wills of their own may be the subject of suspicion. As the nineteenth century wore on, writers became increasingly suspicious of the power that commodities had over consumers. For followers of Marx's theories, there was increasing concern regarding the growing power of the commodity, and the powerlessness of the consumer and the worker. While objects were inherently passive, *things* could be beguiling, treacherous, even dangerous. In children's literature, this is reflected in a growing tension between the child and the commodities around them. In Chapter 4, I examine texts in which child characters prove to be ineffective consumers, unable to master the commodities around them, and texts in which characters break and abuse commodities, or in which commodities turn on their owners. Drawing on Brown's Thing Theory and concentrating on the work of Kenneth Grahame, Beatrix Potter and E. Nesbit, herself a prominent member of the Fabian society, this final chapter examines texts in which child characters and things come into direct – and sometimes violent – conflict.

4

'A disgraceful state of things': Bad consumers and bad commodities

There was no sign of a forced entry or a struggle in Charles Ensley's house. When Ensley's servant found him dead in his sitting room on the afternoon of 16 June 1887, it was clear that the man had been murdered in his sleep. The room seemed undisturbed: Ensley lay curled on the couch as he had been when he lay down for an afternoon nap. A jug of water and a glass stood close by, ready for when he woke. No possessions were missing: the dead man's watch and wallet were still safe inside his pockets. Perversely, the murderer had returned the murder weapon, Ensley's own rifle, to its original position, on a hook over the fireplace. Suspicion immediately fell upon Ensley's cousin and next-of-kin, John Avery, who stood to inherit the bachelor's considerable fortune. But the real killer was only identified three years later when Avery's lawyer reconstructed the scene of the crime. His forensic reconstruction of the scene is the centrepiece of an advertising pamphlet for Mother Seigel's Curative Syrup, a British product sold as a digestive aid. The lawyer's reconstruction of the scene on an August afternoon in 1891 was exacting: he placed a sheet with a charcoal outline of the body on Ensley's couch, replaced the rifle on its hooks, and positioned a jug of water exactly where the dead man had left one. With eight witnesses, the lawyer waited patiently in the room and 'within a few minutes, the rifle, untouched by human hands, went off with a sharp report, the ball striking the outlined form on the sheet' ('Was Charles Ensley Murdered?', 1892: 2). The writer explains: 'As Ensley lay asleep on the couch the direct rays of the sun passing through the jug of water, which acted as a burning glass, struck the cartridge-chamber of the rifle and caused an intense heat, which fired the cartridge' (2). The pamphlet continues in this strange vein, marvelling: 'How curiously a man may come by his death! Who knows what will kill him, or when?' (3). Perhaps unwisely for a pamphlet advertising the virtues of a medicinal syrup, the pamphlet also reports the case of a clergyman who died after accidentally inhaling a cork he held between his teeth as he measured out a spoonful of medicine (3). Ordinary objects could prove lethal.

While stories of dangerous objects were seldom so dramatic and bizarre as the ones recounted by the Seigel's pamphlet, advertisements from this period are full of cautionary tales, warning prospective consumers of the perils of substandard and dangerous commodities. The Carbolic Smoke Ball company cautions customers: 'Beware of Worthless and Fraudulent Imitations' (1891: 1) and a pamphlet for Pears Soap denounces 'Dangerous Soaps' and warns consumers thus: 'arsenic, the acid nitrate of mercury, tartar emetic, and potassa caustic, form part of their ingredients, whilst they are coloured green by the sesquioxide of chromium, or a rose colour by the bisulphuret of mercury' ('Poison in Toilet Soaps!' 1890: 1). These harmful soaps are established as detrimental to the health and well-being of consumers. By contrast, the reader is led to assume, Pears Soap contains only safe, quality ingredients that will nourish the tender skin of the consumer. The Victorian popular press revelled in stories of consumers who were injured by objects. Vicky Holmes observes that there was an exponential increase in the 'somewhat macabre interest in accidents in the late-Victorian era central to which was a concern over domestic dangers' (2014: 126), a concern which was closely connected to 'a rise in press coverage, the formation of various accident-prevention societies, the establishment of the St. John Ambulance service, and a rise in the publication of first-aid manuals indicated an increasing interest in accidents – "their provision, treatment, and avoidance"' (126). Accidents in the home, especially those caused by shoddy commodities such as cheap oil lamps ('The Ancoats Lamp Fatality', 2 December 1899: 12) or badly made cribs ('Two Luckless Babes', 31 August 1894: 1), were common. Rather than apportioning blame to human carelessness, the blame for these numerous domestic accidents fell on the commodities and on the manufacturers of the second-rate commodities (Holmes 2014: 127). Towards the end of the nineteenth century, then, there was a clear sense that not all consumer goods were *good*; some were dangerous and the unwary consumer put themselves in harm's way.[1]

This chapter explores instances of what Scott Herring terms 'material deviance' (2011: n.p.) in late-nineteenth- and early-twentieth-century children's literature, and examines the characters and items that stray outside of their normal positions in the system of objects and consumers. The texts I have discussed up to this point celebrate contemporary commodity culture and position the child as a central participant in the production, consumption and appreciation of goods. Child readers in the texts I have discussed up to this point were presented through a worldview in which consumption is normalized and commodities are benign, helpful and obedient. Towards the end of the period, however, the growing suspicion of commodity culture manifests in the children's literature of the late nineteenth and early twentieth century as an increased tension between child characters and the material goods around them. These texts present children, not as burgeoning consumers immersed in the benign world of goods, but as inept consumers surrounded by unruly and recalcitrant objects. In texts by Kenneth Grahame, Beatrix Potter and E. Nesbit, children (or their animal stand-ins) are shown to have poor relationships with contemporary commodity culture, and they are revealed as unsuccessful and ineffectual consumers, whose lack of expertise leaves them open to exploitation; they are easily duped by advertisements, taken in by unscrupulous shopkeepers, unable to spend their money freely and often left unsatisfied with the purchases they make. While earlier texts sought to accommodate and enculture the naïve consumer, and to guide the child characters – and by extension the child reader – through the complex world of goods, these texts suggest that commodity culture is a devious and dangerous one of which characters – and readers – should be wary.

In the texts I discuss in this chapter, both child consumers and commodities are depicted as deviant in that they deviate or stray from normative material practices. In these texts, I argue, there is an increasing tendency to portray commodities as 'things' rather than 'goods'. While the two terms are often used interchangeably, it is important to distinguish between them: while 'goods' carry connotations of virtue and moral worthiness, 'things' are more ambiguous. Bill Brown suggests that things 'hover over the threshold between the nameable and unnameable, the figurable and unfigurable, the identifiable and unidentifiable' (2001: 5). While goods 'mak[e] visible and stable the categories of culture' (Douglas and Isherwood 1979: 59), things 'stubbornly resis[t] integration into a discursive, systematic order' (Kreienbrock 2013: 2). Commodities become things when they do not fulfil the functions they are expected to fulfil or they eschew the values they are expected to promote. Things reject the use values imposed on them by consumers, either through stubborn inaction or outright rebellion. Frequently, this transformation is made known when an item that had previously been a passive servant or inert commodity suddenly fails to perform as expected. Brown explains that commodities become things 'when they stop working for us … when their flow within the circuits of production and distribution, consumption and exhibition, has been arrested, however momentarily' (2001: 4). Yet Brown's classification of the thing still positions it as passive, as something that is acted upon: the passive construction of the phrase 'has been arrested' attests to this. On the other hand, Karl Marx typifies things as active and agent. He argues that when a commodity pauses within the cycles of circulation, it 'changes into a thing which transcends sensuousness' ([1887] 1990: 163). Moreover, Marx goes on to suggest that the thing is almost vampiric, taking its energy at the expense of the worker's. As Fromm puts it: 'The worker puts his life into the object and his life then belongs no longer to himself but to the object. ... The life which he has given to the object sets itself against him as an alien and hostile force' (1962: 170). Here, the object that moves outside of the cycles of production, exchange and consumption can become actively malevolent. Once things break free from the system of objects, they can disorder and subvert the social and cultural values we link to commodities. So, on the one hand, we have 'goods', stable and well-behaved objects that serve as valued touchstones for cultural and social values; their stability promotes stability in their users. On the other hand, we have 'things', beguiling, treacherous, deviant commodities that subvert cultural and social values, and have a deleterious effect on the user. This chapter examines texts by Nesbit, Potter and Grahame in which characters prove to be ineffective consumers, unable to master the commodities around them, vulnerable to the caprices of things.

Children's literature is a good place to look for things. Jörg Kreienbrock asserts: 'For the child, things are inscribed with a force that goes beyond function and meaning. ... The child entertains a quasi-animistic relationship to the objects in his environment' (2013: 215). This quasi-animistic relationship allows for fluidity in the categorization of subject and object. This, in turn, allows for the increased possibility of agent things that act and express will within children's literature. Furthermore, some critics have traced a connection between children's material deviance (evidenced through playful or naughty misappropriations of objects) and objects that have become things. Jones and Boivin draw direct comparisons between children and things, stating that 'objects acting with their own volition [are] often like cranky people or children' (2010: 334). While Jones and Boivin align children and things, there is often little sympathy between things and children consumers in children's literature.

If objects enshrine and uphold moral and cultural values, the users of these objects should absorb and internalize these values. However, once things break free from the system of objects, they disorder and subvert these values, leading the consumer into material deviance. Just as the good object promotes further goodness, the unstable thing generates further instability. Thus, both the bad consumer and the bad object have a reciprocal role to play in material deviance: each reinforces and furthers the bad behaviour of the other. In this manner, the bad thing and the bad child are simultaneously potential enemies and potential allies, asserting their subjectivity and might in a world of adult-approved commodities and networks of power. In literary texts, bad things and bad consumers disrupt social and material orders, bringing confusion, change and chaos. The texts discussed here are not concerned with inducting the child reader into contemporary material culture but instead revel in characters who largely disregard the social, scientific and moral principles that had been connected to consumption and consumerism. The characters in these texts are depicted as having complex, challenging and difficult relationships with the material objects they interact with. Their fraught interactions with commodities are symptomatic of an increased suspicion of material goods in the Edwardian period, and mark the onset of a new phase in the representation of material culture in children's literature.

Bad consumers in E. Nesbit's work

E. Nesbit had a complicated relationship with consumerism and commodity culture. While she was acknowledged as 'a vigorous socialist and member of the Fabian Society' ('General Gossip of Authors and Writers', September 1889: 196), her contributions to the Society are sometimes overlooked because of the presence of more outspoken and flamboyant men in the group, including Jerome K. Jerome, George Bernard Shaw and Nesbit's husband, the 'dashing' Hubert Bland (Chesterton 1931: 14). Yet Nesbit was a radical in her own right; she was an active member of Charlotte Wilson's 'Karl Marx Club', a radical political study group that met to discuss Marxist and anarchist theory and she tried to bring some of this critical rigour to the Fabians, proposing at a committee meeting in May 1887 that they organize classes in political economy (Fitzsimons 2019: 73). Yet this political radicalism is not often evident in her writing for children. Nesbit was a professional writer who was keenly aware of the need to commodify her work, writing episodes quickly to meet the demands of the periodical market (Briggs 1989: 225), shamelessly borrowing plots from earlier authors, reusing scenes and lines among her own stories and even transforming incidents in the lives of her own children into fodder for her stories.[2] One of these incidents, described by Edgar Jepson, reveals the tensions between her socialist ideals and the practicalities of making a living from her work. Jepson recalls when two of the Blands' children, Rosamund and Fabian, dabbled in 'Big

Business' by dressing in shabby clothes and selling flowers to commuters outside the train station:

> For a while the two children lived happily in an affluence beyond all dreams. Then a meddlesome native informed the Blands that their two youngest had slipped into the sphere of Big Business, and the Blands in a furious annoyance stopped the enterprise. Their annoyance astonished me: it seemed so Victorian, and here we were in the Edwardian age, the age in which Big Business was beginning to get into its stride and press gallantly on. (1937: 24–5).

While Jepson sees the Blands' disapproval of Big Business as anachronistic, their distaste for capitalist enterprise seems to fit closely with their socialist ideals. Paradoxically, Nesbit was not above turning a profit from the incident herself, and reworked her children's experiences as the basis of an episode in *The Story of the Treasure Seekers* (1899) where the narrator Oswald, desperate to earn sixpence to cover the cost of a telegram, sells flowers in penny bunches to commuters. While the real incident was a source of acute embarrassment for the Blands, Nesbit reframes it as an act of supreme selflessness and ingenuity in the novel. This tension between suspicion and celebration of consumerism is a key tenet of Nesbit's writing for children. While many of her child characters demonstrate entrepreneurial spirit, their skills are often sorely lacking, and their efforts to become successful capitalists are misunderstood by adult characters or thwarted by the myriad recalcitrant commodities that surround them.

While Nesbit was a Victorian (born in 1858), she only came to prominence as an author in the Edwardian period. Her literary output, appropriately, has characteristics of both of these periods: while texts like *Five Children and It* (1902) or *The Railway Children* (1906) are superficially influenced by Victorian values and narrative patterns, her work actively engages with modernist sensibilities and playfully undermines the values, particularly the material values, that they initially seem to uphold. Nesbit's biographer Julia Briggs hails her as 'the first modern writer for children' (1989: xi). In both embracing and rejecting Victorian material culture, Nesbit's Bastable stories – *The Story of the Treasure Seekers* (1899), its sequels, *The Wouldbegoods* (1901) and *The New Treasure Seekers* (1904), and the short stories collected within *Oswald Bastable and Others* (1905) – mark the point of transition between Victorian and modernist commodity culture. These texts are centrally concerned with the relationships between people and material objects. The narrative trajectory of the series is a variation of the rags-to-riches story structured around largely self-contained, episodic quests for 'treasure'. For all their apparent structural simplicity, these are complex cross-written texts which engage in a sophisticated way with contemporary material culture, and address the shifting attitudes towards goods and consumption that characterized the *fin de siècle* and the early years of the twentieth century. This liminal temporal position invests the texts, particularly *The Story of the Treasure Seekers*, with extra cultural significance: Anita Moss argues that this text 'stands squarely between Victorian and modern children's literature' (1991: 226), and Claudia Nelson sees *The Story of the Treasure Seekers* as marking 'a watershed in children's culture' (2014: n.p.). This text sits on the boundary between Victorian culture and modernist culture, and presents a nuanced and complex commodity culture – one which characters both readily engage with and reject. The Bastable siblings are, at times, beguiled by goods. At other times, they become deviant users of material goods and battle with the things around them. Nelson argues that this text's 'simultaneous acceptance of the status of commodity and the criticism of the culture of commodification, positions it, Janus-like, on the boundary between past and future' (2014: n.p.). The transitional nature of the text makes it inherently unstable, and Nesbit makes this instability a key feature of the text – both in terms of its style and its thematic concerns. The series employs a unique narrative style, in which Oswald Bastable narrates both in the first and third person, playfully switching between the two. This device allows Nesbit to draw attention to the problems of subjectivity and objectivity within the narrative. Accordingly, the role of objects within these texts becomes especially interesting, as the shifting positions of subject and object open the possibility of objects becoming, however temporarily, agent things.

The Bastable stories are replete with material detail. Seemingly every item in the household is enumerated and detailed, from the nursery furniture to the 'clothes-pegs, dirty dusters, scallop shells, string, penny novelettes, and the dining-room corkscrew' (Nesbit [1904] 1996: 23) crammed into the drawer of the kitchen dresser. *The Story of the Treasure Seekers* is particularly rich in this respect, and the importance of materiality is signalled to the reader through descriptions of objects. Indeed, the absence of objects, and the wear and tear evident on existing objects, is the first indication of the family's deteriorating financial position. Oswald confides:

> Father does not like you to ask for new things. That was one way we had of knowing that the fortunes of the ancient House of Bastable were really fallen. … The carpets got holes in them – and when the legs came off things they were not sent to be mended. … And the silver in the big oak plate-chest that is lined with green baize all went away to the shop to have the dents and scratches taken

out of it, and it never came back. We think Father hadn't enough money to pay the silver man for taking out the dents and scratches. The new spoons and forks were yellowy-white, and not so heavy as the old ones, and they never shone after the first day or two. (Nesbit [1899] 1994: 11–12)

Oswald is an expert in reading objects, or 'things', as he terms them, and he knows that the holes and missing parts serve as outward and visible signs of the gaps within their father's bank account. Poverty is made known through absences – the missing visitors and the lack of pocket money – and by the fact that even the furnishings and household items that remain are incomplete or broken. The holes in the carpet and the dents in the silverware are signs of a greater and deeper hollowness within the home. Oswald has paid close attention to the objects within the home, noting not only what these items look like but also what they are made from. He appraises the new cutlery with an expert eye, noting the difference not only in appearance but also, crucially, in the weight of the spoons and forks. The items are understood corporeally as well as intellectually. The new cutlery is deficient as it lacks the physical properties of the original set. A perfect inversion of this list is found at the end of the story when the generosity of the 'Indian' Uncle and the family's new-found wealth is made known through the influx of goods into the Bastable home: 'I never saw so many beautiful things before. There were carved fans and silver bangles and strings of amber beads, and necklaces of uncut gems – turquoises and garnets, the Uncle said they were – and shawls and scarves of silk, and cabinets of brown and gold, and ivory boxes and silver trays, and brass things' (231–2). Whereas Oswald is very specific about the details of the objects lost from the house, he is imprecise about the new presents – the 'brass things' is especially vague: when there are so many objects, it is suggested, one can afford to pay less attention to each item. These scenes demonstrate Nesbit's apparent adherence to Victorian codes of material representation; the objects function as cultural symbols and outward and visible signs of social status, and Oswald and his siblings are readily able to read and interpret these signs.

As characters who stand on the threshold between the Victorian and the modern, it is only fitting that the Bastables also engage in modern consumer practices. Nelson argues: 'Nesbit's text marks a departure from Victorian norms ... in its recognition and acceptance of advertising, journalism, and related forms of popular culture as part of the modern child's cultural capital' (2014: n.p.). These children 'are always already implicated in the marketplace' (n.p.) and their deep interest in advertisement, in the popular press, in celebrity and in consumption sets them apart from the child characters of earlier children's fiction, who are more concerned with the moral or didactic qualities of commodities. The siblings are experienced and thrifty consumers, able to get good value for their money. In one scene, Oswald informs the reader that 'Dora and H. O. had clubbed their money together and bought a melon; quite a big one, and only a little bit squashy at one end. It was very good, and then we washed the seeds and made things with them and with pins and cotton' (Nesbit [1899] 1994: 38-9). Nelson notes the Bastables' joyful fascination with advertising, and draws particular attention to the wordplay around H. O.'s name: 'His real name is Horace Octavius, but we call him H. O. because of the advertisement, and it's not so very long ago he was afraid to pass the hoarding where it says "Eat H. O." in big letters' (Nesbit [1899] 1994: 15). Nelson notes that this is a reference to a Hornby's Oatmeal advertising campaign of the 1890s (2014: n.p.), and suggests that the children's awareness of the advert – and by extension the implied reader's understanding of the joke – indicates their immersion in a world where consumption and commodities are part of the fabric of everyday life. The advert's slogan even invades H. O.'s dreams, embedding itself deeply into his subconscious. Nelson argues too that the children readily absorb the 'patter' and language of advertisements, and draws attention to the scene where Alice tries to hawk sherry to the butcher as a key example of the way that advertisement and the language of consumerism impacts the children's lives. Alice announces: 'I want to call your attention to a sample of sherry wine I have here. It is called Castilian something or other, and at the price it is unequalled for flavour and bouquet' (Nesbit [1899] 1994: 146). Alice's behaviour here is shocking to the butcher (and to the other adults she tries to sell the sherry to) and may be considered deviant. Like the sherry, this kind of sales patter more properly belongs in the mouth of the adult, and to hear a child parrot it is both surprising and alarming. While Alice is by no means fully adept – she neither fully understands the words she speaks, nor appreciates the product she is selling – her ability to speak the language of the advertiser is precocious and unsettling. This is a signal to the knowing reader that the children's relationship to commodities is skewed and must be corrected. In this narrative, order and orderly consumer behaviour is restored by the intervention of the 'Indian' Uncle, a fantastically rich capitalist who takes the whole family to live with him in his large house and showers the children with gifts. With access to such riches, the children no longer need to engage in inappropriate schemes to make money and their keen interest in advertisements and unsuitable commodities tapers off. They are restored to consumer behaviour that is more appropriate for their age and class. This restoration is brief as the Bastables' consumer behaviour and their encounters with things become comically worse in later books in the series.

Bad things in Nesbit's work

Nesbit's work is full of things. In *Five Children and It* (1902), household objects become things that menace the children and the children in turn menace the household objects, misappropriating items in play, and often damaging and breaking items too. Here, children's toys contain 'sharp convenient wire' (Nesbit [1902] 1993: 74) to stab them, the clocks 'always struck wrong' (78) and the matting on the floor 'always caught your foot' (184). The Lamb (the youngest child) is very nearly strangled by his high chair, an object that is supposed to keep babies safe at the table: 'The baby was particularly lively that morning. He not only wriggled his body through the bar of his high chair, and hung by his head, choking and purple, but he collared a tablespoon with desperate suddenness, hit Cyril heavily on the head with it, and then cried because it was taken away from him' (51). The horrible image of him dangling 'choking and purple' sets the tone for a text in which things are presented as hostile. Only a few sentences later, as Jane bites off the loose ends of a needleful of thread, the narrator interjects to remind the reader: 'Perhaps you don't know that if you bite off ends of cotton and swallow them they wind tight round your heart and kill you?' (53). Even the most ordinary and innocuous of objects can be lethal.

Ordinary commodities are a source of tension in the Bastables stories too. The children Bastables continually break, abuse, misappropriate and damage things and, in retaliation, things hurt and inconvenience the children. In this world, children and things are at odds with one another. Of the three books in the Bastables series, *The Wouldbegoods* is most obviously concerned with the friction between children and things. The text opens with the children attempting to recreate scenes from Rudyard Kipling's *The Jungle Book* (1894) in the garden, and misappropriating household items as substitutes for the landscape and fauna of the jungle: they make a waterfall out of a ladder and a mackintosh; take hunting trophies out of their display cases and set them up around the garden; and use Condy's Fluid (a disinfectant) to paint themselves brown and colour the dog's fur with pencil to disguise him as a tiger. Their game not only destroys the garden, but it also undermines the cohesion of the household: by taking objects out of the house, the children disrupt the material order of the house which, in turn, impacts the social order of the household. The adults attempt to restore order by removing the children to the countryside for the remainder of the summer. Once in this rural purgatory, the children are continually punished for their material deviance by objects that turn against them.

The first indication that objects will start to assert their thingness and make their agency felt is when, during an early exploration of the moat, Dora injures her foot on an old tin can: 'It was indeed terrible. The thing she thought was a shark came up with her foot, and it was a horrid, jagged, old meat-tin, and she had put her foot right into it. Oswald got it off, and directly he did so blood began to pour from the wounds. The tin edges had cut it in several spots' (44). There can be no doubt that this is a moment when an object, as John Plotz puts it, 'steps over a boundary and becomes a thing' (2005: 115). Daniel Miller writes that 'where material forms have consequences for people that are autonomous from human agency, they may be said to possess the agency that causes these effects' (2005: 11). The tin becomes agent and the consequence of this for Dora is a temporary inversion of the usual orders of object and subject. Here, the meat-tin asserts its 'presence and power' (Brown 2001: 3–4) and Dora is reduced, momentarily, to the level of object. The tin is meant for holding meat and, after lying idle and empty, is suddenly full of meat again, albeit the meat of Dora's living foot. The tin reaffirms its purpose and function, and simultaneously injures Dora – impeding her ability to act and function.

The thing's potential for malice is again made clear in 'The Waterworks' chapter of *The Wouldbegoods*, when a cricket ball is the cause of a flood in the house. From the moment the cricket ball is introduced in the narrative, it is ascribed a status unlike that of other objects. It is among the presents Noël receives for his birthday and so it is imbued with special status. James Carrier argues that gifts 'are more than neutral utilities, for they express and recreate a range of social values' (1993: 55). The social values and relationships inscribed in the presents that Alice (Noël's twin) receives are made clear, as each of the gifts and its giver is carefully enumerated in the text. By comparison, the values present in the gifts that Noël receives are obscured, because Oswald's narrative neither reveals what these gifts are nor who has given them. As the only one of Noël's presents that is named at all, the cricket ball is awarded special status.

Its status is threatened when Noël trades the cricket ball with Oswald, swapping it for a coconut, two pencils and a notebook. Oswald's and Noël's deal transforms the gift into a fungible commodity, a 'passive object of transaction' (Mauss 1970: 49), and strips the cricket ball of its gift-given meaning. Carrier, citing Mauss, argues that gifts and commodities exist as polar opposites:

At one pole are gift relations. In these, people are linked to each other and to the things around them in enduring ways. These links are the basis of people's identities and they define people's obligations to each other. At the other pole are commodity relations. In these, people are not linked in any enduring ways to the people and things that surround them. (1993: 55-6)

While commodities can become gifts – through, for example, the acts of removing price tags and wrapping an item in paper to conceal it – this is a one-way process. There is an unspoken cultural agreement that gifts ought not to become commodities. To sell or exchange a gift ruptures the connections between people and the relationships between people and things that are inscribed with acts of gift-giving and gift-receiving. By trading the cricket ball, Noël shifts it from one pole to the other – inverting its status from prized gift to priced commodity.

By disregarding the ball's status as gift, Noël simultaneously shows disregard for the social connections forged by the gifting. This leads to tensions between Noël and his siblings, in a situation where the practice of gifting ought to have promoted social harmony. To compound these problems, Noël is unwilling to stick to the terms of his transaction with Oswald, complaining that the deal was unfair and that he wants the ball back (even though he has already eaten the coconut). Oswald refuses to go back on the exchange, and the social tensions caused by the transaction erupt into violence when the brothers fight over the ball. Oswald goes off to sulk with the cricket ball 'crammed ... into his pocket' (Nesbit [1901] 1995: 87). The verb 'cram' is richly connotative. It suggests that the ball does not properly belong in Oswald's pocket and also pre-empts the way the ball later wedges itself tightly into other spaces where it does not belong. Even though it is concealed in a pocket, the ball makes its presence felt and known. By the time Oswald climbs out onto the roof with it, the ball has become a thing with an agency of its own.

It is not long before the ball asserts its autonomy: 'presently it rolled away, and [Oswald] thought he would get it by-and-by' (88). Although there is something almost gentle in the way it rolls away, there can be no doubt that this is the action taken by the ball itself; it simply rolls off by itself and tucks itself into a drainpipe. By blocking the drainpipe, the ball causes a flood in the house which, significantly, mostly affects the boys' bedroom. The boys are forced to spend the night fighting the flood, bailing water out of the windows and trying to conceal the extent of the damage from the adults in the house.[3] Like the meat-tin, the cricket ball is not merely agent, but spiteful. Because Oswald and Noël do not hold it in the proper regard, it punishes them by disappearing from sight. It is satisfyingly ironic that the ball makes itself noticed by hiding itself.

Even after Oswald discovers the cause of the flood and retrieves the ball from the drainpipe, he 'could not get rid of the feeling that this was [his and Noël's] fault somehow' (96). Despite Dora's accident, Oswald is used to viewing objects as passive and so he is initially unable to imagine that an inanimate object could really be to blame for the flood. Over the course of the day, however, he begins to get a sense of the ball's malignance: 'he could feel the hateful cricket ball heavy and cold against the top of his leg, through the pocket' (103). The word 'hateful' is ambiguous, implying both that the ball inspires hate in Oswald and that it hates Oswald. By suggesting that the ball has emotion, Nesbit makes the reader aware that the ball is something more than a mere object. Its palpable malice discomforts Oswald even further and, overwhelmed by guilt and discomfort, he ends up confessing to causing the flood. This is the ultimate inversion of normative subject-object relationships: Oswald takes the blame for what the ball has done and so he becomes its instrument.

The episode comes to an end when Oswald gives the ball back to Noël. In giving the ball to Noël without receiving anything in return for it, Oswald restores their good relationship and reinstates the ball to its original status as a gift and as a passive object. However, Oswald reveals that his reason for giving the ball back to Noël is not because he wants to uphold fair play or to forge a stronger fraternal relationship: he gives it away because 'it could never be the same to me after what *it* had done and what I had done' (104, emphasis in original). The emphasis on 'it' makes it clear that Oswald now acknowledges the cricket ball as an agent thing, capable of acting of its own volition.

The Enchanted Castle and the live thing

If the malice of things is a recurrent motif in the Bastable stories, it is the driving force behind the narrative of *The Enchanted Castle* (1907). Like many of Nesbit's texts, *The Enchanted Castle* is largely episodic and the plot centres on the efforts of three siblings – Gerald, Cathy and Jimmy, and their friend Mabel – to deal with the repercussions of various unruly things. In this text, the wilful disobedience of things and the potential for things to become agents are foregrounded. The text is peppered with discussions of how ordinary household objects can turn against their users. Nesbit contrasts a good day 'when all the things you want are in their places' with a very bad day:

When your shoelace breaks, your comb is mislaid, your brush spins on its back on the floor and lands under the bed where you can't get at it – you drop the soap, your buttons come off, an eyelash gets into your eye, you have used your last clean handkerchief, your collar is frayed at the edge and cuts your neck, and at the very last moment your suspender breaks, and there is no string. (Nesbit [1907] 1998: 116)

These small inconveniences are cumulative; there is a sort of spreading epidemic of material deviance. The careless consumer, who has used the last clean handkerchief and neglected to wash it or replace it, shares culpability with the bad things, like the hairbrush that hides under the bed, for the bad day. In contrast, the success of the good day depends entirely on things 'being in their places'. This suggests that in this particular text, things have power over people and human happiness is directly influenced by material things and dependent upon the things' willingness to co-operate with their users. Throughout the text, both minor and major things are shown to influence the lives of the human characters, working for them and rewarding them for good behaviour (such as using objects for their intended purpose or abiding by the standard rules of exchange), or working against them and punishing them for any deviation from the standard norms of consumption.

The most important and the most recalcitrant object in the narrative is the magical ring. Like the magic carpet in *The Phoenix and the Carpet* (1904), the ring appears to cause problems because it interprets the children's wishes far too literally: it could be seen as an object that causes trouble because it is *too* obedient. However, as the narrative progresses it becomes clear that the ring has a mind of its own and only obeys orders when it wants to. The ring refuses to settle on one kind of magic – it is sometimes a wishing ring, sometimes a ring of invisibility, sometimes a binding love-token – and so its function and value are in flux. Sometimes it stubbornly refuses to come off the wearer's finger, but at other times it simply slips away unnoticed. Its potency is derived from its inconstancy: without any stable use value, the ring eludes any attempt to assign it a fixed meaning. The ring also has an unstable exchange value, sometimes exacting a payment in return for wishes and sometimes foregoing payment. Its price shifts too; sometimes a wish costs a life, while at other times it comes at the cost of the wisher's sanity, and at others still it chooses not to be a wishing ring and stubbornly refuses to provide service or accept payment. These slippages, both literal and figurative, indicate the ring's refusal to take a fixed place in the system of objects.

The ring is undoubtedly a bad thing and its power impacts both the people and the objects around it. Its most significant effect is the vivification of the Ugly Wuglies. Nesbit rehearsed the horrors of the inanimate object suddenly imbued with life in her 1893 short story 'Man-Size in Marble' where statues in a church come to life and terrorize people in the neighbourhood. She returns to the theme in *The Enchanted Castle* when the Ugly-Wuglies, a group of seven manikins made out of old clothes and household objects, which the children assemble as an audience for a play, come to life as the result of a wish made on the magic ring. As they are made from household objects misappropriated through play, the Ugly-Wuglies are displaced from the ordinary system of objects. As manikins, the Ugly-Wuglies are objects that take the form of people and so occupy the boundary between subjects and objects. Nesbit's narrative skilfully switches between identifying the Ugly-Wuglies as people and revealing the true nature of their composition. Each time Nesbit adds an anthropomorphizing detail – a reference to body parts, for example – she immediately undercuts it by revealing that these body parts are made of household goods:

> The seven members of the audience seated among the wilderness of chairs had, indeed, no insides to speak of. Their bodies were bolsters and rolled-up blankets, their spines were broom-handles, and their arm and leg bones were hockey sticks and umbrellas. Their shoulders were the wooden crosspieces the Mademoiselle used for keeping her jackets in shape; their hands were gloves stuffed out with handkerchiefs; and their faces were the paper masks painted in the afternoon by the untutored brush of Gerald, tied on to the round heads made out of the ends of stuffed bolster-cases. ([1907] 1998: 118–20)

This invests the manikins with an uncanny dualism as the reader is forced to hesitate between categorizing them as objects or as subjects. Indeed, when the children's teacher Mademoiselle first sees the Ugly-Wuglies, she 'half laughed, quite screamed' (118). This ambiguous reaction, which hesitates between amusement and terror, articulates perfectly the uncanny ambiguity of these things.

The blurring of the boundaries between subject and object is completed when the Ugly-Wuglies come to life. The children first become aware of this when, at the end of their pantomime, the things start to applaud. In this moment, the things become the viewing subjects – the audience – and the children become the objects of their gaze. The normal orders of subject and object are totally inverted. In addition to this crisis of categorization, the Ugly-Wuglies also initiate a crisis of language as neither the characters nor the narrator are properly able to articulate what the Ugly-Wuglies really are: the adults in the audience scream and run away, the children are left speechless and even the narrative begins to show signs of fragmentation: 'the hall was crowded with live things, strange things – all horribly short as broomsticks and umbrellas are short. A limp hand gesticulated. A pointed white face with red cheeks looked up at [Gerald], and the wide red lips said something but he could not tell what' (125). The short, disjointed sentences, and the apparently oxymoronic phrase 'live things', encapsulates the uncanny horror of the Ugly-Wuglies. Their unintelligible language reflects their fundamental incomprehensibility. They cannot make the children understand them and the children, momentarily struck dumb in horror, cannot speak back to them. These are 'unspeakable' things that disrupt linguistic, social and material orders.

Gerald is the quickest to recover from his horror and he makes another wish on the ring in a desperate attempt to counteract this disaster. He envisions 'Mabel's wish undone, and the empty hall strewed with limp bolsters, hats, umbrellas, coats and gloves, prone abject properties from which the brief life had gone out forever' (125). His wish is to fragment the Ugly-Wuglies and reduce them once again to their component parts; to make them a collection of nameable commodities rather than unified beings. It is significant that he wishes for them to become abject as well as object. Gerald's wish is more than just a desire to kill the creatures; it is a desire to reassert his power as consumer and their inferior status as 'properties' that can be owned and controlled. He wants to regain control of his material agency. The failure of Gerald's wish reminds the reader of the unruliness of things in this narrative; neither the Ugly-Wuglies nor the magical ring that endowed them with life can be successfully brought under human control. They rise up from their seats and start to wander about, looking for a good hotel. H. R. Millar's illustration of the moment the Ugly-Wuglies leave the makeshift theatre renders the horror of the moment apparent (Figure 4.1).

Gerald stands face-to-face with the animate things, a moment that presents human and thing as of equal stature. The Ugly-Wugly with the bowler hat leans a gloved hand softly on the boy's arm and, while the gesture itself is horribly intimate, it is not overtly threatening. Nevertheless, Gerald pulls away from the hand, his free arm wrapped around a reassuringly inanimate newel-post. Millar's illustration makes much of the grimacing painted faces of the Ugly-Wuglies, particularly the female figure on the left of the frame who stares blankly out at the viewer, her wide mouth slack and expressionless. Her fingers just reach out over the edge of the frame, suggesting that her energy and agency cannot be completely contained.

Figure 4.1 As 'live things', the Ugly-Wuglies threaten the boundary between object and subject. *Source*: *The Enchanted Castle* (Nesbit 1907: 184), illustration by H. R. Millar, 'A Limp Hand Was Laid on His Arm'.

The Ugly-Wuglies present a more direct threat to human characters than any other thing in Nesbit's work. They come into direct conflict with the child characters and even come close to killing the bailiff of the Castle. In keeping with their ambiguous presentation, however, Nesbit is initially unclear as to whether the Ugly-Wuglies are dangerous or not. Even while they are described as 'amiable Ugly-Wuglies' (135), Nesbit foreshadows something darker in them by having Gerald describe them as 'perfectly killing' (130). Although they initially seem harmless and want nothing more than a good hotel to stay in for the night, they become more and more dangerous over the course of the evening until they become absolutely vicious. When Mabel and Gerald are alone with them in the gardens of the Castle, the children realize that 'the Ugly-Wuglies were no longer friendly and commonplace, that a fierce change had come over them' (139). This 'fierce change' lays bare the monstrous power of these things and Gerald, who is accidentally brushed by the groping glove of one Ugly-Wugly, suddenly recognizes that 'if they get out they'll kill us all' (140). Mabel and Gerald try to shut the things up in an underground passageway, hoping that the spell will wear off and the things will become lifeless manikins again, but the Ugly-Wuglies turn on them. The result is a physical struggle, with the children on one side of the door and the things on the other, pushing and striving against one another:

> There were screams for the ladies' voices, the hoarse, determined shouts of strong Ugly-Wuglies roused to resistance and, worse than all, the steady pushing open of that narrow stone door that had almost closed upon the ghastly crew. ... And the tone of their consonantless speech was no longer conciliatory and ordinary; it was threatening, full of the menace of unbearable horrors. (139)

The children hope to imprison the things long enough for the enchantment to fade but when they return in the morning, they find that the spell has not worn off and the things are 'alive indeed – with a vengeance' (149).

The Ugly-Wuglies are powerful and dangerous things. As assemblages or bricolages of many household items, they seem to have the combined potential for malice of each of these things, but are also more than the sum of their parts. The Ugly-Wuglies come closest of any of Nesbit's unruly objects to becoming human subjects and each has a distinct personality, from the 'gushing, girlish' (135) rose-wreathed lady, through the 'respectable' (127) older gentleman, to the tallest of the male figures who is described by other Ugly-Wuglies as 'underbred' (149) and 'not quite a gentleman' (127). Their personalities are not, however, enough to convince the children that they are people. Each time Mabel and Gerald seem to start to accept them as proper people, they are reminded of the awful fact that the Ugly-Wuglies are made up of bolsters and sticks and umbrellas rather than flesh and bone. The characters and the reader are repeatedly confronted with the 'thingness of things'. One Ugly-Wugly even mutters 'something that sounded like "disgraceful state of things"' (129), a self reflexive comment that calls attention to his own haphazard composition and to the Ugly-Wuglies' disruption of material order. The stark materiality of the things makes them less than human, but they are definitely more than objects. As deviant things, they worry the borders between the subject and the object, but they also directly threaten human life. They attack the Castle bailiff and the children find him unconscious and bleeding. While other things hurt characters in Nesbit's work for children, this is the first time a thing threatens a character's life. The Ugly-Wuglies are the culmination of malicious things in Nesbit's work not only because they are the most complex but also because they are the most dangerous.

The Ugly-Wuglies also provide Nesbit with a sophisticated vehicle for criticizing contemporary attitudes to consumerism. They personify many of the issues that Nesbit, as a Fabian and a Marxist, potentially saw as affecting British society. While the stuff they are composed of is perfectly common, the Ugly-Wuglies are definitely bourgeois; they demand to be taken to 'a good hotel' and are clearly interested in class hierarchies. They discriminate among themselves, and the 'older gentleman' blames the assault of the bailiff on an 'underbred' Ugly-Wugly. This 'older gentleman' appears more life-like than the other manikins, and tells the children that he is a businessman and that his main concern is to get back to his offices in London. He tells the children that he is 'frightfully rich' (154) and that he has so much money he 'doesn't know what to do with it' (155). His fundamental lack of imagination reminds the reader that, in spite of his riches, he is still an empty-headed Ugly-Wugly made from old clothes and household items. He functions as an allegory for consumerism. Nesbit suggests that to be wealthy is not merely a matter of owning stuff; it is about being made up of the stuff one owns. The wealthy are possessed by their possessions and so become indistinguishable from these material goods. The Ugly-Wugly's identity, both figuratively and literally, is nothing more than an accumulation of stuff.

While the other children remain horrified by the animate thing, Jimmy falls under the spell of the Ugly-Wugly's riches and wishes, rather foolishly, to be rich like the Ugly-Wugly. Jimmy's transformation into an adult – like that of the Lamb in *Five Children and It* – is hideous. While the Lamb becomes an ordinary, if aloof, young man, Jimmy becomes something less than human:

> By quick but perfectly plain-to-be-seen degrees, Jimmy became rich. ... The whole thing was over in a few seconds. Yet in those few seconds they saw him grow to a youth, a young man, a middle-aged man; and then with a sort of shivering shock, unspeakable horrible and definite, he seemed to settle down into an elderly gentleman, handsomely but rather dowdily dressed, who was looking down at them through spectacles and asking them the way to the railway station. (155)

The narrator refers to this elderly gentleman as 'That-Which-Had-Been-Jimmy' or, more simply 'That', highlighting the fact that Jimmy has become a 'that' rather than a person: he has become an Ugly-Wugly. Jimmy's transformation needs also to be considered alongside the scene when Kathleen is transformed into a statue by the power of the ring. Although the instance of transformation is presented as shocking, at least in Millar's illustration of the scene, her transformation brings her delight and allows her to dance in the moonlight with the other statues in the gardens of the Castle. By contrast, Jimmy is not made happy by his transformation. Nor is he made beautiful, as Kathleen is. Jimmy's desire for riches means that he has to be so fully immersed in the world of goods that he becomes something less than properly human: he becomes a live thing. This is the ultimate moment of material deviance in *The Enchanted Castle*, where the slippages caused by things are rendered visible. Here, the thing and the person, the Ugly-Wugly and the boy, become indistinguishable.

Bad mice and crooked sixpences: Material deviance in Beatrix Potter's work

Like Nesbit, Beatrix Potter is a figure positioned on the boundary between the nineteenth and the twentieth centuries. While some of her stories such as *The Tailor of Gloucester* (1903) and *Little Pig Robinson* (1930) engage directly with a historical past (however vague that history might be), Humphrey Carpenter characterizes Potter's work as 'belong[ing] to the modern age rather than the Victorian' (1989: 296), and Katherine Chandler argues that these 'unobtrusive, seemingly non-revolutionary children's books are texts that quietly challenge Victorian mores and literary styles. They are, actually, harbingers of modernism' (2007: 287). Potter's work is deeply concerned with commodity culture. While her books are filled with detailed illustrations of plants and animals, she also relies on close observational drawings of material objects. The clothes in *The Tailor of Gloucester*, for instance, are modelled closely on items held in the Victoria and Albert Museum, and the embroidery work that the mice complete for the tailor are replicated precisely from an eighteenth-century waistcoat (item 652A-1898) which was acquired by the museum in 1898. Her precise replication of the tiny French knots and the fine satin stitches indicates not only her fine eye for detail, but also her keen interest in this object. There are close observational studies of objects in many of her other books; for instance, in *The Tale of Two Bad Mice* (1904), the doll's house was modelled on one built by Norman Warne for his niece (to whom the book is dedicated) and the toy food was copied from a set bought at Hamleys (Potter, letter to Norman Warne, 24 February [1904] 2012). Her letters and diaries are similarly crammed with commodities. Some, like the old clothes and toys kept in her grandparents' house, hold special memories for her (Potter 1966: 78). Other familiar objects become things – recalcitrant, vexing and playful: books seem to move themselves about on the shelves, thwarting the person who reaches for them (Potter 1966: 38), and rings appear and disappear from locked drawers (Potter 1966: 77). Alongside these tricksy things, there are shopkeepers, small-minded and grasping, who seek to take advantage of the unwary buyer. Potter's letters record her concerns that consumer tastes are 'too much governed by the shop keepers' ([1929] 2012) and feels that retailers took unfair advantage of her and her publishers. In a letter to Norman Warne in 1910, Potter complains, 'I do not see any advantage of having immense sales without a fair profit – if Harrod's [sic] for instance would not pay 9d, for my part I would have let Harrods go without it' ([1910] 2012). Her anxieties around buying and selling, and her sense that neither shopkeepers nor commodities can be fully trusted, indicate that she is immersed, not in Victorian material culture where goods can be safely celebrated, but in modern commodity culture where both objects and consumers can slip up. Chandler argues that 'the "new" quality of Potter's books primarily lay in the fact that they spoke directly to children and granted young readers an opportunity to explore their world and resist the confines of strict obedience', and in the ways that 'she modifies genre, liberates highly wrought illustration from fussiness, simplifies book format, hones writing to sparse precision, celebrates anti-heroes, fashions ironic narrators, surprises with unconventional conclusions, and rejects cultural values of the Victorian age' (2007: 288). It is this final quality – the rejection of earlier cultural values – that interests me here. Among the values that Potter rejects are the material values of the Victorian period. In her books, she creates a world of naïve consumers and recalcitrant commodities, where ordinary goods frequently go bad.

Of all Potter's animal characters, her mice are most obviously placed at the intersection of the domestic and the wild and, as a result, are always poised between civilization and unruliness. They allow Potter to explore ideas of propriety and property and so it is especially fitting that in *The Tale of Two Bad Mice* (1904), two mice, Tom Thumb and Hunca Munca, invade and destroy a doll's house, and in so doing reveal bourgeois consumption as an elaborate sham. The illustrations show the doll's house filled with 'all sorts of delightful objects', from household tools like copper kettles and fire irons, to table linens and napkin rings, and decorative items like rugs and mirrors, which indicate that the dolls 'appear to lead the kind of conventional life that would have been well known to Potter herself' (Kutzer 1997: 209). More than any of Potter's other texts, this narrative teeters on the edge between Victorianism and modernism, apparently promoting the codes of Victorian middle-class life but simultaneously subverting these codes entirely. The text also playfully slips between fantasy and reality, blending fairy-tale motifs with mundane settings. The narrative adeptly parodies the story of Goldilocks and the Three Bears,[4] but while Goldilocks initially finds that the bear's furniture is too large or too small, too hard or too soft, before finally settling on items that are 'just right' for her, Tom Thumb and Hunca Munca, initially, find everything in the doll's house to be a 'convenient' size for them but then discover that none of the items is suited to them at all.

The Tale of Two Bad Mice is about thwarted expectations. Adele Tutter notes that the opening line of the text 'establishes the story's orientation, placing us squarely in "fairyland"' (2014: 140). These fairy-tale connotations, however, are immediately undercut. While the reader might expect the word 'girl' to follow the phrase 'once upon a time there was a very beautiful', the word that Potter supplies is 'doll's-house', allowing the fairy-tale opening to give way almost immediately to the material and the mundane. The description of the doll's house that follows focuses exclusively on the materiality of the building: 'it was red brick with white windows, and it had real muslin curtains and a front door and a chimney' (Potter 1904: 7). The 'real' muslin curtains are a curious detail and one which has, curiously, been overlooked by critical discussions of the text. While on the one hand the 'real' muslin curtains add to the supposed verisimilitude of the house, on the other hand, they detract from it. The fact that 'realness' is a remarkable quality of only the curtains implies that this same quality is lacking in other items in the house, and hints that the inauthenticity of these items will be exposed. Thus, with only a few words and a single image, Potter manages to inject a note of uncertainty into the text, and to draw the reader's attention to the issues of authenticity and misrepresentation that are central to this narrative.

At the start of the text, the mice are presented as outsiders to the world of bourgeois luxury that the doll's house represents. The first image of them, peering through a hole in the skirting board, reflects their low social status via their low position on the page. They are, significantly, poised on a threshold, ready to cross physical borders and, with them, class boundaries. Beguiled by the promise of luxury and comfort that lies inside the doll's house, the mice invade the space. They do not exactly break in – the door 'was not fast' (16) – and so it seems that the house, and the world of consumption it represents, readily admits them.

But when the mice sit down to dinner, they realize that the household goods are not all they appear to be. The food is made of plaster and when Tom Thumb tries to slice the ham, the little knife crumples against the side of the ham and hurts his paw. The mice try other items only to discover that the fish and the fruit is also hard and inedible. While it is actually the knife that has first worked against him, the plaster food, the 'most irritatingly unreal' (Armstrong 1996: 49) element within the doll's house, becomes the focus of Tom Thumb's rage. The mice move from disillusionment to destruction. Realizing that they have been duped, that the food is not edible at all, that the luxury and beauty of the doll's house is nothing but a sham, the mice set about destroying the objects (Potter 1904: 28). Tom Thumb's rage is potent: the image of him standing over the smashed remains of the dinner with the shovel poised mid-swing is particularly violent (Figure 4.2).

Tom Thumb's ferocious outburst echoes Toad's physical passions for the motor car – both characters have forceful physical responses to the fact that they cannot effectively grasp the commodities they desire. Tom Thumb abandons the pretence of being a good consumer and, rather than trying to learn and internalize the values apparently promoted by the doll's house furniture – order, mannerly and social eating – he rages against them. Smashing the sham food is a violent rejection of bourgeois taste – both material and bodily taste – and demonstrates his refusal of all that the food represents. He moves from being a willing potential consumer to being a material deviant.

The material deviance of the two bad mice is compounded and facilitated by the bad things around them. The doll's house is not full of objects at all, but only deceitful things – the sham food, the false fire, the ersatz cutlery – which frustrate the mice and bait them into further bad behaviour. The plaster fish proves particularly resistant to consumption. Its refusal to perform its proper role drives Tom Thumb to ever greater extremes of rage and destruction; he moves from trying to use it to trying to destroy it completely. Potter writes: 'As the fish would not come off the plate, they put it into the red-hot crinkly paper fire in the kitchen; but it would not burn either' (28). Not only does it refuse to be consumed (eaten) by the mice, it will not be consumed (burnt) by the fire. The fish stubbornly refuses to play the role expected of it. Through its recalcitrance, it becomes something more than a passive object. It is no longer an object, but a thing.

Figure 4.2 'Then Tom Thumb lost his temper. He put the ham in the middle of the floor, and hit it with the tongs and with the shovel – bang, bang, smash, smash!'. Source: *The Tale of Two Bad Mice* (Potter 1904: 39), illustration by B. Potter.

As their desire to take part in middle-class life is frustrated, the mice set about destroying the house but, only a couple of pages later, their rage and disappointment comes to an abrupt end when Hunca Munca realizes that looting, rather than vandalism, is a wiser course of action. The mice steal furnishings and clothing from the dolls and set up the loot in their mouse hole. Although Adele Tutter describes the mice as 'discriminating consumers' (2014: 142), it is clear that they are easily beguiled by material objects and are unselective in their tastes. Suzanne Rahn notes that they 'steal not only useful things such as the bolster but also a birdcage and a bookcase which (significantly) will not fit into their mouse-hole' (1984: 80). The birdcage and bookcase have no real use value for the mice. Nevertheless, they desire these things – and the lifestyle and status they seem to represent – and go to great lengths to try to get hold of them. Like Toad, Tom Thumb and Hunca Munca are indiscriminate consumers – they repeatedly fall under the spell of material goods even though experience tells them that these commodities are not all they appear to be. While they do not speak in the language of advertising as Toad does, they are nevertheless beguiled by the promises offered by the objects, enchanted by what these things seem to be rather than what they really are. Their thieving is, like Toad's theft of the motor car in *The Wind in the Willows*, an attempt to possess the ephemeral promises of the objects and a sure sign of their material deviance. Rather than acquiring the goods honestly and so upholding the social codes that surround commodity culture, they disrupt the usual modes of consumption by stealing.

Their theft has largely been forgiven by critics of Potter's work. Rahn argues that the mice 'make their own terms of payment' (1984: 90), and a close look at the illustrations seems to reveal that the mice pay exactly the same price for the food as the dolls did. The box of shavings that the food arrives in is illustrated on pages 9 and 10 of the text with the label 'provisions' and the price – 6d – clearly visible on the side of the box. The sixpence the mice stuff into one of the doll's stockings on Christmas Eve at the end of the narrative seems a just compensation for the plaster food that they have destroyed. However, the text notes that the sixpence is 'crooked' and so makes it clear that this transaction is corrupt. Tom Thumb has only 'found' the money under the hearthrug; it does not properly belong to him at all and so this is not a true reparation for the damage. Besides, the mice do not pay for any of the other goods they have stolen. In failing to pay for the goods they take, Tom Thumb and Hunca Munca are not proper consumers at all – merely thieves. Nevertheless, as Armstrong observes, 'the readers' sympathies are with the mouse intruders' (1996: 49). Potter encourages the reader to identify with the mice rather than with the dolls and, through this identification, to see the mice as victims of a deceit rather than the dolls as victims of vandalism. The mice's 'rage and disappointment' (Potter 1904: 28) is presented as justification for their behaviour, even though their only real disappointment is that the items they plan to use and steal for themselves are not as wonderful as expected. The final line of the story, informing us that 'very early every morning – before anybody is awake – Hunca Munca comes with her dust-pan and her broom to sweep the Dollies' house!' (57) might seem to placate and reassure the reader that some semblance of normative social order has been restored – with the lower-class Hunca Munca now cleaning the house of the middle-class dolls – but the dress that the mouse wears and the dustpan and brush are among the items she has stolen. She is not repentant at all, but flaunts her material deviance. As a mouse, a wild creature living within the domestic space, Hunca Munca cannot be fully inducted into the bourgeois world of the dolls; she consumes on her own terms and undermines the rules of property and ownership through her continued invasions of the dolls' space and her continued use of their possessions.

The (mis)adventures of Mr Toad

If Nesbit's and Potter's work sits somewhat uneasily on the borders between Victorian and modern children's literature, Grahame's *The Wind in the Willows* (1908) 'does not fit comfortably into the history of children's literature, if at all' (Hunt 2010: viii). Hunt observes that its original publishers advertised the book as a sophisticated political satire and many critics, including Barbara Wall, Margaret Blount and Humphrey Carpenter, see the book as one that alludes to childhood but is not for children. Nevertheless, portions of the text were intended to be enjoyed by at least one child reader and have their origins in letters written by Grahame for his son, Alastair (xxi–xxiii). As the central figure in those portions of the narrative that were written for a child reader, Toad is an appropriate exemplar for the problematic relationships between people and things in children's literature in this period. While his experiences bear some resemblance to Mole's (both, for instance, sleep in a hollow tree, both have emotional reunions with their home space), Toad's narrative journey defies conventions of character development. His journey is neither a hero's journey, nor a heroic one: Grahame's repeated references to literary heroes, and especially the wandering Odysseus, are made bathetic by Toad's utter unwillingness to develop, change or grow. His final triumphant return to Toad Hall sees him just as unrepentant and as rascally as ever, thinking not of the great debt that he owes to his loyal friends, but only of how he might impress them next. Toad's refusal to adhere to the expected patterns of character development has led critics to consider that there might be something fundamentally wrong with him. Peter Green even goes so far as to diagnose this fictional character with a real mental disorder, arguing that 'Toad's behaviour is irresistibly suggestive of an adult manic-depressive' (1959: 282). Roger C. Schlobin asserts that Toad manifests 'compulsion and delusion' (1999: 34–41), Jonathan Mattanah claims that Toad 'suffer[s] from a narcissistic personality disorder' (2010: 88), and Sarah Wadsworth identifies Toad as an addict, desperately seeking his next high (2014: 45). These readings fundamentally misunderstand Toad's behaviour because they disregard a key element of his madness. Toad's bizarre behaviours are all connected to and made visible through his interactions with material goods. It is, therefore, only fitting to consider Toad as a material deviant.

Toad's relationships with material goods are eccentric and may even be considered queer. I take my cue in using this term from Herring who, building on the work of Sara Ahmed, employs *queer* 'as a term that applies not only to accounts of sexual nonconformity but also to other non-normative identities' (Herring 2014: 2). Ahmed argues that queer theory 'can contest not only heteronormative assumptions, but also social conventions and orthodoxies in general' (2006: 78). For Herring, this opens up a new way 'to think further about how possessions and their usage also become queer via discourses of contemporary object relations' (2014: 2). In this sense, queer object relations are any material behaviours that do not correspond to or conform to established norms of production or consumption. A community may uphold and promote certain kinds of consumer practices as forms of normative, proper, orderly, lawful and even morally correct behaviour. Any behaviour that deviates from these standards may be viewed as suspicious, and may be ridiculed or even reviled. By engaging in material practices such as hoarding and stealing, which are openly derided by the other characters, and by refusing to conform to the standards set by the River-Bank community, Toad is established as a queer consumer.

Toad's material deviance is thrown into stark relief by the orderly material practices of the other characters in Grahame's novel. In *The World of Goods*, Mary Douglas and Baron Isherwood argue that material goods 'make and maintain social relationships' (1979: 60). To a large extent, the material objects seen in *The Wind in the Willows* make the social and moral ideologies of this fictional world legible to the reader. Seth Lerer argues that the household goods in Grahame's novel convey 'a kind of effortless esprit, as well as an essential "Englishness"' (2009: 51), and demonstrates that the furnishings in each character's homes encourage the reader to make inferences about the character and their ideals: their national, social and moral values are expressed through the material items that they value (58). Badger's ancient home speaks eloquently of the importance of heritage, hospitality and comfort. While Mole does not have access to this sort of heritage, he emulates it as best he can with plaster imitations: he literally and figuratively 'buys in' to the appearance of these old-world values. Lerer argues that Mole's 'catalog-bought' (59) statuettes of Queen Victoria and Giuseppe Garibaldi reveal his deep longing to belong among the River-Bankers and to shape his home according to the 'ideal of a middle-class, commodity aesthetic for the late Victorian era' (59). Even though Mole's décor is cheap and mass produced, it has, at least, the right appearance and this gains him the approval of Ratty – the reader's and Mole's touchstone for the tastes of the River Bank. In this world where domestic décor is largely antique, generational, conservative and respectable, Toad is an outlier. His material behaviour deviates from the standards of the River Bank community. In spurning the rules of consumer behaviour that the other animals uphold, he also rejects the moral codes that the others adhere to. If, as Herring observes, orderly engagement with material goods can offer, or appear to offer, 'cultural stability, purposefulness, vivification, psychic self-anchoring, and social well-being … sanity, sound mental health, naturalness, and orderliness' (2014: 4), then Toad's irregular and disorderly engagement with objects foreshadow crisis, instability and his apparently 'unnatural' behaviour in the novel.

But Toad has not simply put aside the moral codes that the other characters uphold. He never shared their values in the first place. For starters, Toad's home does not express his personality or personal values. While the other characters are largely topophiles, in the sense that their lives are deeply rooted in and revolve around their home spaces, Toad is topophobic, restlessly and relentlessly moving beyond the influence of the home space (Kuznets 1978: 115–19). Although he has inherited a fine house from his father, he does not think about it in terms of family heritage or any emotional value. When he is asked about his home by the gaoler's daughter, he describes it through the kind of language more suited to advertising – telling her it is 'an eligible self-contained gentleman's residence very unique; dating in part from the fourteenth century, but replete with every modern convenience. Up-to-date sanitation. Five minutes from church, post-office, and golf-links, Suitable for——'. The gaoler's daughter, laughing, interrupts him to say 'I don't want to TAKE it. Tell me something REAL about it' (Grahame [1908] 2010: 83). This strikes at the heart of Toad's problem: Toad cannot properly distinguish between the real and the imaginary, between actual objects and fantastic ideas about them as presented in advertisements.

While Toad is a deviant consumer because he does not adhere to the normative rules of the River Bank, in another sense, he is a consumer *par excellence*: he believes absolutely in the elusive and illusive joy that new commodities promise. His quest for material satisfaction leads him to purchase a series of vehicles – first boats, then a caravan, then a motor car – which offer him not merely a means of transport, but a means by which to be transported out of the everyday. By doing so, Toad moves through a series of purchases that become more and more modern and less and less in tune with the environment occupied by his friends. When Toad speaks about these objects, he slips lithely into the language of advertising, extolling not the physical qualities of the items or their practical function, but the fleeting experiences and emotions they can unlock for him. While Nesbit's Bastable children also speak the language of advertising, Toad goes further because he has the financial capital available to convert these fetishized dreams into real purchases. When he shows Mole and Rat his new yellow caravan, he exclaims:

> There's real life for you, embodied in that little cart. The open road, the dusty highway, the heath, the common, the hedgerows, the rolling downs! Camps, villages, towns, cities! Here to-day, up and off to somewhere else to-morrow! Travel, change, interest, excitement! The whole world before you, and a horizon that's always changing! And mind! this is the very finest cart of its sort that was ever built, without any exception. Come inside and look at the arrangements. Planned 'em all myself, I did! (19)

Here, his syntax collapses into a series of unconnected nouns, echoing the pared-back, punchy language of the commercial. The phrase 'The whole world before you, and a horizon that's always changing!' reads as a slogan, a jingle from an advert intended to lure the unwitting purchaser. And, of course, Toad is *selling* the caravan, or at least the possibility of taking a holiday in it, to Mole. Rat, who is savvy enough to see through Toad's patter, is not taken in by the spiel and mostly ignores what is happening. Toad, by comparison, has no such self-awareness or self-control. Rather than internalizing the social values that the caravan should uphold (a traditional way of life, a return to simplicity and a slow pace) or reflecting critically on what benefits the caravan might bring to his life, Toad has internalized only the promise of happiness as advertised.

Once the thrill of the new wears off, Toad is ready to move on to the next commodity. This is clearly illustrated in the scene where a passing motor car runs the caravan off the road. The motor car is a thoroughly modern commodity, one that symbolically and figuratively overtakes the caravan, pushing it, and the traditional values it represents, aside. Even as the motor car is described in largely impressionistic terms as 'a dark centre of energy' (22) and as something 'immense, breath-snatching, passionate' (22), the caravan becomes, by contrast, lumpenly mundane. While the motor car flies by, a glittering embodiment of speed and dynamism, the caravan ends up lying 'on its side in the ditch, an irredeemable wreck' (23). One vehicle is whole and swift, the other broken and static. At this moment, the caravan's 'fairy' qualities are diminished and Toad loses all interest in it. By destroying the caravan, the motor car reveals itself not as a 'good', but as a bad thing. As a thing, the car disrupts 'the circuits of production and distribution, consumption and exhibition' (Brown 2001: 4). Unlike the ordinary goods that are made to meekly serve the consumer, the motor car is a thing that asserts its own power over the consumer.

The motor car has a will of its own and Toad becomes its devotee. The very second he sees the motor car, he is enthralled by it:

> 'Glorious, stirring sight!' murmured Toad, never offering to move. 'The poetry of motion! The REAL way to travel! The ONLY way to travel! Here to-day – in next week to-morrow! Villages skipped, towns and cities jumped – always somebody else's horizon! O bliss! O poop-poop! O my! O my!' … 'And to think I never KNEW!' went on the Toad in a dreamy monotone. 'All those wasted years that lie behind me, I never knew, never even DREAMT! But NOW – but now that I know, now that I fully realise! O what a flowery track lies spread before me, henceforth! What dust-clouds shall spring up behind me as I speed on my reckless way! What carts I shall fling carelessly into the ditch in the wake of my magnificent onset! Horrid little carts – common carts – canary-coloured carts!' (Grahame [1908] 2010: 24)

He lapses once more into the language of the advert, extolling 'the poetry of motion!', holding the motor car up as more authentic, more 'REAL' than the caravan could ever be. The ephemeral joy of the car comes in direct opposition to the dull physicality of the caravan which he now reviles as 'horrid', 'little' and 'common'. By embracing the car, Toad also embraces values that are in direct opposition to the values promulgated by the more traditional River-Bankers. If they value quiet, slow living, tradition and heritage, Toad is enraptured by noise, speed and the new. If we read this initial encounter with the motor car as a moment of rapture, or to borrow Barthes's term, as 'ravishment', a moment of instantaneous enthrallment with a love object (see Heath 1982: 100–6), we can understand Toad's interest in motor cars as obsessive and lustful, blurring the lines between material and sexual fetishes. This 'libidinal overinvestment in non-genital sexual objects' (Herring 2014: 6) later causes Toad to have 'violent paroxysms' that reach a 'climax' only when he re-enacts a car accident, throwing himself bodily on the floor of his bedroom (Grahame [1908] 2010: 65).

The motor car is the apex of Toad's material deviance and spurs him into ever more reckless behaviour. Even when he has wrecked the cars, he does not dispose of their carcasses, but hoards them in his coach house. Rat laments that the coach house is 'piled up – literally piled up to the roof – with fragments of motor-cars, none of them bigger than your hat!' (39). That Toad decides to keep, rather than properly dispose of, the broken remains of the cars, further testifies to his material deviance. While the other characters keep myriad items in their homes, they arrange the objects carefully and with a view to the aesthetic; Toad simply piles the junk out of sight. His hoarding is an outward and visible sign of his unwillingness to adhere to the material or social values upheld by the other characters (Herring 2014: 3). Toad's material deviance reaches a new low – or a new high, depending on one's view – when he steals a motor car and goes joyriding (Figure 4.3). E. H. Shepard's illustration captures perfectly the energy and glee of this episode; the horizontal lines streaming out behind Toad and his scarf whipping in the wind convey a sense of the speed and movement he associates with the car, yet we know from the human figures who hold on to the car that the vehicle cannot actually be moving at any great speed.

Toad takes the car without going through the proper process by which objects are lawfully acquired and his spree only stops when he is arrested. Yet Toad

Figure 4.3 Toad's material deviance finds its fullest expression in the motor car. *Source: The Wind in the Willows* (Grahame [1908] 1931), illustration by E. H. Shepard, 'The Rush of Air in His Face, the Hum of the Engine'.

remains wholly unrepentant. When Badger confronts him about his reckless driving and his prodigal spending, rather than being 'very easily converted' (63) as his friends hope, Toad remains stoutly intractable:

> 'No!' he said, a little sullenly, but stoutly; 'I'm NOT sorry. And it wasn't folly at all! It was simply glorious!'
>
> 'What?' cried the Badger, greatly scandalised. 'You backsliding animal, didn't you tell me just now, in there——'
>
> 'Oh, yes, yes, in THERE,' said Toad impatiently. 'I'd have said anything in THERE. You're so eloquent, dear Badger, and so moving, and so convincing, and put all your points so frightfully well – you can do what you like with me in THERE, and you know it. But I've been searching my mind since, and going over things in it, and I find that I'm not a bit sorry or repentant really, so it's no earthly good saying I am; now, is it?' (64)

Badger has fundamentally misunderstood the problem at the heart of Toad's wild materialism: while Badger believes a 'poison' has entered Toad's system and infected him, he does not consider that Toad's issue is not a presence, but an absence. Toad is driven by want, by the need to pursue something that he cannot fully grasp. He does not treat commodities as possessions, but as gateways to feelings and experiences. The motor car offers the promise of something but, as a thing, never quite fulfils that promise. Moreover, Toad lacks the basic rules of consumerism that Ratty, Mole and Badger espouse and remains unwilling to learn these rules or to internalize the moral codes that they entail. He is unable and unwilling to be encultured as a proper, normative consumer.

Conclusion

While Toad's behaviour makes him unique among the River-Bankers, he is by no means exceptional in the broader context of children's literature in this period. In fact, Toad is one of a number of materially deviant characters that emerge in children's texts in the early twentieth century and *The Wind in the Willows* is 'nothing if not a book of its time' (Hunt 2010: xxv). These texts, including those by E. Nesbit and by Beatrix Potter that I have discussed here, move away from the material-culture trends presented by and inculcated within nineteenth-century children's literature. In moving away from Victorian mores, Nesbit, Potter and Grahame's work marks a movement away from Victorian commodity culture and from the enthusiasm for material stuff that characterized that period. Their texts manifest the growing suspicion of commodity culture as a mounting tension between child characters and the material goods around them. The characters in their texts are often ineffective consumers who have fraught relationships with the objects around them. Likewise, the objects in their texts frequently become things that are 'recalcitrant, obtrusive, and vexing' (Kreienbrock 2013: 1) and act against the human characters.

By moving away from Victorian material values, the characters created by Grahame, Nesbit and Potter may be considered deviant. The Bastables, the Bad Mice and Toad are beguiled by the objects around them and become frustrated when the things refuse to live up to the advertisements. While the Bastables engage enthusiastically in the world of advertising and commerce, they are still vulnerable to the whims of the recalcitrant things that surround them. They do not live up to the expectations of child consumers; their ability to imitate the adult language of advertising unsettles many of the adults they encounter and suggests that they eschew the values typically inculcated through material culture. Likewise, Toad rejects the material values of his community and pursues his desire for ever-more thrilling vehicles that will bring him hurtling away from the static world of ornaments and household décor so loved by the other River-Bankers.

But in these texts, there is also a clear sense that commodities are not passive objects that can be neatly overlaid with moral, social and cultural values. They are things that shrug off or subvert the expectations, and the values, of the people who try to use them. Toad's motor car; the obstinate plaster food in the doll's house; the tin can that grasps Dora's foot; the cricket ball that floods the house; the magic ring that slides from fingers or refuses to budge; these are things rather than goods and they do not bend to the will of the consumer. These things do not serve to provide object lessons or to teach the child consumer about the origins and manufacture of goods, nor about the proper circulation of goods within society. Nevertheless, these things do serve to enculture the child reader into a modern sort of consumerism, a world in which advertisements are not to be trusted, in which commodities can – and do – turn on the consumer.

These texts pave the way for other literary depictions of things that turn against consumers in the twentieth century. The tension between people and things can be played for humorous or horrifying effect. For instance, in M. R. James's short story 'The Malice of Inanimate Objects' (1933), everyday items become sinister characters. The narrator muses that it is not 'life' or living beings that turn on us, but 'the things that do not speak or work or hold congresses and conferences. It includes such beings as the collar stud, the inkstand, the fire, the razor, and, as age increases, the extra step on the staircase which leads you either to expect or not to expect it' (James [1933] 2011: 397). In the story, Mr Burton is menaced by a dozen small encounters with things, culminating in a run-in with a kite, painted with a pair of ugly eyes and bearing the legend 'I. C. U'. Burton is later murdered and, while the connection between the kite and the murder is never fully explained, the reader is encouraged to connect the sense of unease caused by the kite's apparent omniscience with his sudden and violent death. In a more humorous vein, Paul Jennings's facetious essay 'Report on Resistentialism' (1950) claims 'Les choses sont contre nous'. 'Things are against us' ([1950] 1959: 147). Though Jennings is playing with the conventions of philosophy and, particularly, with the convoluted language of twentieth-century European philosophy, he nevertheless sites the origins of Resistentialism in the latter years of the nineteenth century, claiming that the word 'Resistentialism' entered language – and consciousness – in 1894 (150). The central theme of Resistentialism, that ordinary things are spiteful and find ways to trouble and inconvenience people, is easy to understand. Jennings's examples – pencils that fall to the floor and land tantalizingly out of reach, marmalade toast that unerringly lands marmalade-side-down on expensive carpets – are all about things that slip out of our grasp or evade our possession. Indeed, this is the crux of thing theory too. Objects become things when they elude us, both literally, figuratively and linguistically – when they slip from our hands, or when we can't quite fix on the correct name for an item, or when we find we have no words to properly describe the sense of unease some things inspire in us. If goods 'mak[e] visible and stable the categories of culture' (Douglas and Isherwood 1979: 59), things slip outside of these categories, unsettling both the objects and our expectations of them. This runs counter to the ways commodities are presented in Victorian children's literature. There, objects are used to help the child reader make sense of the world, to help them understand social and material networks, to help them learn about how goods are made and how they are used. What marks writers like Grahame, Potter and Nesbit as modern is the way they treat commodities and consumerism. The bad things and the bad consumers in their texts offer a different kind of material culture, one that resists, challenges and plays with our expectations.

Conclusions: Failed palaces and magic cities

In May 1914, an exhibition that was set to rival the Great Exhibition of 1851 didn't happen. Surprisingly, it wasn't the spectre of war on the European mainland that thwarted the Universal Exhibition but a lack of interest from the British public.

The Universal Exhibition (1914) Nottingham had got off to a good start. It had prestigious patrons and an impressive committee: the Duke of Portland was president, the Dukes of Rutland and Somerset and the Mayor of Nottingham were the vice-presidents, and the committee included the composer Edward Elgar and the painter Edward John Poynter. It was hailed as 'one of the most imposing industrial and art exhibitions ever held in the provinces' ('To Cost £130,000: International Exhibition in Nottingham', 11 August 1913: 5). The *Nottingham Evening Post* declared that there was 'nothing that thought, time, or money can suggest to make the project a success being left undone' ('Next Year's Exhibition in Nottingham', 7 October 1913: 5). The plans for the Universal Exhibition were laudably ambitious. During its six-month opening, the exhibition was expected to attract 'an attendance of between 3 and 4 million people' ('To Cost £130,000: International Exhibition in Nottingham'). By October, the *Nottingham Evening Post* was able to describe the proposed buildings in some detail, indicating that the plans were well developed by this point:

> Directly to the right and left of the main entrance from the Victoria Embankment will be the two great 'Palaces of Industry', each 300 feet long by 160 feet wide in which will be displayed the products of the great industrial centres of the world. Beyond these, to the left, will be the 'Palace of Fine Arts', 200 feet long and 90 feet wide, in which will be displayed a collection of modern oil paintings drawn from every country in Europe. Quality rather than quantity will be aimed at in the selection of these pictures, and the merit of the collection will be beyond question. … Opposite the Fine Arts Section, and divided from it by a series of gardens designed and maintained by leading horticultural firms, will be

the 'Women's Palace' and associated with it a Child Life Section. ('Next Year's Exhibition in Nottingham')

The exhibition's emphasis on quality over quantity suggests a movement away from the busy, crammed displays of the Great Exhibition of 1851, where the visitor risked being overwhelmed by the sheer volume and diversity of the goods on display. The Universal Exhibition promised order and discernment, a curated display rather than the chaotic bazaar that faced Charlotte Brontë and the other visitors at that earlier exhibition. The Universal Exhibition also promised to showcase the best of modern technology. In addition to the displays of industry and art, there were plans for a 'Palace of Light', 'which will be a masterpiece of the designer's art ... illuminated by countless lamps, illustrative of every departure in artificial lighting – electricity, gas, acetylene, petrol, &c.' ('To Cost £130,000: International Exhibition in Nottingham') with shadowy passageways between each of the areas 'to represent the dimly-lighted streets of bygone times' ('Next Year's Exhibition in Nottingham'). The past, this scheme implied, was murky and unpleasant, the future, bright and clear. This exhibition would bring together modern ideas and modern design and present them for all to see.

But the Universal Exhibition did not capture the public interest. Though there were adverts placed in newspapers by Charles Ouzman (the organizing secretary of Amusements and Attractions) and Walter Stenning (the organizing secretary of Home Exhibits), the exhibition failed to attract the vendors and exhibitors necessary to make it a viable enterprise. Though there was a grand sod-cutting ceremony and much fanfare in the local press about the labour the exhibition would create and the business it would bring to the area ('Nottingham's Exhibition: Big Scheme on a Business Basis', 5 November 1913: 3), the scheme did not generate interest among local businesses. The enormous buildings were never completed and by March, the organizers called the exhibition off though hoping that the event would merely be postponed ('Nottingham Exhibition: The Enterprise Abandoned for This Year', 24 March 1914: 3). By 9 May 1914, the *Nottingham Journal* declared the exhibition a 'fiasco', noting that the building had been stripped of materials in an effort to recoup some of the expenses but 'not more than £30 worth of timber was disposed of at the recent auction sale' ('Exhibition Fiasco: Birds Find Skeleton of "Palace of Industries" Useful': 3). Not even the materials held any interest or value for the general public. And so, in May 1914, the age of Britain's great exhibitions came to an ignoble end.

But there were some smaller exhibitions with tighter thematic focus that fared better, at least initially. In the winter of 1912–13, the Children's Welfare

Exhibition at London's Olympia drew large crowds. An advert in the *Pall Mall Gazette* captures something of the energy of the event and the excitement it promised to visitors (Figure C.1). The advert shows a well-dressed crowd hurrying to the Exhibition. Significantly, the people at the front of the crowd are children. A young girl holding a baby in her arms leads the way, behind her stride two boys, one wearing a top hat, one carrying a kite, behind them, a toddler with a hand in her mouth is carried by a woman with another young girl at her side. Here, children lead the way both literally and figuratively.

The text of the advert makes it clear that this Exhibition counts children among its primary audience, declaring 'every boy and girl who wants to enjoy

Figure C.1 Children leading the way to the Exhibition. *Source*: 'The Children's Welfare Exhibition at Olympia Dec. 31 to Jan. 11', advertisement, *Pall Mall Gazette*, 30 December 1912: 9.

the Christmas holidays should go to Olympia'. Notably, there was a separate admission price for children. While the Commissioners for the Great Exhibition of 1851 dithered over creating special children's tickets, the organizers of the Children's Welfare Exhibition sold half-price tickets to children under fifteen. This shows that they expected children to attend in large numbers and also that they accepted children as a distinct market group. In addition to the lectures and discussions and the displays of modern nursery furnishings which were intended to attract parents, carers and educators, the Children's Welfare Exhibition had a number of special events and displays which were aimed squarely at a child audience. The daily 'fairy pageant', motorized carnival rides and 'the biggest Christmas tree in the world' were, no doubt, intended to amuse younger visitors.

Among the displays and exhibits, children's books played an important role. Not only are books listed first among the 'books, pictures, toys and dolls' that would be on show, but there was also a series of readings by famous authors, including G. K. Chesterton, H. G. Wells and E. Nesbit. Jenny Bavidge argues that 'literature was co-opted by those concerned with the lives of Edwardian children, and helped to define categories of childhood around welfare issues' (2009: 125) and while the Exhibition of 1912–14 and the later exhibition in April–May 1913 'cannot be claimed to have been landmark events' (126), they are nevertheless significant for the way they cemented the connection between childhood and the literature for and about children. One of the star attractions of the Exhibition was 'The Magic City', a strange hybrid of children's book and commodities created by E. Nesbit.

Nesbit used her stall at the Children's Welfare Exhibition as a space to promote her novel *The Magic City* (1910) in which the protagonist, Philip, creates a fantastic city out of objects he finds in his house. This was not the first time she had attempted such a promotional stunt: earlier she had tried to mount 'a small exhibition in Selfridges' to promote her novel but 'the store manager had been horrified how many bricks she had taken from the toy department. When he refused to allow her any more, she took umbrage and left' (Fitzsimons 2019: 252). Her stall at the Children's Welfare Exhibition proved a better space to advertise her wares. In addition to reading excerpts from her work to the crowds of children who attended the event, and offering copies of *The Magic City* for sale at the stall (Fitzsimons 2019: 252), Nesbit created a 'magic city' out of ordinary commodities – 'with bricks and toys and little things such as a child may find and use' (Nesbit 1913: vii) – to display to the visitors. The 'magic city' was made 'with elaborate palaces and towers, delicate bridges and lush gardens, all fashioned from common household items: cotton reels, biscuit tins, saucepan lids and chessmen' (Fitzsimons 2019: 252). By pressing ordinary objects into service as a means to advertise her novel, she blurs the line between text and commodity, transforming her imagined and intangible city into a physical and tangible one.

The Magic City was enormously popular with the crowds who attended the Exhibition. Nesbit, always alert to commercial opportunity, used this display as the basis of a new non-fiction book *Wings and the Child, or, The Building of Magic Cities* (1913), a piece that is part-child psychology and part-guidebook to creating ornamental cities from household bric-a-brac. In it, she argues that children need to be given the means and opportunities to engage in imaginative, creative play. Her discussion of children's innate ludic instincts centres on the ways that children interact with commodities:

> The five-year-old will lay a dozen wooden bricks and four cotton reels together, set a broken cup on the top of them, and tell you it is a steam-engine. And it is. He has created the engine which he sees, and you don't see, and the pile of bricks and cotton reels is the symbol of his creation. He will silently borrow your best scissors and cut a serrated band of newspaper, which he will fasten round his head (with your best brooch, if he cannot find a pin), hang another newspaper from his shoulders, and sit in state holding the hearth-brush. He will tell you that he is a king – and he is. He has created crown, robes, sceptre, and kingship. The paper and the rest of it are but symbols. (Nesbit 1913: 18–19)

For Nesbit, the child sees commodities as symbols, not as the literal, physical things that they are. She argues, then, that the best objects to supply a child with are those that lend themselves readily to such symbolic interpretations. The child's experience of commodity culture is, Nesbit argues, separate to and even antithetical to the 'ordinary' experiences of adults who come into contact with these same objects. Like the bad consumers in her novels, Nesbit encourages the child at play to take ordinary objects and use them in new and unexpected ways. This approach was not universally popular. A report of her Magic City display from the *Westminster Gazette* describes the problem with this sort of enthusiastic appropriation of household stuff:

> There are ebony elephants and brass knobs and sugar castors and gilded wastepaper baskets and a massive brass inkstand. China bowls and copper bowls roof the palaces, dominoes flag the paths. And if your city aspires to a monolith (and if mother is musical as well as sympathetic) what better, what more utterly splendid and inspiring than the metronome case? An avenue of trees, needless to say, you must have: annex the cribbage-board and insert in the holes thereof

sprigs of laurel, or of what-you-please annexed from mamma's sympathetic new hat. ('The Magic City. E. Nesbit's Table Game for The Children. Testing Parental Sympathy', 3 January 1913: 5)

Here, the child who builds the 'magic city' is juxtaposed with the parents whose wardrobes, cabinets and desks are stripped of their valuables. The child's desire to play with these items is at odds with the adult desire to use them and to keep them in their proper places. The game, the article suggests, is likely to 'test parental sympathy', not only because the domestic commodities are displaced through the game, but also because these elaborate edifices are likely to remain in place for days on end as the city is completed piece by piece. Here, children's experiences of commodity culture are set in direct opposition to adults' experiences of commodity culture: the use and enjoyment one has of an object prevents the other from using or enjoying it at all. Children's commodity culture is, therefore, presented as distinct, discrete and troublesome.

Especially troublesome is the question of class and privilege that lurks beneath the surface of the Children's Welfare Exhibition. As Bavidge notes, the Exhibition assumed a certain 'flexibility of the category of childhood, particularly around debates about child labour' which 'becomes apparent when reports of the Exhibition's many charms are printed alongside news reports of criminal activity and dramatic incidents involving children' (Bavidge 2009: 130). Nesbit tried, unsuccessfully, to address the experiences of poor children who came from homes that were not so replete with inessential commodities that could be used to build elaborate cities. Like Oswald Bastable, Nesbit equates poverty with the absence of material wealth, lamenting that some children lived in 'poor homes, where there were none of the pretty things – candlesticks, brass bowls, silver ash-trays, chessmen, draughts, well-bound books, and all the rest of it' (1913: 178). The solutions she offers are bizarre: children should collect what objects they can and club together to create a city among them. And besides,

> in most schools there will be some children not quite so poor who can afford a penny or so for tinsel paper and the few things – colours, paints, and so on – that do not occur naturally in a house, even a well-to-do house. These, let us hope, will be able to furnish a few old chessmen, for there is nothing like chessmen for giving an air of elegance to domes and minarets. (181)

The poor child can play at magic cities only if they are enabled to do so by other, not-so-poor children. She cannot see how unlikely it is to have 'a few old chessmen' lying about spare in a house that has very little by way of excess commodities. While she holds some radical and modern views of children's education and welfare, Nesbit's view of the domestic space is firmly rooted in the Victorian middle class full of rooms groaning under the weight of ornaments, draperies and knick-knacks. Nesbit, and the wider Children's Welfare Exhibition, concentrated their focus on a privileged middle-class audience. In failing to address children of other backgrounds or different kinds of childhood experience in any meaningful way, the Exhibition restricted its audience and limited its potential reach. Bavidge summarizes thus: 'Both City and Exhibition express the difficulty of trying to establish a view of child development which cannot allow itself to abandon the assertion of the unsayable magical mystery of childhood, and particularly of doing so within a commercial setting' (2009: 135). The Exhibition looked backwards rather than forwards and spoke to and of values that were rapidly becoming dated. Though it was successful enough to run twice in 1913, the Exhibition did not run again in 1914. It fell victim to the same lack of interest that caused the Universal Exhibition to fail before it had even opened.

The year 1914 marks the end of a particular period in children's commodity culture. Throughout the latter half of the nineteenth century and the early years of the twentieth century, children's literature was closely intertwined with children's experiences of material culture, helping to instruct and induct young readers in the nuances of contemporary consumption, revealing the science and the magic behind common commodities, and modelling ways to consume well or badly. My study has been largely chronological though I must note that there are some temporal overlaps among the texts discussed here so that the chapters group together texts with thematic as well as historical commonalities.

The object lessons of Chapter 1 inculcate the child reader in a world of consumption: the child readers of the texts about the Great Exhibition are encouraged to marvel at and enjoy a wide range of commodities. The implied child reader of many of these non-fiction works is one who is not yet properly inducted into contemporary consumer culture and who needs to be taught how to appreciate the commodities on display in the Exhibition. Authors, like Newcombe, used the model of the object lesson to teach their readers how to examine commodities carefully, using all of their senses, in order to become an informed, impartial consumer. In many of the texts about the Great Exhibition, the end product is divorced from the process of production and the economic and social truths underlying the production of goods such as coal or cotton are elided in favour of a celebration of the usefulness or attractiveness of the finished commodity. However, as I have shown, some authors sought to draw their readers' attention to the networks of production, trade and consumption behind the commodities on display. The 'it-narratives' discussed in Chapter 2 take the interest in the production and circulation of goods to a new level. Rather than being second-rate imitations of eighteenth-century novels of circulation aimed at adult readers, I have argued that children's it-narratives of the nineteenth century are distinctive for their focus on child characters, and on scientific content. These texts are a hybrid of fact and fiction and embed information about the ways that familiar commodities, such as matches, needles and table salt, are produced.

Chapter 3 discussed the connections between children's fantasy and commodity culture, drawing connections between the rise of children's fantasy literature and the growing interest in magic and Spiritualism in the middle of the nineteenth century. In these texts, ordinary household objects such as tables, chairs and clocks, are imbued with other-worldly powers and become animated. These texts present fictional worlds in which commodities interact with – and even talk to – child characters. If Chapter 2 focuses on science, the focus of Chapter 3 is magic though I have resisted presenting these as a pair of opposites because, in truth, science and magic existed in harmony rather than in tension, at least within the world of children's texts where the 'magic' of Andersen's and of Perkins's books on 'parlour magic' draws just as much simple scientific experiments as it does on sleights of hand.

If Chapter 3 focuses on texts in which children and objects can become interlocutors, even equals, Chapter 4 examines texts in which children and commodities are at odds. The texts discussed here feature objects that have become things. Unlike the objects I discussed in Chapter 1, which uphold and clarify cultural and social values within children's texts, these deviant items expose the fractures and instabilities within the world of goods. What the former promotes, the latter subverts. Likewise, the child characters who encounter these things are not figured as burgeoning consumers ready to take their place in the world of trade and exchange, but hapless victims of consumer culture, susceptible to advertising and liable to misuse commodities and to be hurt as a result.

In his survey of Victorian commodity culture *Victorian Things*, Asa Briggs acknowledges the difficulty, and even the futility, of trying to pin down the subject of Victorian material culture:

Such a concept of 'material culture' has been described as 'wondrous and gargantuan', 'with everything thrown in except the kitchen sink'; and more recently the kitchen sink has been thrown in too, along with the grate and the hearth. ... As a concept, it clearly needs refinement, if not narrowing of scope. (1993: 30)

There has been no narrowing of scope since Briggs's publication – if anything, the topic has grown in both popularity and range. This book goes a small way towards addressing this topic. It is limited both temporally and geographically, and my sample texts speak generally to privileged, white, middle-class, Anglophone readers and so my discussion generally speaks of these same privileged children. There is scope for much more investigation, particularly into the lives of children who were not only consumers but also makers of commodities in their own right. Their experiences, like their labour, is so commonly overlooked as to be difficult to see clearly at first and this is an area of childhood experience that could usefully be brought to light.

In coming to the end of this book, I find myself returning to E. Nesbit's words at the end of *Wings and the Child*: 'I feel that I have only been touching the fringe of the greatest problem in the world: that there is very much which I have left unsaid, or which I might have said differently, and better' (1913: 197). Children's literature and material culture is a wide topic and I have reached out to touch the fringes of it here. While some objects produced during this period have obvious monetary and cultural value, like the materials from the Great Exhibition of 1851 that formed the basis of the collections of the Victoria and Albert Museum, the majority of the items I have discussed here are so common as to be overlooked: the needles and pins, tinderboxes and china cups, clocks and chairs, cricket balls and doll's furniture. These items have a material reality and, within the children's texts discussed here, they also have a textual reality and there are many complex intersections between the real and the fictional, the material and the imagined.

The children's texts produced between 1850 and 1914 reflect contemporary ideas about and anxieties around consumption, tracing a range of attitudes towards commodity culture, from celebration to suspicion. These texts reflect the flexibility, range and power of children's engagements with commodity culture in this period, presenting child characters as naïve consumers beguiled by objects, as apprentice consumers in need of enculturation, as adept consumers confident in their own desires and tastes, and as material deviants. The texts I have selected for discussion bring ordinary objects into focus, making them narrators or characters, or using them as narrative devices, or transforming them into antagonists for child characters to strive against. These are not commodities to be pointed at with an index finger, or slipped into a pocket, or balanced on the palm of the hand. These are commodities to be thought. The representation of material objects in children's literature does not only 'make visible and stable the categories of culture' as Douglas and Isherwood suggest (1979: 61), but also makes these ideas tangible to us, however briefly, even at the great remove of the twenty-first century. Our task as readers is no less 'wondrous and gargantuan' than the topic of material culture itself; we have to read carefully, to consider the objects we are presented with as literary devices, and to consider them as objects, to understand them as fictional representations of real items with economic value, social significance and material properties. The golden age of children's literature was also a golden age of consumerism and we may reach a richer understanding of both if we acknowledge the close, complex connections between children's literature and commodity culture.

Notes

Chapter 1

1 Dickens sat on the Working Classes Central Committee but moved to dissolve it on 7 June 1850 because it could 'neither effectively render the services it seeks to perform, nor command the confidence of the Working Classes' (*Minutes of the Proceedings of Her Majesty's Commissioners for the Exhibition of 1851, 11th January 1850–24th April 1852*, Appendix H: 16–17).
2 Charlotte Brontë undoubtedly knew Thackeray's novel as he had sent her an inscribed copy in 1848 before he was aware of her real identity. He called on her on 12 June 1850 when she was in London and she lectured him on his literary shortcomings. The meeting 'ended in decent amity' and later that day she attended a dinner at his London home (Brontë [1850] 1908: 143–4).
3 E. Whimper's name is sometimes recorded in error as Whymper, possibly as a result of being confused with Edward Whymper (1840–1911), mountaineer, landscape painter and illustrator. Edward Whymper would have been only eleven years old at the time of the Great Exhibition and so it seems rather unlikely he is the commercial artist behind the illustrations in Newcombe's work.

Chapter 3

1 The translation of this particular passage is complex. Here, I have followed Moore and Aveling's translation because of their inclusion of the term 'table-turning', a richly evocative phrase in the context of late Victorian parlour magic and fantasy literature. Fowkes completes the line as 'far more wonderful than if it were to begin dancing of its own free will' (Marx [1887] 1990: 163–4). Either way, the table's sudden movements, and its agency, are presented as surprising and uncanny. Moore and Aveling also include the following explanatory note which explicitly connects the image of the capering table in Marx's *Capital* to the rise of the Spiritualist movement:

> In the German edition, there is the following footnote here: 'One may recall that China and the tables began to dance when the rest of the world appeared to be standing still – *pour encourager les autres* [to encourage the

others].' The defeat of the 1848–49 revolutions was followed by a period of dismal political reaction in Europe. At that time, spiritualism, especially table-turning, became the rage among the European aristocracy. (56)

Chapter 4

1 That The Society for Checking the Abuses of Public Advertising (SCAPA) was founded in 1898 suggests that there was a need for careful monitoring and regulation of advertisements and the unfounded claims made by unscrupulous manufacturers.
2 Valerie Sanders observes that incidents from Ada J. Graves's *The House by the Railway* (1896) are reworked for *The Railway Children*, and Julia Briggs has suggested that Nesbit plagiarized elements of F. Antsey's *The Brass Bottle* (1900) in both *Five Children and It* and in *The Phoenix and the Carpet*. Nesbit also reuses the line 'Daddy, Oh My Daddy!' in both *The House of Arden* and *The Railway Children*. Similarly, Nesbit used and reused a series of domestic disasters that occurred when the Blands moved into Well Hall at Eltham as the basis for scenes in her novels for adults and children. See Sanders (2013).
3 This scene is reprised in a similar incident in *The Red House* (1902), a text written for an adult audience in which the Bastables also make an appearance. Julia Briggs notes that these flood scenes, along with other minor crises, are based on a series of domestic disasters that really occurred when the Blands moved into Well Hall at Eltham (Briggs 1989: 202–4).
4 The original story called 'The Three Bears' was published by Southey in *The Doctor &c*. The story features not a golden-haired girl, but an old woman (Southey 1848).

References

'A Natural History Reading Room' (1899), *Times*, 6 February: 10.
'A Visit to Messrs Liberty's' (1897), London: Liberty.
'Beautiful Soap' (1871), Pears Soap, Bodleian Library, University of Oxford 2010, John Johnson Collection, Soap 7 (11a).
'Beware of Worthless and Fraudulent Imitations' (1891), The Carbolic Smoke Ball Company, Bodleian Library, John Johnson Collection, Patent Medicines 8 (34a).
'Children's Welfare' (1913), *Gloucester Journal*, 4 January: 9.
'Danziger's "Ouija", or, The Wonderful Talking Board' (1891), *Pittsburgh Dispatch*, 1 February: 12.
Eastern Carpets and Rugs: India, China, and Japan Merchants (1897), London: Liberty.
'Exhibition Fiasco: Birds Find Skeleton of "Palace of Industries" Useful' (1914), *Nottingham Journal*, 9 May: 3.
Fans, Ancient and Modern, Eastern and Western: A Brief Sketch of Their Origin and Use (1894), London: Liberty.
'General Gossip of Authors and Writers' (1889), *Current Opinion*, September.
Information on Common Objects for the Use of Infant and Juvenile Schools and Nursery Governesses (1845), London: Darton and Clark.
'List of Articles and Money Found in the Exhibition, Hyde Park, Remaining Unclaimed in Possession of the Police' (1852), MEPOL 2/106, National Archives, Kew.
'List of Statuary and Other Objects of Interest Placed in the Main Avenues of the Building' (1851), *Official Catalogue of the Great Exhibition of the Worlds of Industry of All Nations, 1851*, 8–9, London: Spicer.
Little Polly's Doll's House (n.d.), London: George Routledge.
Mamma's Visit with Her Little Ones to the Great Exhibition (1852), London: Darton.
Minutes of the Proceedings of Her Majesty's Commissioners for the Exhibition of 1851, 11 January 1850–24 April 1852 (1852), Appendix H, London: W. Clowes & Sons.
Model Lessons for Infant School Teachers and Nursery Governesses (1838), London: R. B. Seeley and W. Burnside.
'Next Year's Exhibition in Nottingham' (1913), *Nottingham Evening Post*, 7 October: 5.
'Nottingham's Exhibition: Big Scheme on a Business Basis' (1913), *Nottingham Evening Post*, 5 November: 3.
'Nottingham Exhibition: The Enterprise Abandoned for This Year' (1914), *Nottingham Evening Post*, 24 March: 3.
'Poison in Toilet Soaps!' (1890), Pears Soap, Bodleian Library, University of Oxford 2010, John Johnson Collection, Soap 8 (36).

'Return of Schools Reported to the Executive Committee as Having Entered the Building' (1852), *Report of the Royal Commission to Parliament*, Appendix XVIII, 92. London: W. Clowes & Sons.

'Return Showing the Quantity of Provisions of Each Kind Reported to Have Been Consumed in the Refreshment Courts during the Whole Time of the Exhibition' (1852), *Report of the Commissioners for the Great Exhibition of 1851, Vol. 1*, Appendix XXIX, 150, London: W. Clowes & Sons.

'Return Showing the Temperature of the Building for Each Day during the Time of the Exhibition' (1852), *Report of the Commissioners for the Great Exhibition of 1851, Vol. 1*, Appendix X, 67–8, London: W. Clowes & Sons.

'Spirits and Spirit-Rapping' (1858), *Westminster Review*, XXV (January): 29–66.

'Statement of the Materials Supplied for the Construction of the Building – Continued' (1852), *Report of the Commissioners for the Great Exhibition of 1851, Vol. 1*, Appendix XI, 70–1, London: W. Clowes & Sons.

'Table-Turning and Table-Talking' (1854), *Launceston Examiner*, 18 April: 2.

'The Adventures of a Gold-Ring', *Rambler's Magazine*, 1 (March 1783), 84–7; (April 1783), 128–30; (May 1783), 167–9; (June 1783), 207–9; (July 1783), 254–6. Reprinted in Blackwell et al. (2012), *British It-Narratives 1750–1830, Vol. 4*, 81–94, London: Pickering & Chatto.

The Adventures of a Pin, Supposed to be Related by Himself, Herself, or Itself (1796), London: John Lee.

'The Ancoats Lamp Fatality' (1899), *Manchester Guardian*, 2 December: 12.

The Boy's Own Conjuring Book: Being a Complete Hand-Book of Parlour Magic (1860), New York: Dick & Fitzgerald.

'The Comical Creatures from Wurtemberg' (1851), *Morning Chronicle*, 12 August: 6.

The Comical Creatures from Wurtemberg: Including the Story of Reynard the Fox with Twenty Illustrations, Drawn from the Stuffed Animals Contributed by Herrmann Ploucquet of Stuttgart to the Great Exhibition (1851), London: David Bogue.

The Crystal Palace: A Little Book for Little Boys, for 1851 (1851), London: James Nisbet.

The Dream of the Rood (2004), trans. M. Swanton, Exeter: University of Exeter Press.

The Fine Crystal Palace the Prince Built (n.d.), London: Dean & Son.

The House That Jack Built: Also, The History of Mrs. Williams, and Her Plumb Cake, Which She Mathematically Divided among Her Pupils, according to Their Merit: The Story of Little Red Riding Hood (1790), Boston: Joseph White and Charles Cambridge near Charles-River Bridge.

'The Magic City. E. Nesbit's Table Game for The Children. Testing Parental Sympathy' (1913), *Westminster Gazette*, 3 January: 5.

'The Magic City' (1913), *Gentlewoman*, 4 January: 20.

The Victoria Alphabet (n.d.), London: George Routledge.

The World's Fair: Or, Children's Prize Gift Book of the Great Exhibition of 1851: Describing the Beautiful Inventions and Manufactures Exhibited Therein: With Pretty Stories about the People Who Have Made and Sent Them: And How They Live When at Home (1851), London: Thomas Dean and Son.

'Three May Days in London [iii]: The May Palace 1851' (1851), *Household Words*, 3 May: 121–4.

'To Cost £130,000: International Exhibition in Nottingham' (1913), *Nottingham Evening Post*, 11 August: 5.

'Two Luckless Babes' (1894), *Washington Post*, 31 August: 1.

Uncle Nimrod's First Visit to the Great Exhibition (n.d.), London: George Routledge.

Uncle Nimrod's Second Visit to the Great Exhibition (n.d.), London: George Routledge.

Uncle Nimrod's Third Visit to the Great Exhibition (n.d.), London: George Routledge.

'Was Charles Ensley Murdered?' (1892), A. J. White Ltd., Bodleian Library, John Johnson Collection, Patent Medicines 12 (38).

A.L.O.E. [C. M. Tucker] (1858), *The Story of a Needle*, London: T. Nelson and Sons.

Ackerman, S. L. (2008), *Behind the Looking Glass*, Newcastle: Cambridge Scholars.

Ahmed, S. (2006), *Queer Phenomenology: Orientations, Objects, Others*, Durham, NC: Duke University Press.

Andersen, J. H. (1839), *The Fashionable Science of Parlour Magic: Being the Newest Tricks of Deception, Developed and Illustrated*, London: R. S. Francis.

Andrews, E. (1798), *The History of a Pin as Related by Itself*, London: Newbery.

Appadurai, A. (1986), 'Introduction: Commodities and the Politics of Value', in A. Appadurai (ed.), *The Social Life of Things: Commodities in Cultural Perspective*, 3–63, Cambridge: Cambridge University Press.

Armstrong, F. (1996), 'The Doll House as Ludic Space 1690–1920', *Children's Literature*, 24: 23–54.

Barthes, R. ([1975] 1989), 'The Reality Effect', in R. Howard (trans.), *The Rustle of Language*, 141–8, Berkeley: University of California Press.

Baum, L. F. (1900), *The Art of Decorating Dry Goods Windows and Interiors: A Complete Manual of Window Trimming, Designed as an Educator in All the Details of the Art, according to the Best Accepted Methods, and Treating Fully Every Important Subject*, Chicago: Show Window.

Baum, L. F. (2012), *The Complete Stories of Oz*, Ware: Wordsworth.

Bavidge, J. (2009), 'Exhibiting Childhood: E. Nesbit and the Children's Welfare Exhibitions', in A. Gavin and A. F. Humphries (eds), *Childhood in Edwardian Fiction: Worlds Enough and Time*, 125–42, New York: Palgrave Macmillan.

Beaudry, M. C. (2006), *Findings: The Material Culture of Needlework and Sewing*, New Haven, CT: Yale University Press.

Bellamy, L. (2007), 'It-Narrators and Circulation: Defining a Subgenre', in M. Blackwell (ed.), *The Secret Life of Things: Animals, Objects, and It-Narratives in Eighteenth-Century England*, 134–44, Lewisburg, PA: Bucknell University Press.

Bernaerts, L., M. Caracciolo, L. Herman and B. Vervaeck (2014), 'The Storied Lives of Non-Human Narrators', *NARRATIVE*, 22 (1): 68–93.

Bernstein, R. (2013), 'Toys Are Good for Us: Why We Should Embrace the Historical Integration of Children's Literature, Material Culture, and Play', *Children's Literature Association Quarterly*, 38 (4): 458–63.

Berry, C. (1876), *Experiences in Spiritualism: A Record of Extraordinary Phenomena, Witnessed through the Most Powerful Mediums: With Some Historical Fragments Relating to Semiramide, Given by the Spirit of an Egyptian Who Lived Contemporary with Her*, London: James Burns.

Blackwell, M. (ed.) (2007), *The Secret Life of Things: Animals, Objects, and It-Narratives in Eighteenth-Century England*, Lewisburg, PA: Bucknell University Press.

Blackwell, M. (2012), 'General Introduction', *British It-Narratives, 1750–1830, Vol. 1*, ed. L. Bellamy, vii–xxviii, London: Pickering & Chatto.

Blackwell, M., L. Bellamy, C. Upton and H. Keenleyside (eds) (2012), *British It-Narratives, 1750–1830*, London: Pickering & Chatto.

Blanchard, S. L. (1851), 'Biography of a Bad Shilling', *Household Words*, 25 January: 420–6.

Bourget, P. (1895), *Outre-Mer: Impressions of America*, New York: C. Scribner's Sons.

Bowlby, R. (1985), *Just Looking: Consumer Culture in Dreiser, Gissing, and Zola*, London: Methuen.

Boyle, M., and C. Dickens (1851), 'My Mahogany Friend', *Household Words*, 8 March: 558–62.

Brenda (1875), *Froggy's Little Brother*, London: Shaw.

Briefel, A. (2017), '"Freaks of Furniture": The Useless Energy of Haunted Things', *Victorian Studies*, 59 (2): 209–34.

Briggs, A. (1993), *Victorian Things*, London: Penguin.

Briggs, J. (1989), *A Woman of Passion: The Life of E. Nesbit, 1858–1924*, London: Penguin.

Brontë, C. ([1850] 1908), Letter to Ellen Nussey, 12 June, in C. Shorter (ed.), *The Brontës' Life and Letters, Vol. 2*, 143–4, London: Hodder and Staughton.

Brontë, C. ([1851a] 1908), Letter to Patrick Bronte, 30 May, in C. Shorter (ed.), *The Brontës Life and Letters, Vol. 2*, 212–13, London: Hodder and Staughton.

Brontë, C. ([1851b] 1908), Letter to Ellen Nussey, 2 June, in C. Shorter (ed.), *The Brontës Life and Letters, Vol. 2*, 214–15, London: Hodder and Staughton.

Brontë, C. ([1851c] 1908), Letter to Patrick Bronte, 7 June, in C. Shorter (ed.), *The Brontës Life and Letters, Vol. 2*, 215–16, London: Hodder and Staughton.

Brontë, C. ([1851d] 1908), Letter to Miss Wooler, 14 July, in C. Shorter (ed.), *The Brontës Life and Letters, Vol. 2*, 223–4, London: Hodder and Staughton.

Brown, B. (1998), 'How to Do Things with Things (A Toy Story)', *Critical Inquiry*, 24 (4): 935–64.

Brown, B. (2001), 'Thing Theory', *Critical Inquiry*, 28 (1): 1–22.

Brown, B. (2003), *A Sense of Things: The Object Matter of American Literature*, Chicago: University of Chicago Press.

Brown, B. (2009), 'The Secret Life of Things: Animals, Objects, and It-Narratives in Eighteenth-Century England (review)', *Eighteenth Century Fiction*, 21 (4): 631–8.
Brown, B. (2016), 'The Bodies of Things', in K. Boehm (ed.), *Bodies and Things in Nineteenth-Century Literature and Culture*, 221–8, Basingstoke: Palgrave Macmillan.
Browne, F. (1857), *Granny's Wonderful Chair and Its Tales of Fairy Times*, London: Griffith and Farran.
Buckingham, D., and V. Tingstad (eds) (2014), *Childhood and Consumer Culture*, Basingstoke: Palgrave Macmillan.
Buck-Morss, S. (1989), *The Dialectics of Seeing: Walter Benjamin and the Arcades Project*, Cambridge, MA: MIT Press.
Bunyan, J. ([1678] 1996), *The Pilgrim's Progress*, ed. S. Sim, London: Wordsworth.
Burnett, F. H. (1893), *The One I Knew the Best of All: A Memory of the Mind of a Child*, New York: Scribner's.
Buzard, J., J. W. Childers and E. Gillooly (eds) (2007), *Victorian Prism: Refractions of the Crystal Palace*, Charlottesville: University of Virginia Press.
Byrd, W. (1800), *Cock Robin, The House That Jack Built, History of an Apple Pye, and Other Entertainments*, Stockton: n.p.
Capron, E. W. ([1855] 1976), *Modern Spiritualism: Its Facts and Fanaticisms, Its Consistencies and Contradictions*, New York: Arno Press.
Carey, A. (1870), *Autobiographies of a Lump of Coal, a Grain of Salt, a Drop of Water, a Bit of Old Iron, a Piece of Flint*, London: Cassell, Petter and Galpin.
Carey, A. (1872), *Threads of Knowledge Drawn from a Cambric Handkerchief, a Brussels Carpet, a Print Dress, a Kid Glove, a Sheet of Paper*, London: Cassell, Petter and Galpin.
Carey, A. (1880), *The Wonders of Common Things*, London: Cassell.
Carpenter, H. (1989), 'Excessively Impertinent Bunnies: The Subversive Element in Beatrix Potter', in G. Avery and J. Briggs (eds), *Children and Their Books: A Celebration of the Work of Iona and Peter Opie*, 271–98, Oxford: Oxford University Press.
Carpenter, H. (2012), *Secret Gardens: A Study of the Golden Age of Children's Literature*, London: Faber & Faber.
Carrier, J. G. (1993), 'The Rituals of Christmas Giving', in D. Miller (ed.), *Unwrapping Christmas*, 55–74, Oxford: Clarendon Press.
Carroll, J. S. (2020), 'Girlhood and Space in Nineteenth-Century Orphan Literature', in L. Peters and D. Warren (eds), *Rereading Orphanhood: Texts, Inheritance, Kin*, 186–205, Edinburgh: Edinburgh University Press.
Carroll, L. ([1865] 1971), *Alice's Adventures in Wonderland*, illus. J. Tenniel in M. Gardner (ed.), *Alice's Adventures in Wonderland* and *Through the Looking Glass and What Alice Found There*, 17–164, Harmondsworth: Penguin.
Carroll, L. ([1869] 1911), *Phantasmagoria and Other Poems*, illus. A. B. Frost, London: Macmillan.

Carroll, L. ([1871] 1971), *Through the Looking-Glass and What Alice Found There*, illus. J. Tenniel in M. Gardner (ed.), *Alice's Adventures in Wonderland* and *Through the Looking Glass And What Alice Found There*, 166–345, Harmondsworth: Penguin.

Carroll, L. ([1882] 1978), Letter to James Langton Clarke, 4 December, in L. Carroll, *The Letters of Lewis Carroll, Vol. I*, ed. M. N. Cohen and R. Lancelyn Green, 471–2, New York: Oxford University Press.

Carroll, L. ([1892] 1989), Letter to Alice Hargreaves, 7 January, in L. Carroll, *The Selected Letters of Lewis Carroll*, ed. Morton N. Cohen, New York: Springer.

Carroll, L. ([1898] 1920), 'Preface to the Eighty-Six Thousand', Christmas 1896 in *Alice's Adventures in Wonderland*, New York: Macmillan.

Carroll, L. (1989), *The Selected Letters of Lewis Carroll*, ed. Morton N. Cohen, New York: Springer.

Chandler, K. R. (2007), 'Thoroughly Post-Victorian, Pre-Modern Beatrix', *Children's Literature Association Quarterly*, 32 (4): 287–307.

Cheang, S. (2007), 'Selling China: Class, Gender and Orientalism at the Department Store', *Journal of Design History*, 20 (1): 1–16, 1.

Chesterton, A. (1931), *The Chestertons*, London: George G. Harrap.

Cluckie, L. (2008), *The Rise and Fall of Art Needlework: Its Socio-Economic and Cultural Aspects*, Bury St. Edmunds: Arena Books.

Codell, J. (2018), 'Introduction: Domesticity, Culture, and the Victorian Press', *Victorian Periodicals Review*, 51 (2): 215–29.

Collingwood, S. D. (1898), *The Life and Letters of Lewis Carroll (Rev. C.L. Dodgson)*, London: T. F. Unwin.

Commissioners of the Great Exhibition (1851), *Minutes of the 41st Meeting of the Commissioners*, 10 May 1851, Unpublished Minutes, Royal Commission for the Exhibition of 1851, Imperial College, London.

Commissioners of the Great Exhibition (1852), *Minutes of the Proceedings of Her Majesty's Commissioners for the Exhibition of 1851, 11th January 1850–24th April 1852*, Royal Commission for the Exhibition of 1851, Imperial College, London.

Cook, D. T. (2014), 'Commercial Enculturation: Moving beyond Consumer Socialization', in D. Buckingham and V. Tingstad (eds), *Childhood and Consumer Culture*, 63–79, Basingstoke: Palgrave Macmillan.

Crowe, C. (1850), *The Night Side of Nature, or, Ghosts and Ghost-Seers*, New York: J. S. Redfield.

De Morgan, A. (1863), 'Preface' to Sophia De Morgan, *From Matter to Spirit: Ten Years' Experience of Spirit Manifestations, Intended as a Guide to Enquirers*, London: Longman, Green, Longman, Roberts & Green.

De Morgan, S. (1863), *From Matter to Spirit: Ten Years' Experience of Spirit Manifestations, Intended as a Guide to Enquirers*, London: Longman, Green, Longman, Roberts & Green.

Denisoff, D. (2016a), 'Introduction', in D. Denisoff (ed.), *The Nineteenth Century Child and Consumer Culture*, 1–25, London: Routledge.

Denisoff, D. (ed.) (2016b), *The Nineteenth-Century Child and Consumer Culture*, London: Routledge.

Dickens, C. ([1851] 2012), Letter to Lavinia Watson, 11 July, in J. Hartley (ed.), *The Selected Letters of Charles Dickens*, 233–5, Oxford: Oxford University Press.

Dickinsons' Comprehensive Pictures of the Great Exhibition of 1851: From the Originals Painted for H.R.H. Prince Albert, Vol. 1 (1854), London: Dickinson Brothers.

Dixon, W. (1852), Letter to Metropolitan Police, 27 January, MEPOL 2/106, National Archives, Kew.

Dolls and Sights of the Great Exhibition (n.d.), London: George Routledge.

Douglas, A. (2007), 'Britannia's Rule and the It-Narrator', in M. Blackwell (ed.), *The Secret Life of Things: Animals, Objects, and It-Narratives in Eighteenth-Century England*, 147–61, Lewisburg, PA: Bucknell University Press.

Douglas, M., and B. Isherwood (1979), *The World of Goods towards an Anthropology of Consumption*, New York: Basic Books.

Du Maurier, G. ([1886] 1897), *English Society Sketched by George Du Maurier*, London: Osgood, McIlvaine.

Eliot, G. (1860), *The Mill on the Floss, Vol. 2*, New York. Harper.

Festa, L. (2007), 'Moral Ends of Eighteenth- and Nineteenth-Century Object Narratives', in Mark Blackwell (ed.), *The Secret Life of Things: Animals, Objects, and It-Narratives in Eighteenth-Century England*, 309–28, Lewisburg, PA: Bucknell University Press.

Field, H. (2019), *Playing with the Book: Victorian Movable Picture Books and the Child Reader*, Minneapolis: University of Minnesota Press.

First Report of the Commissioners for the Exhibition of 1851 (1852), London: W. Clowes & Sons.

Fitzsimons, E. (2019), *The Life and Loves of Edith Nesbit: Author of the Railway Children*, London: Duckworth.

Flanders, J. (2003), *The Victorian House: Domestic Life from Childbirth to Deathbed*, London: HarperCollins.

Freedgood, E. (2010), *Ideas in Things: Fugitive Meaning in the Victorian Novel*, Chicago: University of Chicago Press.

Fromm, E. (1962), *Beyond the Chains of Illusion: My Encounter with Marx and Freud*, New York: Touchstone.

Garrison, W. L. ([1867] 1972), Letter to Frank J. Garrison, 18 January, Boston Public Library, quoted in R. L. Moore, 'Spiritualism and Science: Reflections on the First Decade of the Spirit Rappings', *American Quarterly*, 24 (4): 474–500.

Gourard, J. (1864), *The Adventures of a Watch*, Dublin: James Duffy.

Grahame, K. ([1908] 2010), *The Wind in the Willows*, ed. P. Hunt, Oxford: Oxford University Press.

Grandpapa's Walking Stick (1873), London: S. W. Partridge.

Green, P. (1959), *Kenneth Grahame: A Biography*, Cleveland, OH: World.

Grenby, M. O. (2008), *Children's Literature*, Edinburgh: Edinburgh University Press.

Gubar, M. (2009), *Artful Dodgers: Reconceiving the Golden Age of Children's Literature*, Oxford: Oxford University Press.

Gurney, P. (2007), '"A Palace for the People"? The Crystal Palace and Consumer Culture in Victorian England', in James Buzard, Joseph W. Childers and Eileen Gillooly (eds), *Victorian Prism: Refractions of the Crystal Palace*, 138–50, Charlottesville: University of Virginia Press.

Hartley, J. (2012), *The Selected Letters of Charles Dickens*, Oxford: Oxford University Press.

Haskell, F. (2000), *The Ephemeral Museum: Old Master Paintings and the Rise of the Art Exhibition*, New Haven, CT: Yale University Press.

Heath, S. (1982), 'Barthes on Love', *SubStance*, 11/12 (4/1): 100–6.

Herring, S. (2011), 'Material Deviance: Theorizing Queer Objecthood', *Postmodern Culture*, 21(2). Available online: doi:10.1353/pmc.2011.0009.

Herring, S. (2014), *The Hoarders: Material Deviance in Modern American Culture*, Chicago: University of Chicago Press.

Hicks, D., and M. Beaudry (eds) (2010), *The Oxford Handbook of Material Culture Studies*, Oxford: Oxford University Press.

Holmes, V. (2014), 'Penny Death Traps: The Press, the Poor, Parliament, and the "Perilous" Penny Paraffin Lamp', *Victorian Review*, 40 (2): 125–42.

Horne, R. H., and C. Dickens (1851), 'The Great Exhibition and the Little One', *Household Words*, 5 July: 356–60.

Hunt, P. (1987), 'Landscapes and Journeys, Metaphors and Maps: The Distinctive Feature of English Fantasy', *Children's Literature Association Quarterly*, 12 (1): 11–14.

Hunt, P. (2010), 'Introduction', in K. Grahame, *The Wind in the Willows*, vii–xxxii, Oxford: Oxford University Press.

James, M. R. ([1933] 2011), 'The Malice of Inanimate Objects', in D. Jones (ed.), *Collected Ghost Stories*, 397–400, Oxford: Oxford University Press.

Jenkins, A. (2013), 'Getting to Utopia: Railways and Heterotopia in Children's Literature', in C. Hintz and E. Ostry (eds), *Utopian and Dystopian Writing for Children and Young Adults*, 23–37, New York: Routledge.

Jenks, C. (1996), *Childhood*, London: Routledge.

Jennings, P. ([1950] 1959), 'Report on Resistentialism', *Oddly Enough*, 147–64, London: Max Reinhardt.

Jepson, E. (1937), *Memories of an Edwardian and Neo-Georgian*, London: Richards.

Johnson, S. L. (2018), 'Christina Rossetti's Ghosts, Soul-Sleep, and Victorian Death Culture', *Victorian Literature and Culture*, 46 (2): 381–402.

Johnstone, C. (1760), *Chrysal: The Adventures of a Guinea*, London: T. Becket.

Jones, A. M., and N. Boivin (2010), 'The Malice of Inanimate Objects: Material Agency', in D. Hicks and M. Beaudry (eds), *The Oxford Handbook of Material Culture Studies*, 333–51, Oxford: Oxford University Press.

Katson, A. (1998), 'Speaking Pictures: The Fantastic World of Christina Rossetti and Arthur Hughes', *Journal of Narrative Technique*, 28 (3): 305–28.

Keenan, H. T. (1988), 'Molesworth, M.L.S. 1839-1921', in J. M. Bingham (ed.), *Writers for Children: Critical Studies of Major Authors since the Seventeenth Century*, 407-13, New York: Charles Scribner's Sons.
King, C. K. (2014), 'A History of Inanimate Minds', *The Eighteenth Century*, 55 (4): 451-3.
Kipling, R. ([1901] 2011), *Kim*, London: Puffin.
Kline, S. (1993), *Out of the Garden: Toys, TV, and Children's Culture in the Age of Marketing*, New York: Verso.
Kohlt, F. (2019), '"More Than a Figment of Scientific Fancy": Dreams and Visions in Victorian Psychology and Fantastic Literature, 1858-1900', PhD diss., University of Oxford.
Kreienbrock, J. (2013), *Malicious Objects, Anger Management and the Question of Modern Literature*, New York: Fordham University Press.
Kutzer, M. D. (1997), 'A Wildness Inside: Domestic Space in the Work of Beatrix Potter', *The Lion and the Unicorn*, 21 (2): 204-14.
Kuznets, L. R. (1978), 'Toad Hall Revisited', *Children's Literature*, 7 (1): 11528.
Lake, C. B. (2013), 'Feeling Things: The Novel Objectives of Sentimental Objects', *The Eighteenth Century*, 54 (2): 183-93.
Lamb, J. (2001), 'Modern Metamorphoses and Disgraceful Tales', *Critical Inquiry*, 28 (1): 133-66.
Lambert, F. (1843), *Hand-Book of Needlework*, London: John Murray.
Lambert, J. A. (2020a), *The Art of Advertising*, Oxford: Bodleian Library.
Lambert, J. A. (2020b), 'Art and Commerce', in J. A. Lambert (ed.), *The Art of Advertising*, 80-3, Oxford: Bodleian Library.
Lambert, J. A. (2020c), 'Ways and Means', in J. A. Lambert (ed.), *The Art of Advertising*, 99-125, Oxford: Bodleian Library.
Lastoria, A. (2019), 'Lewis Carroll, Art Director: Recovering the Design and Production Rationales for Victorian Editions of Alice's Adventures in Wonderland', *Book History*, 22: 196-225.
Lathey, G. (2017), 'Figuring the World: Representing Children's Encounters with Other Peoples and Cultures at the Great Exhibition of 1851', in E. O'Sullivan and A. Immel (eds), *Imagining Sameness and Difference in Children's Literature: From the Enlightenment to the Present Day*, 71-88, London: Palgrave MacMillan.
Lear, L. (2007), *Beatrix Potter: A Life in Nature*, London: Allan Lane.
Ledbetter, K. (2012), *Victorian Needlework*, Santa Barbara, CA: ABC-CLIO.
Leech, J. (1886), 'Memorials of the Great Exhibition', in *Leech's Pictures of Life and Character, Volume I (Of III) from the Collection of 'Mr. Punch'*, 228-40, London: Bradbury, Agnew.
Lehman, A. (2014), *Victorian Women and the Theatre of Trance: Mediums, Spiritualists and Mesmerists in Performance*, Jefferson, NC: McFarland.
Lerer, S. (2009), 'Style and the Mole: Domestic Aesthetics in "The Wind in the Willows"', *Journal of Aesthetic Education*, 43 (2): 51-63.

Lindner, C. (2003), *Fictions of Commodity Culture: From the Victorian to the Postmodern*, London: Ashgate.
Linton, E. L. (1860), 'Modern Magic', *All the Year Round*, 28 July: 370–4.
Loeb, L. A. (1994), *Consuming Angels: Advertising and Victorian Women*, New York: Oxford University Press.
Logan, T. (2001), *The Victorian Parlour: A Cultural Study*, Cambridge: Cambridge University Press.
Lucas, E. V. (1899), *The Book of Shops*, illus. F. D. Bedford, London: Grant Richards.
Lutz, D. (2015), *Relics of Death in Victorian Literature and Culture*, Cambridge: Cambridge University Press.
Lyell, C. (1830–3), *Principles of Geology, Being an Attempt to Explain the Former Changes of the Earth's Surface, by References to Causes Now in Operation, Vols. 1–3*, London: John Murray.
Martineau, H. (1852), 'What There Is in a Button', *Household Words*, 17 April: 106–12.
Marx, K. ([1887] 1990), *Capital: A Critique of Political Economy, Vol. 1*, trans. B. Fowkes, London: Penguin.
Marx, K. ([1887] 2015), *Capital: A Critique of Political Economy, Vol. I*, trans. S. Moore and E. Aveling, Moscow: Progress.
Masschelein, A. (2002), 'The Concept as Ghost: Conceptualization of the Uncanny in Late-Twentieth-Century Theory', *Mosaic: An Interdisciplinary Critical Journal*, 35 (1): 53–68.
Matéaux, C. L. (1884), *The Wonderland of Work*, New York: Cassell.
Mattanah, J. (2010), 'A Contemporary Psychological Understanding of Mr. Toad and His Relationships in *The Wind in the Willows*', in J. C. Horne and D. White (eds), *Kenneth Grahame's The Wind in the Willows: A Children's Classic at 100*, 87–108, Lanham, MD: The Children's Literature Association.
Mauss, M. (1970), *The Gift: Forms and Functions of Exchange in Archaic Societies*, trans. Ian Cunnison, London: Cohen & West.
McCorristine, S. (2010), *Spectres of the Self: Thinking about Ghosts and Ghost-Seeing in England, 1750–1920*, Cambridge: Cambridge University Press.
McRobbie, L. R. (2013), 'The Strange and Mysterious History of the Ouija Board', *Smithsonian Magazine*, 27 October, n.p. Available online: https://www.smithsonianmag.com/history/the-strange-and-mysterious-history-of-the-ouija-board-5860627/ (accessed 4 March 2020).
McRobbie, L. R. (2016), 'How Novels Came to Be Written in the Voice of Coins, Stuffed Animals and Other Random Objects', *Atlas Obscura*, 12 May. Available online: https://www.atlasobscura.com/articles/how-novels-came-to-be-written-in-the-voice-of-coins-stuffed-animals-and-other-random-objects (accessed 7 July 2020).
Melech, A. (2008), *Servants of the Supernatural: The Night Side of the Victorian Mind*, London: William Heinemann.

Miller, A. H. (1995), *Novels behind Glass: Commodity Culture and Victorian Narrative*, Cambridge: Cambridge University Press.

Miller, D. (2005), *Materiality*, Durham, NC: Duke University Press.

Miller, J. H. (2009), *The Medium Is the Maker: Browning, Freud, Derrida, and the New Telepathic Ecotechnologies*, Eastbourne: Sussex Academic Press.

Molesworth, M. L. (1877), *The Cuckoo Clock*, London: Macmillan.

Moore, R. L. (1972), 'Spiritualism and Science: Reflections on the First Decade of the Spirit Rappings', *American Quarterly*, 24 (4): 474–500.

Morrall, M. T. ([1854] 1862), *The History and Description of Needlemaking*, Manchester: n.p.

Morris, W. (1883), 'The Beauty of Life', in W. Morris, *Hopes and Fears for Art: Five Lectures Delivered in Birmingham, London, and Nottingham, 1878–1881*, 71–113, London: Ellis and White.

Moss, A. (1988), 'Mrs Molesworth: Victorian Visionary', *The Lion and the Unicorn*, 12 (1): 105–10.

Moss, A. (1991), 'E. Nesbit's Romantic Child in Modern Dress', in J. H. McGavran (ed.), *Romanticism and Children's Literature in 19th Century England*, 225–45, Athens: University of Georgia Press.

Murché, V. T. (1895), *Object Lessons for Infants, Vol. 1*, London: Macmillan.

Nash, J., From *Dickinsons' Comprehensive Pictures of the Great Exhibition of 1851: From the Originals Painted for H.R.H. Prince Albert, Vol. I* (London, 1854), pl. 24, The Getty Research Institute, 90-B9947.

Nelson, C. (2014), 'Mass Media Meets Children's Literature, 1899: E. Nesbit's *The Story of the Treasure Seekers*', in Dino Franco Felluga (ed.), *BRANCH: Britain, Representation and Nineteenth Century History*, extension of *Romanticism and Victorianism on the Net*. Available online: http://www.branchcollective.org/?ps_articles=claudia-nelson-mass-media-meets-childrens-literature-1899-e-nesbits-the-story-of-the-treasure-seekers (accessed 25 September 2017).

Nelson, C. (2016), 'Adult Children's Literature in Victorian Britain', in D. Denisoff (ed.), *The Nineteenth Century Child and Consumer Culture*, 137–49, London: Routledge.

Nesbit, E. ([1899] 1994), *The Story of the Treasure Seekers*, London: Puffin.

Nesbit, E. ([1901] 1995), *The Wouldbegoods*, London: Puffin.

Nesbit, E. ([1902] 1993), *Five Children and It*, Ware: Wordsworth Classics.

Nesbit, E. ([1904] 1987), *The Phoenix and the Carpet*, Harmondsworth: Puffin.

Nesbit, E. ([1904] 1996), *The New Treasure Seekers*, London: Puffin.

Nesbit, E. (1905), *Oswald Bastable and Others*, London: Wells Gardner, Darton.

Nesbit, E. ([1907] 1998), *The Enchanted Castle*, Ware: Wordsworth Classics.

Nesbit, E. (1910), *The Magic City*, London: Macmillan.

Nesbit, E. (1913), *Wings and the Child, or, The Building of Magic Cities*, New York: Hodder and Stoughton.

Newcombe, S. P. (1850–3), *Pleasant Pages*, London: Houlston and Stoneman.

Newcombe, S. P. (1851a), *Little Henry's Holiday at the Great Exhibition, by the Editor of 'Pleasant Pages'*, London: Houlston and Stoneman.

Newcombe, S. P. (1851b), *The Royal Road to Reading through the Great Exhibition in Which Those Who Were Too Young to Visit the Exhibition May Learn to Read about It*, London: Houlston and Stoneman.

Newcombe, S. P. (1851c), *Fireside Facts from the Great Exhibition, Being an Amusing Series of Object Lessons on the Food and Clothing of All the Nations in the Year 1851*, London: Houlston and Stoneman.

Newcombe, S. P. (1852), *Little Henry's Records of His Life-Time, Old 1851*, London: Houlston and Stoneman.

Newcombe, S. P. (1860), *A Book about All Kinds of Things Which We Eat, Drink and Wear: Being a Series of Object Lessons, Formally Entitled Fireside Facts from the Great Exhibition*, London: Houlston and Wright.

Norcia, M. A. (2013), 'The London Shopscape: Educating the Child Consumer in the Stories of Mary Wollstonecraft, Maria Edgeworth, and Mary Martha Sherwood', *Children's Literature*, 41: 28–56.

Opie, I., and P. Opie ([1951] 1997), *The Oxford Dictionary of Nursery Rhymes*, Oxford: Oxford University Press.

Ovid (2008), *Metamorphoses*, trans. A. D. Melville, Oxford: Oxford University Press.

Pagani, C. (1998), 'Chinese Material Culture and British Perceptions of China in the Mid-Nineteenth Century', in T. Barringer and T. Flynn (eds), *Colonialism and the Object: Empire, Material Culture and the Museum*, 28–40, Abingdon: Routledge.

Parker, R. ([1984] 2012), *The Subversive Stitch: Embroidery and the Making of the Feminine*, London: I. B. Tauris.

Parkes, C. (2012), *Children's Literature and Capitalism: Fictions of Social Mobility in Britain, 1850–1914*, Basingstoke: Palgrave Macmillan.

Perkins, H. (1838), *Parlour Magic*, Philadelphia: H. Perkins.

Pestalozzi, J. H. (1984), *How Gertrude Teaches Her Children: An Attempt to Help Mothers to Teach Their Own Children and an Account of the Method*, trans. Lucy E. Holland and Frances C. Turner, ed. Ebenezer Cooke, London: Swan Sonnenschein.

Picard, L. (2009), 'The Great Exhibition', *The British Library*, 14 October. Available online: https://www.bl.uk/victorian-britain/articles/the-great-exhibition (accessed 4 August 2016).

Pietz, W. (1985), 'The Problem of the Fetish I', *RES Anthropology and Aesthetics*, 9: 5–17.

Pietz, W. (2003), 'Fetish', in R. S. Nelson and R. Shiff (eds), *Critical Terms for Art History*, 306–17, Chicago: University of Chicago Press.

Pimple, K. D. (1995), 'Ghosts, Spirits, and Scholars: The Origins of Modern Spiritualism', in B. Walker (ed.), *Out of the Ordinary: Folklore and the Supernatural*, 75–89, Boulder: University Press of Colorado.

Plotz, J. (2005), 'Can the Sofa Speak?: A Look at Thing Theory', *Criticism*, 47 (1): 109–18.

Plotz, J. (2008), *Portable Property: Victorian Culture on the Move*, Princeton: Princeton University Press.

Porter, D. H. (1998), *The Thames Embankment: Environment, Technology, and Society in Victorian London*, Akron, OH: University of Akron Press.

Potter, B. ([1904] 2012), Letter to Norman Warne, 24 February, in J. Taylor (ed.), *Beatrix Potter's Letters*, London: Frederick Warne.

Potter, B. (1904), *The Tale of Two Bad Mice*, London: Frederick Warne.

Potter, B. ([1910] 2012), Letter to Norman Warne, 15 July, in J. Taylor (ed.), *Beatrix Potter's Letters*, London: Frederick Warne.

Potter, B. ([1929] 2012), Letter to Mrs J. Templeton Coolidge, 9 December, in J. Taylor (ed.), *Beatrix Potter's Letters*, London: Frederick Warne.

Potter, B. (1966), *The Journal of Beatrix Potter from 1881 to 1897*, transcribed by L. Linder, London: Frederick Warne.

Potter, B. (2012), *Beatrix Potter's Letters*, ed. J. Taylor, London: Frederick Warne.

Price, L. (2009), 'From *The History of a Book* to a "History of the Book"', *Representations*, 108 (1):120–38.

Pringle, P. (2010), 'Scampering Sofas and "Skuttling" Tables: The Entertaining Interior', *Interiors*, 1 (3): 219–43.

Rahn, S. (1984), 'Tailpiece: *The Tale of Two Bad Mice*', *Children's Literature*, 12: 78–91.

Richards, T. (1990), *Commodity Culture of Victorian England: Advertising and Spectacle 1851–1914*, Stanford: Stanford University Press.

Rodgers, B. (2016), *Adolescent Girlhood and Literary Culture at the Fin de Siècle: Daughters of Today*, New York: Palgrave Macmillan.

Rosenthal, L. (1986), 'Writing Her Own Story: The Integration of the Self in the Fourth Dimension of Mrs Molesworth's *The Cuckoo Clock*', *Children's Literature Association Quarterly*, 10 (4): 187–91.

Rossetti, C. (1874), *Speaking Likenesses*, London: Macmillan.

Ruskin, J. ([1885] 2012), *Praeterita*, Oxford: Oxford World Classics.

Said, E. (2003), *Orientalism*, London: Penguin.

Sanders, V. (2013), *Records of Girlhood: Volume Two: An Anthology of Nineteenth-Century Women's Childhoods*, Farnham: Ashgate.

Saunders, G. (2002), *Wallpaper in Interior Decoration*, London: V & A.

Schlobin, R. C. (1999), 'Danger and Compulsion in *The Wind in the Willows*, or Toad and Hyde Together at Last', in E. E. Smith and R. Haas (eds), *The Haunted Mind: The Supernatural in Victorian Literature*, 31–8, Lanham, MD: The Scarecrow Press.

Shorter, C. (1908), *The Brontës' Life and Letters, Vol. II*, London: Hodder and Stoughton.

Sircar, S. (1984a), 'Other Alices and Alternative Wonderlands: An Exercise in Literary History', *Jabberwocky: The Journal of the Lewis Carroll Society*, 13 (2): 23–48.

Sircar, S. (1984b), 'A Select List of Previously Unlisted "Alice" Imitations', *Jabberwocky: The Journal of the Lewis Carroll Society*, 13 (3): 59–67.

Smith, L. (2004), 'Domestic Fantasy: Real Gardens with Imaginary Toads', in P. Hunt (ed.), *International Companion Encyclopedia of Children's Literature*, 447–54, New York: Routledge.

Smollett, T. (1781), *The Critical Review: Or, Annals of Literature*, Vol. 52, London: W. Simpkin and R. Marshall.

Sotheby's (2001), *Lewis Carroll's Alice: The Photographs, Books, Papers and Person Effects of Alice Liddell and Her Family, London Wednesday 6 June 2001*, London: Sotheby's.

Soul, J. (1851), Letter to Prince Albert, 9 May, Letter Number 262, Archives of the Royal Commission for the Great Exhibition, Imperial College, London.

Southey, R. (1848), 'The Story of the Three Bears', in *The Doctor, &c.*, 327–9, London: Longman, Brown, Green and Longmans.

Stewart, S. (1993), *On Longing: Narratives of the Miniature, the Gigantic, the Souvenir, the Collection*, Durham, NC: Duke University Press.

Stirling, E. M. ([1861] 1868), *The History of a Pin; or, The Changes and Chances of an Eventful Life*, London: T. Nelson and Sons.

Strassavuso The Prevalent (1851), 'Visits to the Great Exhibition of Industry', *The Spectator*, 24, 10 May: 445–6.

Susina, J. (2009), *The Place of Lewis Carroll in Children's Literature*, New York: Routledge.

Tallis, J. (1852), *Tallis's History and Description of the Crystal Palace, and the Exhibition of the World's Industry in 1851, Vol. III*, London: John Tallis.

Tarr, C. (2018), 'The Tables Turned: Curious Commodities in Victorian Children's Literature', *Journal of Victorian Culture*, 23 (1): 25–44.

Taylor, J. (1852), Letter to Metropolitan Police, 5 June, MEPOL 2/106, National Archives, Kew.

Thornbury, W. (1878), *Old and New London, Vol. 2*, London: Cassell, Petter & Galpin.

Tidy, C. M. (1897), *The Story of a Tinder Box: A Course of Lectures Delivered before a Juvenile Auditory at the London Institution during the Christmas Holidays of 1888-89*, London: Society for Promoting Christian Knowledge.

Tilley, C., W. Keane, S. Küchler, M. Rowlands and P. Spyer (2006), *The Handbook of Material Culture*, London: Sage.

Timbs, J. (1855), *Curiosities of London: Exhibiting the Most Rare and Remarkable Objects of Interest in the Metropolis*, 368, London: David Bogue.

Todorov, T. (1975), *The Fantastic: A Structural Approach to a Literary Genre*, trans. R. Howard, Ithaca, NY: Cornell University Press.

Trentmann, F. (2017), *Empire of Things*, London: Penguin.

Trowbridge, J. T. (1908), 'Early Investigations in Spiritualism', *North American Review*, 188 (635): 526–38.

Tutter, A. (2014), '"To Half Believe and Wholly Play": Dialectics of Reality in Beatrix Potter's *The Tale of Two Bad Mice*', *American Imago*, 71 (2): 133–60.

Veblen, T. ([1899] 2007), *The Theory of the Leisure Class*, ed. M. Banta, Oxford: Oxford University Press.

Victoria (1851), Diary Entry, 16 May, *Queen Victoria's Journals*. Available online: http://www.queenvictoriasjournals.org/home.do (accessed 13 December 2017).

Vidler, A. (1987), 'The Architecture of the Uncanny: The Unhomely Houses of the Romantic Sublime', *Assemblage*, 3: 6–29.

Volkhovsky, F. (1898), *A China Cup and Other Stories for Children*, London: T. Fisher Unwin.

Wadsworth, S. (2014), '"When the Cup Has Been Drained": Addiction and Recovery in *The Wind in the Willows*', *Children's Literature*, 42: 42–70.

Wall, C. S. (2006), *The Prose of Things: Transformations of Description in the Eighteenth Century*, Chicago: University of Chicago Press.

Wallace, A. R. (1875), *On Miracles and Modern Spiritualism: Three Essays*, London: James Burn.

Weston, R. (2001), *Modernism*, London: Phaidon.

Willburn, S. A. (2006), *Possessed Victorians: Extra Spheres in Nineteenth-Century Mystical Writings*, New York: Routledge.

Wilson, J. L. (1856), *Western Africa: Its History, Condition, and Prospects*, New York: Harper & Brothers.

Winter, A. (1998), *Mesmerized: Powers of Mind in Victorian Britain*, Chicago: University of Chicago Press.

Work, H. C. (1876), 'Grandfather's Clock', New York: C. M. Cady.

Žižek, S. (2018), '200 Years Later, We Can Say That Marx Was Very Often Right – but in a Much More Literal Way Than He Intended', *The Independent*, 4 May. Available online: https://www.independent.co.uk/voices/karl-marx-200-years-uk-politics-elections-working-class-slavoj-zizek-a8335931.html (accessed 21 April 2019).

Index

accidents 63, 123–4, 135, 150, 52
adverts and advertising 7, 9–10, 84
    for Carbolic Smoke Ball company 124
    as deceptive, 155
    for Eyebright Polish 58
    for Mother Seigel's Curative
        Syrup 123–4
    in Nesbit's *The Story of the Treasure
        Seekers* 130–1
    for Pears Soap 9–11, 115, 124
    slogans, 131, 151
A.L.O.E, *The Story of a Needle* 67, 70–3
anthropomorphism 70, 78–9, 80, 88, 100, 137
Arts and Crafts movement 111–12, *see also* Morris, William
Aunt Mavor's series 33–4
    *Dolls and Sights of the Great
        Exhibition* 34–5
    Little Polly's Doll's House 34
    *Uncle Nimrod's First Visit to the
        Exhibition* 35–6, 45–6
    *Uncle Nimrod's Second Visit to the
        Exhibition* 35–6
    *Uncle Nimrod's Third Visit to the
        Exhibition* 35–6
    The Victoria Alphabet 45

ball 3, 8, 133–5
Barks, Roland xi
Barthes, Roland
    ravishment 152
    reality effect 12
Baum, L. Frank 92–3
Berry, Catherine, *Experiences in Spiritualism* 96
Bildungsroman 56, 70, 76
books (as commodities) 2, 3–11, 16, 32, 34–5, 51
Brenda, *Froggy's Little Brother* 12
British Empire 26, 44, 49, 94, 101

Brontë, Charlotte 23–4, 27, 158
Bunyan, John, *The Pilgrim's Progress* 27–8
Burnett, Frances Hodgson 1–2
    A Little Princess 113
buttons 8–9, 43

Caldecott, Randolph 32
capitalism 4, 13, 51, 108
    and Spiritualism 90–1
    see also commodity
Carey, Annie, *The Wonder of Common Things*, 15, 77–81
Carroll, Lewis
    Alice's Adventures in Wonderland 2, 8, 46, 109
        price of first edition 9
        commercial tie-ins to 8–9
        in Pears Soap advert 9–11
        auction of memorabilia 8
    The Nursery Alice 9
    Phantasmagoria and Other Poems 103–4
    and Psychical Society 102
    Through the Looking Glass and What Alice Found There 99, 104–9
        and commodities 107–9
        domestic setting of 104–5
        and Spiritualism 102–7
child labour 44–5, 69, 162, 165
Children's Welfare Exhibition (1914) 158–63
    advert for 159
    and children's literature 160, *see also* E. Nesbit
    price of admittance 160
    venue 159
China and Chinese Commodities 94
    and the Great Exhibition 24–5, 33
    in *The Cuckoo Clock* 101, 118–19
China Cup 74–7
    manufacture of 75

class 7, 11, 66, 76, 162
    middle class 49, 101, 143, 150, 163
    working class 45, 74, 162
clothing 8, 12, 71
coal 45–6
    in Carey's *The Wonders of Common Things* 79–81
    mining of 45–6
Comical Creatures from Wurtemberg, The 33
commodity
    emotional value of 77, 92–3, 135
    fetishism of 2, 50–1, 84, 90–5, 108, 120
    shifting values of 63–4, 77, 80–1, 136
conspicuous consumption 58
consumer enculturation 3–6, 7, 46, 48–9, 51, 125, 154–5, 165
cotton 9
    global trade of 43, 163
    as thread 132
Crane, Walter 32
    advertisements by 115–16
    illustrations for *The Cuckoo Clock* 115–17
Crowe, Catherine, *The Night Side of Nature, or, Ghosts and Ghost-Seers* 96
Cruikshank, George 32
Crystal Palace *see* Great Exhibition (1851)
Crystal Palace: A Little Book for Little Boys, for 1851, The 46–7

De Morgan, Sophia *from Matter to Spirit: Ten Years' Experience of Spirit Manifestations, Intended as a Guide to Enquirers* 96
desire 1–2, 31, 38, 74–5, 77, 92–3
Dickens, Charles
    and the Great Exhibition 24, 27–8
    Household Words 38, 58
    'My Mahogany Friend' 58
disorientation 27–8, 104
Dodgson, Charles *see* Carroll, Lewis
Doll's House, 143–8, 155
Dolls 2, 7, 47, 143–4
domestic fantasy (genre), 84, 99–102, 110, 113
domestic space 41, 64, 67, 71
    decoration of 8, 68, 111, 149–50, 163
    haunted, 83–4, 103, 90

parlour as narrative setting 64, 73, 85, 97, 100, 104
parlour as setting for séance 85, 88–90
drawing-room *see* domestic space
Du Maurier, George, *English Society* 68

Edgeworth, Maria
    Practical Education 4
    'The Purple Jar' 5
education 4, 7, 38–9, 79
    education of girls 66, 73, 75
    and the Great Exhibition 46–7
    through Object Lessons 37–9
Edwardian period 128
    and children's literature 160
Eliot, George 60
    The Mill on the Floss 92
envelopes 44–5

Fabian Society 14
    Nesbit's involvement in 127
factories 65, 73
    Factory reform 111
fairy-tale (genre) 144
Faraday, Michael 53, 85
fetish 91, 108
    in *The Mill on the Floss* 92
    sexual 152
    in West African culture 91–2
    see also commodity
fin de siècle 129
food
    cake 7
    butter and oil 48
    at the Great Exhibition 18, 20, 49
    toy food 142–3, 145, 147
    see also taste
Fox sisters 83–4, 96
Frost, Arthur B. 103

ghosts *see* spirits
gifts 131, 133–4
gold 72–3
Golden Age of Children's Literature 2, 8, 102
Gourard, Julie, *The Adventures of a Watch* 63–4
Grahame, Kenneth, *The Wind in the Willows* 148–55
    decoration of houses within 149–50

Toad
    as anti-hero 148
    as deviant consumer 150, 155
    and mental illness 148–9, 154
    Toad's caravan 151–2
    Toad's motor car 151–4
Great Exhibition (1851)
    building and design, 22, 27, 50
    child visitors to 19–22
    display in 22–7, 31–2, 5, 40
        impact on display practices 22, 49–50
        workers on display at 44–5
    lectures about 29–30
    lost property at 17–19
    organisation of 22–3, 27–8
    policing of 17–19, 22
    price of admission 20
    souvenirs of 31–3
Greenaway, Kate 8

handkerchiefs 8–9, 31, 78, 136
Hargreaves, Alice (nee Liddell), auction of personal items 8–9
Hayden, Maria B. 85–7
hoarding 149, 153
Hodgson, Frances Eliza *see* Burnett, Frances Hodgson
Hughes, Arthur 110–11, 112

imperialism 94
Industrial Revolution 3, 45
iron
    in Carey's *The Wonders of Common Things* 78, 79–80
    ironwork in the Crystal Palace 22, 27, 50
    in manufacture of needles 70
it-narrative (genre)
    children's it-narratives, 55–6, 60–4
    and consumer culture 57, 60
    eighteenth-century tradition 55–8
    features of 55–6

James, M. R., 'The Malice of Inanimate Objects' 155–6
Jennings, Paul, 'Report on Resistentialism' 156

Karl Marx Club 127
Kipling, Rudyard
    Kim 11

The Jungle Book 132
Koh-i-Noor 35, 40

labour
    gendered division of 65, 71
    working conditions 43–4 *see also* child labour
Leech, John 20–1, 29, 44, 88–9, 111
Liddell, Alice *see* Hargreaves, Alice
Linton, Eliza Lynn, 'Modern Magic' 87
literacy rates 2
lost children 19, 28–9
lost property 17–19, 56
Lucas, E. V. *The Book of Shops* 6–7
Lyell, Charles 80

magic 84, 91–3, 110, 115
    magic tricks 97–8, 163
    magical objects 91–3, 99–102, 108, 120, 136
    see also fetish
Mamma's Visit with Her Little Ones to the Great Exhibition 28, 36
Martineau, Harriet, 'What There Is in a Button' 62
Marx, Karl
    Capital 50–1, 91
    on commodities, 60, 74, 125–6
    on commodity fetishism 90–2
matches 54–5
Matéaux, Clara L. *Wonderland of Work* 45–6
material deviance 126, 129
    in Grahame, *The Wind in the Willows* 149–54
    in Nesbit's work 130–1, 133, 136
    in Potter, *The Tale of Two Bad Mice* 142–8
mediums 84, 85–6, 88, 91, 95–6, 113 *see also* Fox sisters *and* Hayden, Maria
melodrama, 66
mesmerism 96, 98, 113–14
    in *The Cuckoo Clock* 115
Millar, H. R. 138–9, 142
Milne, A. A. *Winnie-the-Pooh* 2
mirror 105, 107
modernism 128–9, 142, 144
    modern consumer practices 130–1
Molesworth, Maria Louisa, *The Cuckoo Clock* 98, 112–19

and Chinese commodities 101, 118–19
illustration of 116–17
and mesmerism 115
and Spiritualism 112–15
money 141, 147
  coins 29
  pocket money 1–2, 130–1
morality 15, 30, 35, 46–8, 60, 99, 126–7
  and commodities 131, 149–50, 154
  in domestic fantasy 99, 120
  in it-narratives 60–1, 71, 76
Morris, William, 'On the Beauty of Life', 112
motor car 151–4

needle
  in A.L.O.E's *The Story of a Needle* 70–3
  manufacture of, 69, 70
needlework 45, 64–5, 68
Nesbit, E(dith)
  and Children's Welfare Exhibition (1914) 160–3
  The Enchanted Castle 135–42
    Ugly-Wuglies as things 137–42
    Ugly-Wuglies and class 141–2
  The Phoenix and the Carpet 136
  The Story of the Amulet 12
  Fabianism 127, 141
  The Story of the Treasure Seekers 128–32
    and advertising 130–1
    and poverty 129–30
  Wings and the Child, or, The Building of Magic Cities 161–3
  The Wouldbegoods 132–5
    gifts within 133–4
    and things 133–5
    as uncanny 137–8
Newbery, *A Little Pretty Pocket-Book* 3, 7
Newcombe, Samuel Prout 29, 37–42
  Fireside Facts of the Great Exhibition 38, 39–40, 41, 42, 45, 47
  and Horniman Museum and Garden collections 37
  Little Henry's Holiday at the Great Exhibition 14, 29, 38, 40–1, 43, 47, 78
  The Royal Road to Reading through the Great Exhibition 38, 39–40, 41
noise 23, 36, 83, 85, 106, 152

Nottingham, Universal Exhibition (1914) 157–8
novels of circulation *see* it-narrative

object lessons 37–42, 47, 51
orientalism, 94–5
Orphans Working School 29–30
Ouija board 97–8

Paxton, Joseph 27, 41
periodicals
  All the Year Round 87
  Household Words 28, 46, 58
  Illustrated London News 28
  The Launceston Examiner 91
  Nottingham Evening Post 157
  Nottingham Journal 158
  Pall Mall Gazette 159
  The Pittsburgh Dispatch 97
  Punch 20, 44, 88, 106
  The Spectator 27, 30, 44
  The Westminster Review 88
Pestalozzi, Johann Heinrich 37
pincushion 3, 8
pins, manufacture of, 65
pocket watch 56, 63
Postage-Stamps 9, 29
Potter, Beatrix 142–3
  Little Pig Robinson 142
  Peter Rabbit doll 8
  The Tailor of Gloucester 142
  The Tale of Two Bad Mice 142–8
    class issues within 143, 144–6
    mice as deviant consumers 142–8
    violence 145
power 26, 46
  buying power 1, 6–7, 26, 58, 60, 76–7
  power of consumers over commodities 109, 138
  power of commodities over consumers 91–2, 94, 120–1, 136–7, 140, 152
  supernatural power 86–8, 91, 103, 142
Psychical Society 102–3

Queen Victoria 29, 33
Queer Theory 149

Resistentialism 156
Rossetti, Christina
  and Arts and Crafts movement 111–12

Speaking Likenesses 109–12
   and spiritualism 111
rubbish 74–5
Ruskin, John 50, 104

salt
   in Carey's *The Wonders of Common
      Things* 78–81
satire 82, 148
science 163
séance 88, 89, 105
   children participating in 96
   see also mediums
second-hand trade 66–7
servants 88–9, 101
sewing machine 45
Sherwood, *A Drive in a Coach through the
     Streets of London* 5
shops, 1, 5–7, 65–6, 75, 119, 143
   children as shoppers 1, 75–6, 108
   department stores 22–3
      Fenwick 93
      Hamley's 143
      Harrods 93, 143
      Liberty's of London 8, 93, 94–5, 111
      Morris & Co. 93, 111
      Selfridge's 116, 160
      Whiteley's 94
   Sheep's Shop in *Through the Looking
      Glass*, 107–8
   shop display and window-dressing
      92–4, 101, 119
   shopping 22–3, 92–3, 95
   window-shopping 24
sight 27, 31, 34, 36, 40
   focused looking 22–4, 35, 36
slavery 43–4
smell 94
Society for Promoting Christian
     Knowledge 54, 61
souvenirs 31–3

spirits
   as childlike 96–7
   as noisy 83
   spirit-rapping, 84–6
Spiritualism 84–5, 87, 98
   and capitalism, 90
   and fiction 95–6
Spyri, Johanna, *Heidi* 113
Stirling, E. M., *The History of a Pin* 64–7
sugar 43

tables, moving and otherwise 86, 88
taste 3, 18, 25, 33, 37, 48–9, 57, 58, 68, 94,
     112, 143, 145, 147, 150
taxidermy 33, 37
Tenniel, John 105–6
textile manufacture 42–3, 65
theft 5, 146–7, 149, 153
thimbles 17, 18, 72
Thing Theory 108, 125–7, 156
Tidy, Charles Meymott 53–4, 69, 82
tinderbox 54
touch 12, 22, 24–5, 38, 40–1
trade, 42, 81
   global economy 51, 81
trance novel (genre) 96
   see also mesmerism
Tucker, C. M. *see* A.L.O.E.

uncanny, 83, 86–7, 92, 95, 99–100, 110,
     113, 116–19, 120, 137–8
Universal Exhibition Nottingham (1914)
     3, 16, 157–8

vandalism 146–7
Victoria and Albert Museum 142
Volkhovsky, Felix, 'A China Cup', 73–7

William Morris Society 73

www.ingramcontent.com/pod-product-compliance
Lightning Source LLC
Chambersburg PA
CBHW061832300426
44115CB00013B/2345